The Regions of Italy

VALLE
D'AOSTA

TRENTINO-
ALTO
ADIGE

FRIULI-
VENEZIA
GIULIA

LOMBARDY

PIEDMONT

VENETO

LIGURIA

EMILIA-ROMAGNA

TUSCANY

MARCHE

UMBRIA

LAZIO

ABRUZZO

MOLISE

SARDINIA

CAMPANIA

APULIA

BASILICATA

CALABRIA

SICILY

Weight Watchers®

Simply the Best

Italian

More Than 250 Classic Recipes
From the Kitchens of Italy

Macmillan • USA

MACMILLAN

A Pearson Education Macmillan Company
1633 Broadway
New York, NY 10019

Macmillan General Reference books may be purchased for business or sales promotional use.
For information, please write: Special Markets Department, Macmillan General Reference,
1633 Broadway, New York, NY 10019

A WORD ABOUT WEIGHT WATCHERS

Since 1963, Weight Watchers has grown from a handful of people to millions of enrollees annually.
Today, Weight Watchers is recognized as the leading name in safe and sensible weight control.
Weight Watchers members form a diverse group, from youths to senior citizens,
attending meetings virtually around the globe.

Weight-loss and weight-management results vary by individual, but we recommend
that you attend Weight Watchers meetings, follow the Weight Watchers food plan, and participate
in regular physical activity. For the Weight Watchers meeting nearest you, call 1-800-651-6000.
Or visit us at our Web site at www.weightwatchers.com.

WEIGHT WATCHERS PUBLISHING GROUP

Editorial Director: Nancy Gagliardi
Senior Editor: Martha Schueneman, CCP
Senior Editor: Christine Senft, M.S.
Publishing Assistant: Jenny Laboy-Brace
Recipe Developers: Barry Bluestein and Kevin Morrissey,
Barbara Posner Beltrami, Linda Romanelli Leahy
Writer: Joyce Hendley
Photographer: Rita Maas
Food Stylist: Mariann Sauvion
Assistant Food Stylist: Rebecca Adams
Prop Stylist: Cathy Cook

Library of Congress Cataloging-in-Publication Data
Weight Watchers simply the best : Italian
    p.   cm.
    Includes index.
    ISBN 0-02-863526-4 (alk. paper)
    1. Reducing diets Recipes. 2. Cookery, Italian. I. Weight
Watchers International. II. Title: Simply the best.
    RM222.2.W3263   1999
    641.5'635–dc21   99-39033
                                                        CIP

Manufactured in the United States of America

10 9 8 7 6 5 4 3 2 1

contents

recipe symbols

One Pot

Make Ahead

Rush Hour

Vegetarian

No Cook

introduction

The Sistine Chapel. The statue of David. The Colosseum. A plate of *pasta con aglio e olio*. As with all great works of art, Italian cuisine is created with thought and care; ultimately, it is something to be shared, savored, and enjoyed. At first glance, many Italian dishes appear deceptively simple, yet with a closer look (and taste), one soon discovers that she is in the presence of greatness.

North Americans have come to understand this greatness: We rank Italian food as our favorite "ethnic" cuisine. In fact, Italian food has found a comfortable and welcome spot at our table: Pasta is a weeknight staple for busy families, as is pizza, be it take-out or "homemade" (from packaged, refrigerated dough). However, if spaghetti with bottled sauce or a take-out cheese pie are your idea of Italian food, then you've only scratched the surface of this fine cuisine.

To truly understand Italian fare, it helps to know a not-so-secret credo of the Italian kitchen: Start with only the finest and freshest ingredients. Unlike some of the world's other cuisines—where herbs or an intricate blend of spices define the dishes—the food, plain and simple, is the star. This is probably because Italians have long held a stellar reputation as excellent farmers—and with good reason. In Italy, no piece of land was left untouched; even the most mountainous areas were coaxed and cultivated into producing luscious fare. Through years of trial and error, these masters of the elements discovered the perfect balance of sun, earth, and water for producing some of the world's finest fruits and vegetables—not to mention cheeses, meats, oils, vinegars, and wines.

Yet Italian food would still be an oddity to our North American palate if it weren't for the Italian immigrants who journeyed across the ocean. We must give a respectful nod to these twentieth-century pioneers as they adapted to their new lives, all the while holding onto the traditions of home. The immigrant focus on family, hard work, and frugality melded well with our Puritan roots and sensibility. To this day, there is little waste in the Italian kitchen: Leftover pasta may become an ingredient in tomorrow's frittata; day-old bread transforms into a robust *panzanella;* and whatever vegetables are in the garden are tossed into a simmering pot of minestrone.

Simply the Best Italian hopes to broaden your understanding of Italian cuisine and make you a more intuitive Italian cook. We've included over 250 fine recipes that are (for the most part) true Italian fare; signature dishes of many of the regions of Italy are included. We've also supplied historical facts and fanciful lore, as well as a wide range of cook's tricks to make your job in the kitchen more creative, easier, and as authentic as an Italian's.

A final note: While it's true that few Italians have earned international acclaim as master chefs, we contend that Italy has thousands of great chefs—each cooking at home, day after day, for family and friends. And their "nothing fancy" sensibility has produced one the world's finest, and most accessible, cuisines.

Salute!

NANCY GAGLIARDI
Editorial Director

one

antipasti

Fennel with Balsamic Vinegar and Parmesan

Fennel is a popular vegetable in Italy. Sometimes called anise, fennel is often served between courses or after dinner because of its healthful digestive properties.

Makes 4 servings

2 fennel bulbs, cut into slices

4 teaspoons extra-virgin olive oil

2 teaspoons balsamic vinegar

1 ounce Parmesan cheese

Freshly ground pepper, to taste

1. Divide the fennel among 4 salad plates. Drizzle with the oil and vinegar.

2. Shave the cheese into very thin slices with a vegetable peeler or the slicing side of a box grater. Divide the cheese over the fennel, then sprinkle with the pepper. Serve at room temperature or slightly chilled.

Per serving: 82 Calories, 6 g Total Fat, 2 g Saturated Fat, 4 mg Cholesterol, 201 mg Sodium, 3 g Total Carbohydrate, 1 g Dietary Fiber, 3 g Protein, 123 mg Calcium.

POINTS per serving: 2.

D i G i o r n o   To trim the fennel, cut off the feathery tops (save them for a garnish, or use them as you would dill in another recipe). Cut off any bruised or yellowed outer leaves, then halve the bulb from stem to base. Cut out the core, then place the halves, cut-side down, on a board and cut crosswise into thin slices.

Antipasto platter: Roasted Pepper and Mozzarella Bocconcini, (page 4);
Fennel with Balsamic Vinegar and Parmesan (page 2);
Goat Cheese, Tomato, and Basil Crostini (page 12)

Roasted Pepper and Mozzarella Bocconcini

Bocconcini, or "little mouthfuls," are the small balls of mozzarella cheese that are often available at Italian markets (though rarely in skim-milk form). Smoky-sweet peppers, creamy cheese, and pungent herbs make this an irresistible appetizer.

Makes 4 servings

1 green bell pepper

1 red bell pepper

1 yellow bell pepper

1 tablespoon dry white wine

2 teaspoons olive oil

1 teaspoon dried oregano

1 teaspoon dried basil

1 teaspoon dried thyme leaves

1 teaspoon white-wine vinegar

1 garlic clove, minced

Freshly ground pepper, to taste

6 ounces skim-milk mozzarella cheese, cut into 24 cubes

1. Preheat the broiler. Line a baking sheet with foil and set the bell peppers on the foil. Broil the peppers 5 inches from the heat, turning frequently with tongs, until lightly charred. Fold up the foil to cover the peppers and let steam 10 minutes. Set a strainer over a bowl; peel, seed, and devein the peppers over the strainer. Discard the peels and seeds. Cut each pepper into 8 strips and add them to the juices.

2. Stir the wine, oil, oregano, basil, thyme, vinegar, garlic, and ground pepper into the pepper juices. Add the mozzarella and toss to coat. Cover and let stand 30 minutes.

3. Drain the mozzarella and discard the liquid. Wrap each cube with a pepper strip and secure with a toothpick. Arrange on serving platter.

Per serving: 106 Calories, 2 g Total Fat, 0 g Saturated Fat, 4 mg Cholesterol, 317 mg Sodium, 7 g Total Carbohydrate, 1 g Dietary Fiber, 14 g Protein, 329 mg Calcium.

POINTS per serving: 2.

D i G i o r n o   When the cheese is the focus of the dish, as it is here, avoid the packaged mozzarella in your supermarket's dairy case. For a real treat, look for *mozzarella di bufala* in a cheese shop or Italian grocery. Made from the milk of water buffalo, it has a depth of flavor that cow's-milk mozzarella simply can't match.

Whole Roasted Garlic

Could one person eat a whole bulb of garlic? Absolutely, if it's gently cooked until it's nutty brown, creamy in texture, and mellow in flavor. To eat roasted garlic, simply squeeze a clove and spread the pulp onto bread. If you thin it with a little chicken broth, you'll have a tasty pasta sauce; thinned with a bit of vinegar, water, and oil, it makes a sublime creamy-garlic salad dressing. Toss in some chopped basil and pine nuts to make a light pesto.

Makes 4 servings

4 garlic bulbs

1/2 cup low-sodium chicken broth

2 teaspoons olive oil

2–3 sprigs thyme

1–2 sprigs rosemary

Freshly ground pepper, to taste

1. Preheat the oven to 400°F. Cut about 1/4-inch from the top of the garlic, exposing the tips of the cloves. Combine the garlic, broth, oil, thyme, rosemary, and pepper in a shallow baking dish, tossing to coat the garlic. Cover with foil and bake until golden brown and very soft, 1–1 1/4 hours; check the amount of liquid in the baking dish occasionally and add a little more broth if necessary. Remove the foil and bake 10 minutes longer.

2. Cool the garlic to room temperature, then serve, drizzled with the pan juices.

Per serving: 68 Calories, 3 g Total Fat, 0 g Saturated Fat, 0 mg Cholesterol, 19 mg Sodium, 10 g Total Carbohydrate, 1 g Dietary Fiber, 2 g Protein, 57 mg Calcium.

POINTS per serving: 1.

D i G i o r n o   We use roasted garlic in many recipes throughout this book. Make a batch when you have the time, then refrigerate in an airtight glass jar for up to ten days.

Roasted Garlic and Parmesan Flans

These savory flans, called *sformati* in Italy, are popular in Piedmont; there, however, the custards would be made using heavy cream, not evaporated fat-free milk. For the best flans, use the best cheese—authentic Parmigiano-Reggiano—and freshly grate the cheese each time you use it.

Makes 4 servings

8 garlic cloves, roasted (page 5) and peeled

1 (12-ounce) can evaporated fat-free milk

1 tablespoon all-purpose flour

2 eggs

2 egg whites

3 tablespoons grated Parmesan cheese

1. Preheat the oven to 375°F. Spray four 6-ounce ramekins with nonstick spray.

2. Puree the garlic and $1/2$ cup of the milk in a food processor. Transfer the puree to a saucepan. Whisk in the remaining milk and the flour and cook over medium heat, whisking constantly, until steamy, about 5 minutes. Whisk in the eggs, egg whites, and cheese. Divide among the ramekins and set them in a baking dish. Fill the dish with enough water to reach halfway up the sides of the ramekins. Bake until the flans are firm and a knife tip inserted into the center of one comes out clean, about 30 minutes. Cool 5 minutes, then invert onto plates.

Per serving: 158 Calories, 4 g Total Fat, 2 g Saturated Fat, 117 mg Cholesterol, 252 mg Sodium, 13 g Total Carbohydrate, 0 g Dietary Fiber, 13 g Protein, 89 mg Calcium.

POINTS per serving: 3.

D i G i o r n o   Did you know that you can control how garlicky a dish tastes by how small you chop the cloves? Mincing, pureeing, pressing, and finely chopping release more of the garlic's essential oils; bruising, slicing, and coarsely chopping expose less, so not as much passes into the dish.

Bruschetta

Originally, bruschetta (called *fettunta* in Tuscany) was invented as a way to salvage bread that was going stale: The bread was toasted, then rubbed with the cut side of a garlic clove and drizzled with or soaked in olive oil. In this dish, use your best extra-virgin olive oil.

Makes 4 servings

4 ounces crusty Italian peasant bread, cut into 4 slices and toasted

1 large garlic clove, halved

2 teaspoons extra-virgin olive oil

2 teaspoons grated Parmesan cheese

2 teaspoons minced flat-leaf parsley

Freshly ground pepper, to taste

While it is still warm, rub each slice of toast with a cut side of the garlic clove. Drizzle the toast with the oil, then sprinkle evenly with the cheese, parsley, and pepper.

Per serving: 103 Calories, 4 g Total Fat, 1 g Saturated Fat, 1 mg Cholesterol, 185 mg Sodium, 15 g Total Carbohydrate, 1 g Dietary Fiber, 3 g Protein, 39 mg Calcium.

POINTS per serving: 2.

Savory Spinach Timballini

If you would rather make one large *timballo*, or molded pie, as the Tuscans would do, use an 8-inch glass pie plate or a 4-cup soufflé dish instead of the ramekins.

Makes 4 servings

1 (10-ounce) box frozen chopped spinach, thawed and squeezed dry

2 garlic cloves, peeled

2 eggs

1/2 cup fat-free milk

1 1/2 tablespoons all-purpose flour

1/2 teaspoon salt

1/4 teaspoon freshly ground pepper

6 drops green hot pepper sauce

1. Preheat the oven to 375°F. Spray four 6-ounce ramekins with non-stick spray.

2. Combine the spinach, garlic, eggs, and 1/4 cup of the milk in a food processor and process until the spinach is finely chopped.

3. Combine the remaining 1/4 cup of milk and the flour in a small saucepan. Cook over medium heat, stirring constantly, until steamy, about 2 minutes. Stir in the spinach mixture, the salt, pepper, and hot pepper sauce. Divide among the ramekins and set them in a baking dish. Fill the dish with enough water to reach halfway up the sides of the ramekins. Bake until the custards are firm and a knife tip inserted into the center of one comes out clean, about 30 minutes. Cool 5 minutes, then invert onto plates.

Per serving: 41 Calories, 0 g Total Fat, 0 g Saturated Fat, 1 mg Cholesterol, 367 mg Sodium, 7 g Total Carbohydrate, 2 g Dietary Fiber, 4 g Protein, 121 mg Calcium.

POINTS *per serving: 0.*

D i G i o r n o   For a smashing presentation, serve each custard on a bed of bitter greens that have been tossed lightly in balsamic vinegar.

Savory Spinach Timballini

Fresh Tomato Crostini

Tuscan in origin, crostini are little rounds of toasted bread with any of a variety of chopped toppings. Here, the ingredients—crusty bread, tomatoes, garlic, and parsley—evoke picnics in the Italian country-side. Serve these with some fresh fruit and wine or sparkling mineral water.

Makes 4 servings

4–6 plum tomatoes, chopped

1/4 cup minced flat-leaf parsley or basil

2 teaspoons extra-virgin olive oil

1 garlic clove, minced

Freshly ground pepper, to taste

4 ounces crusty Italian peasant bread, cut into 4 slices and toasted

1. Combine the tomatoes, parsley, oil, garlic, and pepper. Cover and let stand 30 minutes.

2. Divide the tomato mixture, with any juices, among the toast. Serve at room temperature.

Per serving: 115 Calories, 4 g Total Fat, 1 g Saturated Fat, 0 mg Cholesterol, 174 mg Sodium, 18 g Total Carbohydrate, 2 g Dietary Fiber, 3 g Protein, 32 mg Calcium.

POINTS per serving: 2.

Di Giorno   Plum tomatoes contain much less water than common supermarket tomatoes. If you can't find plum tomatoes, chop what's available and combine it in a bowl with about 1/2 teaspoon of salt, then let it stand for about 30 minutes. The salt will extract some of the water from the tomatoes, which you can drain off before you combine with the other ingredients. (Don't worry, though—the tomatoes will still be juicy.)

Sun-Dried Tomato Crostini

Try this version of crostini when fresh tomatoes aren't in season—or if you can't get enough of sun-dried tomatoes, make it year-round.

Makes 4 servings

16 sun-dried tomato halves (not packed in oil)

1/2 cup boiling water

1/2 cup flat-leaf parsley leaves

2 garlic cloves

2 teaspoons olive oil

1/4 teaspoon salt

4 ounces crusty Italian peasant bread, cut into 8 slices and toasted

1. Combine the tomatoes and water; soak until softened, 10–15 minutes. Drain the tomatoes; reserve the liquid separately.

2. Puree the tomatoes, parsley, 1 garlic clove, and 1 tablespoon of the tomato liquid in a food processor or blender, scraping down the sides of the bowl if necessary. Stir in the oil and salt.

3. Cut the remaining garlic in half; rub the toast with the cut side of the garlic. Divide the tomato mixture among the toast and serve.

Per serving: 131 Calories, 3 g Total Fat, 1 g Saturated Fat, 0 mg Cholesterol, 314 mg Sodium, 21 g Total Carbohydrate, 3 g Dietary Fiber, 5 g Protein, 35 mg Calcium.

POINTS per serving: 2.

Goat Cheese, Tomato, and Basil Crostini

You might think of goat cheese as French, but feta is Greece's famous version, and the Italians enjoy many different goat cheeses; they are a specialty of the Piedmont region in northwestern Italy. Use any fresh goat cheese (*caprino*) without a rind: Look for *Novarigo* or *Castagneto*.

Makes 4 servings

4 ounces crusty Italian bread, cut into 8 slices and toasted

1 1/2 ounces goat cheese

4 plum tomatoes, sliced

1/4 teaspoon salt

Freshly ground pepper, to taste

8 basil leaves

Spread the toast slices with half of the goat cheese; top each with 2 slices of the tomato, slightly overlapping if necessary. Sprinkle with the salt and pepper, and top each with a basil leaf and some of the remaining goat cheese. Serve at room temperature.

Per serving: 121 Calories, 4 g Total Fat, 2 g Saturated Fat, 8 mg Cholesterol, 358 mg Sodium, 16 g Total Carbohydrate, 1 g Dietary Fiber, 5 g Protein, 60 mg Calcium.

POINTS per serving: 3.

Crab Crostini

If crabmeat is out of your price range, surimi makes an excellent substitute. Or use a can of the highest quality canned crabmeat (expect to pay about five dollars per can)—look for the words *fancy lump jumbo* on the label and rinse it under cold water to remove any taste from the can. Lobster, rock shrimp, or a large-flaked whitefish work well, too.

Makes 4 servings

1/4 **pound fresh or thawed frozen crabmeat**

2 **tablespoons minced celery**

1 **tablespoon slivered basil**

1 **tablespoon fresh lemon juice**

2 **teaspoons extra-virgin olive oil**

1/4 **teaspoon salt**

1/8 **teaspoon cayenne**

4 **ounces Italian bread, cut into 8 slices and toasted**

1. Combine the crabmeat, celery, basil, lemon juice, oil, salt, and cayenne. Cover and refrigerate 2 hours; remove from the refrigerator 1 hour before serving.

2. Divide the crab mixture among the toast and serve.

Per serving: 128 Calories, 4 g Total Fat, 1 g Saturated Fat, 28 mg Cholesterol, 383 mg Sodium, 15 g Total Carbohydrate, 1 g Dietary Fiber, 8 g Protein, 60 mg Calcium.

POINTS per serving: 3.

Artichoke "Crostini"

For an elegant variation, we've opted to mound the artichoke topping on premade polenta, available in 24-ounce rolls in many supermarkets. It has a softer texture and richer taste than bread does.

Makes 12 servings

4 teaspoons olive oil

2 garlic cloves, minced

1 (9-ounce) box frozen artichoke hearts, thawed

2 plum tomatoes, seeded and chopped

1/2 tablespoon anchovy paste

1/4 cup dry white wine

1 tablespoon fresh lemon juice

12 ounces polenta, cut into 1/2-inch slices

1 tablespoon grated Parmesan cheese

1. Preheat the broiler.

2. Heat a nonstick skillet. Swirl in the oil, then add the garlic. Sauté until fragrant, then stir in the artichoke hearts, tomatoes, anchovy paste, and wine. Cook, stirring constantly, until the wine evaporates and the tomatoes break down, 4–5 minutes. Stir in the lemon juice and remove from the heat.

3. Set the polenta slices on a broiler rack and broil until browned, about 4 minutes. Turn the slices over, then top with the artichoke mixture and a sprinkle of cheese. Broil until lightly browned, about 2 minutes.

Per serving: 75 Calories, 3 g Total Fat, 1 g Saturated Fat, 8 mg Cholesterol, 126 mg Sodium, 9 g Total Carbohydrate, 2 g Dietary Fiber, 3 g Protein, 62 mg Calcium.

POINTS per serving: 1.

D i G i o r n o   This topping has a chunky consistency; for a smoother, spreadlike consistency, process the artichoke mixture to a chunky puree in the food processor after removing it from the heat.

Artichoke "Crostini"

Clams Casino

If you can find them, use cherrystone or littleneck clams—they're the smallest of the hard-shell variety, and they have better flavor than larger clams.

Makes 4 servings

12 clams, scrubbed

1/4 cup dry white wine

2 teaspoons olive oil

1 Italian frying pepper, seeded and minced (see Di Giorno, page 137)

1 small onion, minced

1 garlic clove, minced

1 plum tomato, chopped

3 tablespoons plain dried bread crumbs

2 tablespoons minced flat-leaf parsley

1 tablespoon minced oregano, or 1/2 teaspoon dried

1 tablespoon minced fresh basil, or 1/2 teaspoon dried

Freshly ground pepper, to taste

3 slices bacon, crisp-cooked and crumbled

4 lemon wedges

1. Line a 9 × 13-inch baking pan with foil, shiny side up. Preheat the broiler.

2. Put the clams and wine in a saucepan over medium heat. Cover and cook until the clams open, 4–5 minutes; discard any clams that do not open. When cool enough to handle, remove the clams from their shells and coarsely chop. Reserve 12 shells; reserve the cooking liquid separately.

3. Heat a nonstick skillet. Swirl in the oil, then add the frying pepper, onion, and garlic. Sauté until the onion is golden, about 5 minutes.

4. Put the clams, 1/4 cup of the cooking liquid, the tomato, bread crumbs, parsley, oregano, basil, and ground pepper in a food processor. Pulse 4–5 times, just enough to chop the clams coarsely and blend the ingredients. Stir in the bacon and the sautéed vegetables. Divide the mixture among the shells. Set the shells in the baking pan and broil until the filling is browned and crisp, about 5 minutes. Serve, garnished with lemon wedges.

Per serving: 114 Calories, 5 g Total Fat, 1 g Saturated Fat, 14 mg Cholesterol, 139 mg Sodium, 8 g Total Carbohydrate, 1 g Dietary Fiber, 6 g Protein, 43 mg Calcium.

POINTS per serving: 2.

Di Giorno   Clams must be alive when you purchase them. Their shells should either be tightly closed, or should snap shut if you tap them. Don't store them wrapped in plastic or in water. Just set them in the refrigerator and use them as soon as possible.

Clams Oreganato

This recipe, which minimizes the bread crumbs and maximizes the briny flavor of the clams, will make some of the best baked clams you've ever had. Don't look at this just as an appetizer: Try it as a light luncheon with Orange and Fennel Salad (page 144).

Makes 4 servings

12 cherrystone clams, scrubbed

1/4 cup dry white wine

2 plum tomatoes, chopped

1/4 cup chopped mushrooms

3 tablespoons plain dried bread crumbs

2 tablespoons minced flat-leaf parsley

2 tablespoons fresh lemon juice

4 teaspoons olive oil

1 tablespoon minced fresh oregano, or 1/2 teaspoon dried

1 tablespoon fresh thyme leaves, or 1/2 teaspoon dried

2 garlic cloves, minced

Freshly ground pepper, to taste

2 teaspoons grated Parmesan cheese

4 lemon wedges

1. Line a 9 × 13-inch baking pan with foil, shiny side up. Preheat the broiler.

2. Put the clams and wine in a saucepan over medium heat. Cover and cook until the clams open, 4–5 minutes; discard any clams that don't open. When cool enough to handle, remove the clams from their shells. Reserve 12 shells; reserve the cooking liquid separately.

3. Put the clams, 2 tablespoons of the cooking liquid, the tomatoes, mushrooms, bread crumbs, parsley, lemon juice, oil, oregano, thyme, garlic, and pepper in a food processor. Pulse 4–5 times, just enough to chop the clams coarsely and blend the ingredients. If the mixture seems too dry, pulse in 1–2 tablespoons of the cooking liquid until the mixture reaches the desired consistency. Press the filling into the shells; sprinkle with the cheese. Set the shells in the baking pan and broil until the filling is browned and crisp, about 5 minutes. Serve, garnished with lemon wedges.

Per serving: 109 Calories, 5 g Total Fat, 1 g Saturated Fat, 10 mg Cholesterol, 83 mg Sodium, 8 g Total Carbohydrate, 1 g Dietary Fiber, 5 g Protein, 54 mg Calcium.

POINTS *per serving: 2.*

Chilled Polpetti Salad

Polpetti are baby octopus; you'll find them in many Mediterranean, Asian, and Caribbean markets. They come already cleaned and frozen, which tenderizes them.

Makes 6 servings

1/2 pound baby octopus

1 bay leaf

3 tablespoons fresh lemon juice

1 tablespoon olive oil

1/4 teaspoon crushed red pepper

1/3 cup chopped seeded red bell pepper

1/4 cup chopped celery

1 tablespoon capers, drained and chopped

1/4 teaspoon salt

1. Bring a large pot of water to a boil, then add the octopus and bay leaf. Reduce the heat to low and simmer, covered, until fork-tender, about 45 minutes. Transfer the octopus to a colander and rinse under cold water; discard the bay leaf. Coarsely chop the octopus.

2. Combine the lemon juice, oil, and crushed red pepper in a bowl. Add the octopus, bell pepper, celery, capers, and salt; toss to combine. Cover and refrigerate at least 1 hour to allow the flavors to blend.

Per serving: 57 Calories, 3 g Total Fat, 0 g Saturated Fat, 18 mg Cholesterol, 241 mg Sodium, 2 g Total Carbohydrate, 0 g Dietary Fiber, 6 g Protein, 26 mg Calcium.

POINTS per serving: 1.

D i   G i o r n o   If all you can find is *polpo* (adult octopus), feel free to use that instead; some stores sell *polpo* parboiled, in which case you can omit Step 1. Or use 1/2 pound of calamari: Cut the bodies into 1/2-inch rings; rather than simmer them, boil the bodies and tentacles until they turn opaque, about 1 minute.

Anchovy Spread

Mayonnaise tempers the anchovy in this spread, so it has a mild, subtle anchovy taste. The anchovies are salty, so taste this before you add salt; you'll probably find it doesn't need any. This appetizer is a natural as part of an *antipasto misto.* Serve it with crisp crackers, or look for *carta di musica,* the crisp Sardinian flatbread that's so thin it resembles "sheet music."

Makes 20 servings

2 garlic cloves, peeled

1/2 cup packed flat-leaf parsley leaves

2 ounces anchovy fillets (about 15), rinsed and dried

1/4 cup low-fat mayonnaise

20 slices Italian bread

Puree the garlic, parsley, anchovies, and mayonnaise in a food processor. Spread about 1 teaspoon on each slice of bread.

Per serving: 93 Calories, 2 g Total Fat, 1 g Saturated Fat, 3 mg Cholesterol, 288 mg Sodium, 15 g Total Carbohydrate, 1 g Dietary Fiber, 4 g Protein, 33 mg Calcium.

POINTS per serving: 2.

D i   G i o r n o   Look for anchovies imported from Italy or other Mediterranean countries, which are the only producers of real anchovies (in other parts of the world, other little silver fish are often sold as anchovies). Most anchovies sold in the United States come packed in oil; occasionally you'll find them packed in salt.

Chicken Liver Pâté

Although pâtés are rare in most of Italy, they are very popular in Piedmont, the region that borders France and whose cuisine has a decidedly French influence. This creamy, smooth spread is very versatile: Use it to top crostini (use about 1 tablespoon for each slice of toast) or to stuff ravioli (use about 1 teaspoon for each).

Makes 18 servings

1/4 teaspoon olive oil

1 onion, sliced

1 tablespoon coarsely chopped sage

3/4 pound chicken livers, trimmed of all visible fat and rinsed

2 garlic cloves, chopped

1/2 teaspoon salt

1/4 teaspoon crushed red pepper

1/4 cup dry Marsala wine

1/4 cup plain dried bread crumbs

1/4 cup nonfat ricotta cheese

1. Heat a nonstick skillet. Swirl in the oil, then add the onion and sage. Sauté until the onion turns golden, then add the chicken livers. Cook, stirring constantly, until they are no longer pink. Add the garlic, salt, crushed red pepper, and wine. Cook, covered, over medium-low heat until the livers are cooked through, about 5 minutes.

2. Transfer to a food processor. Add the bread crumbs and ricotta and puree. Scrape the pâté into a bowl, cover, and refrigerate at least 1 hour to allow the flavors to blend.

Per serving (2 tablespoons): 49 Calories, 1 g Total Fat, 0 g Saturated Fat, 119 mg Cholesterol, 90 mg Sodium, 3 g Total Carbohydrate, 0 g Dietary Fiber, 5 g Protein, 13 mg Calcium.

POINTS per serving: 1.

Caponata

This robust dish gets its name from the word in Sicilian dialect meaning sailor's tavern (*caupone*). Sailors ate it with bread, but it's also great as a spread for a grilled chicken breast sandwich or, thinned with a little broth, as a pasta sauce.

Makes 4 servings

4 teaspoons olive oil

2 celery stalks, chopped

2 onions, chopped

1 garlic clove, minced

1 (1 1/2-pound) eggplant, coarsely chopped (do not peel)

4 plum tomatoes, chopped

1 cup low-sodium tomato juice

1 cup hot water

20 small black olives, pitted and chopped

2 tablespoons capers, drained

3 tablespoons red-wine vinegar

2 tablespoons sugar

1/4 teaspoon salt

Freshly ground pepper, to taste

1. Heat the oil in a nonstick skillet, then add the celery, onions, and garlic. Sauté until the onion is softened, about 3 minutes. Add the eggplant, tomatoes, tomato juice, water, olives, and capers; cover and cook, stirring frequently and adding 1/2 cup water at a time if necessary, until the vegetables are tender and the sauce thickens, 20–30 minutes.

2. Stir in the vinegar, sugar, salt, and pepper; reduce the heat and simmer, stirring frequently, 5 minutes. Serve at room temperature, or refrigerate for up to 5 days.

Per serving (3/4 cup): 212 Calories, 10 g Total Fat, 1 g Saturated Fat, 0 mg Cholesterol, 653 mg Sodium, 30 g Total Carbohydrate, 7 g Dietary Fiber, 4 g Protein, 50 mg Calcium.

POINTS per serving: 4.

Secrets of the Real Italian Kitchen

You don't need to spend a fortune on exotic ingredients to cook like an Italian grandmother. Her secret: a few well-chosen utensils and high-quality packaged goods—and a trip to the market every day for bread, meat or fish, garden-fresh produce, and other perishables. Here, a list of basics and staples you might want to start keeping on hand:

In the refrigerator:

Italian-style turkey sausage
Pancetta
Parmigiano-Reggiano
Part-skim mozzarella cheese
Pecorino Romano
Part-skim ricotta cheese
Pine nuts
Prosciutto di Parma
Turkey pepperoni

In the pantry:

Arborio rice
Balsamic vinegar
Bread crumbs
Canned and dried beans (chickpeas, cannellini, lentils)
Canned plum tomatoes
Capers
Cornmeal
Crushed red pepper
Dry red wine
Dry white wine
Garlic
Jars of olives (packed in brine)
Jars of roasted red peppers
Marsala wine
Olive oil
Onions
Pastas
Peperoncini
Tubes of tomato paste, olive paste, and anchovy paste

Equipment:

Heavy saucepan
Heavy skillet
Large pasta pot
Large strainer or colander
Meat mallet
Pasta fork
Pasta maker
Rotary grater

From the garden or greengrocer:

Arugula
Artichokes
Basil
Bell peppers
Broccoli rabe
Eggplant
Fennel
Flat-leaf parsley
Frying peppers
Green beans
Lemons
Mint
Mushrooms (cremini, porcini, portobello)
New potatoes
Oregano
Plum tomatoes
Rosemary
Sage
Thyme
Zucchini

Cannellini and Rosemary Spread

Cannellini are the white kidney beans popular throughout Italy, but you could easily substitute another white bean like navy or great Northern. For a milder spread, replace the hot sauce with $1/4$ teaspoon ground white pepper. Spread this on crackers or crusty bread (try it instead of mayonnaise on a chicken sandwich), or use as a dip for vegetables.

Makes 21 servings

1 (19-ounce) can cannellini beans, rinsed and drained

2 tablespoons fresh lemon juice

2 tablespoons rosemary leaves

5 drops hot pepper sauce

Puree the beans, lemon juice, rosemary, and hot pepper sauce in a food processor. Scrape into a bowl, cover, and refrigerate 15 minutes to allow the flavors to blend.

Per serving (1 tablespoon): 22 Calories, 0 g Total Fat, 0 g Saturated Fat, 0 mg Cholesterol, 55 mg Sodium, 4 g Total Carbohydrate, 1 g Dietary Fiber, 1 g Protein, 16 mg Calcium.

POINTS *per serving: 0.*

Cheese Fricos

Fricos, the crisp yet creamy cheese wafers popular in the northeastern region of Friuli, are served plain as an antipasto or on a bed of greens as a main-course salad. They should be a very pale gold—take care not to overcook them because they become chewy as they cool. Serve only two of these elegant "little trifles" per person, as they are extremely rich.

Makes 16 servings

6 ounces Montasio or Parmesan cheese, grated (about 2 cups)

Heat a large nonstick skillet over medium-low heat. Drop the cheese by the tablespoon into the skillet, then lightly flatten each with the back of a spatula. Cook until the cheese melts and is bubbling around the edge, 2–3 minutes. With two pliable rubber spatulas, carefully flip each frico over and cook 1 minute longer. Lift each out of the skillet with one of the spatulas and scrape onto a plate with the second. While the fricos are still hot, pat each into a circle. Repeat with the remaining cheese to make 32 fricos.

Per serving: 51 Calories, 4 g Total Fat, 2 g Saturated Fat, 12 mg Cholesterol, 35 mg Sodium, 0 g Total Carbohydrate, 0 g Dietary Fiber, 4 g Protein, 130 mg Calcium.

POINTS per serving: 1.

D i G i o r n o   When you make fricos, watch the heat like a hawk. If the pan is too hot, the cheese will brown too quickly; if it's not hot enough, the frico won't become properly crisp. When a single strand of cheese placed into the pan sizzles and bubbles in seconds, the temperature is just right, but adjust it as necessary while the fricos cook.

Potato Frico

Montasio is a sharp, hard Friulian cheese that is aged for 6 to 12 months; if you have a choice, opt for a younger cheese, or use Parmesan if you can't find Montasio.

Makes 8 servings

1 small red potato

3 ounces Montasio or Parmesan cheese, grated (about 1 cup)

1. Bring the potato and water to cover to a boil. Reduce the heat and simmer, covered, until just fork-tender, about 15 minutes. Drain and let cool, then peel and thinly slice crosswise.

2. Heat an 8-inch nonstick skillet over medium-low heat. Sprinkle half of the cheese into the pan, covering the bottom. Place the potato rounds in a single layer over the cheese, then top with the remaining cheese. Cook until the cheese melts and is bubbling around the edge, 4–6 minutes. With a pliable rubber spatula, slide the frico onto a plate. Invert the frico back into the pan and cook until the cheese is bubbling around the edge, 4–6 minutes longer. Slide onto the plate and cut into wedges.

Per serving: 60 Calories, 4 g Total Fat, 2 g Saturated Fat, 12 mg Cholesterol, 36 mg Sodium, 3 g Total Carbohydrate, 0 g Dietary Fiber, 4 g Protein, 131 mg Calcium.

***POINTS** per serving: 2.*

D i G i o r n o   Montasio's rind is inedible, so cut it off before you grate the cheese.

Sausage and Cauliflower Frico

Most supermarkets sell Italian-style turkey sausage in both link and bulk form, but it's so easy to make your own: Just finely grind 2 ounces turkey breast tenderloin, $1/4$ teaspoon fennel seed, and $1/2$ teaspoon Italian seasoning in a food processor.

Makes 8 servings

2 teaspoons olive oil

2 ounces Italian-style turkey sausage, crumbled (about $1/4$ cup)

$1/2$ cup chopped cauliflower florets

3 ounces Montasio or Parmesan cheese, grated (about 1 cup)

1. Heat the oil in a nonstick skillet. Sauté the sausage and cauliflower until the sausage is browned and the cauliflower is fork-tender, 7–10 minutes.

2. Heat an 8-inch nonstick skillet over medium-low heat. Sprinkle half of the cheese into the pan, covering the bottom. Spoon the sausage and cauliflower mixture over the cheese, then top with the remaining cheese. Cook until the cheese melts and is bubbling around the edge, 4–6 minutes. With a pliable rubber spatula, slide the frico onto a plate. Invert the frico back into the pan and cook until the cheese is bubbling around the edge, 4–6 minutes longer. Slide onto the plate and cut into wedges.

Per serving: 74 Calories, 6 g Total Fat, 3 g Saturated Fat, 18 mg Cholesterol, 80 mg Sodium, 1 g Total Carbohydrate, 0 g Dietary Fiber, 5 g Protein, 134 mg Calcium.

POINTS per serving: 2.

two

soups

Ribollita

Ribollita means "boiled again," and as with any soup worthy of such a name, it is much better the day after it's made. Authentic ribollita includes *cavalo nero*, a strongly flavored black kale originally from Tuscany. *Cavalo nero* is virtually unavailable in the United States, but kale makes a fine substitute.

Makes 8 servings

2 teaspoons olive oil

2 onions, chopped

1 slice Canadian bacon, julienned

2 garlic cloves, minced

1 (28-ounce) can Italian plum tomatoes (no salt added), chopped

4 celery stalks, chopped

1 carrot, sliced

2 (19-ounce) cans cannellini beans, rinsed and drained

1 bunch kale, cleaned and chopped

8 cups water

2 tablespoons minced sage leaves, or 2 teaspoons dried

1/4 teaspoon salt

Freshly ground pepper, to taste

2 tablespoons extra-virgin olive oil

1. Heat the oil in a nonstick saucepan, then add the onions, bacon, and garlic. Sauté until the onions are softened. Stir in the tomatoes, celery, and carrot. Reduce the heat and simmer until the celery and carrot are softened. Stir in the beans, kale, water, sage, salt, and pepper; bring to a boil. Reduce the heat and simmer, stirring frequently, until the kale is very tender and the soup thickens. Cool to room temperature; cover and refrigerate several hours or overnight.

2. Thirty minutes before serving, reheat the soup over low heat. Serve, drizzling each portion with 3/4 teaspoon extra-virgin oil.

Per serving: 263 Calories, 6 g Total Fat, 1 g Saturated Fat, 2 mg Cholesterol, 191 mg Sodium, 41 g Total Carbohydrate, 11 g Dietary Fiber, 15 g Protein, 202 mg Calcium.

POINTS per serving: 4.

Di Giorno   An easy, not-too-messy way to chop canned tomatoes: Insert kitchen scissors into the opened can and snip away.

Bean and Basil Soup

Friuli is a region known for its fine soups; there, bean and basil is a popular soup combination. Traditionally the soup is made with dried cranberry beans. However, in soups where the beans are pureed, we omit the time-consuming process of soaking and cooking dried beans by using canned beans. Great Northern beans (or any small white beans) are readily available in cans, but if you find canned cranberry beans, by all means use them instead.

Makes 4 servings

2 teaspoons olive oil

1 onion, finely chopped

3 garlic cloves, minced

1 large carrot, chopped

1 (15 1/2-ounce) can great Northern beans, rinsed and drained

3 cups chicken broth

1/3 cup finely chopped basil

1/2 teaspoon ground white pepper

1. Heat the oil in a nonstick saucepan, then add the onion. Sauté until softened. Add the garlic, carrot, and beans, then stir in the broth and bring to a boil. Reduce the heat and simmer, covered, until the vegetables are tender and can easily be mashed, about 15 minutes.

2. Transfer the soup to a food processor and puree. Return to the saucepan, stir in the basil and pepper, and heat to serving temperature.

Per serving: 203 Calories, 6 g Total Fat, 1 g Saturated Fat, 4 mg Cholesterol, 762 mg Sodium, 29 g Total Carbohydrate, 7 g Dietary Fiber, 10 g Protein, 81 mg Calcium.

POINTS per serving: 3.

D i G i o r n o   This soup is sometimes made with barley. If you'd like to make this heartier variation, stir in 1/3 cup of quick-cooking barley along with the broth, and do not puree the soup.

Minestrone

There are as many recipes for minestrone as there are cooks. Onions, carrots, potatoes, celery, and tomatoes are traditionally included, as well as three or four other vegetables, and small pasta. When cooked, dried beans have a firmer texture than canned beans, so they hold up better in a long-simmered soup like this one.

Makes 8 servings

1 cup dried cannellini beans, picked over, rinsed, and drained

8 cups low-sodium beef broth

$1/4$ teaspoon salt

Freshly ground pepper, to taste

2 teaspoons olive oil

2 onions, chopped

1 carrot, sliced

2 celery stalks, sliced

1 garlic clove, minced

1 (28-ounce) can Italian plum tomatoes (no salt added), chopped

$1/2$ cup minced parsley

3 cups coarsely chopped green cabbage

2 small zucchini, diced

$1/2$ cup ditalini or other small pasta

4 teaspoons grated Parmesan cheese

1. Combine the beans with cold water to cover by 2–3 inches; soak overnight.

2. Drain and rinse the beans, then put them in a large saucepan. Add the broth, salt, and pepper; bring to a simmer. Cover and cook until just tender, about 1 hour.

3. Meanwhile, heat the oil in a nonstick skillet, then add the onions, carrot, celery, and garlic. Sauté until the onions are softened. Stir the vegetables into the beans, then add the tomatoes and parsley. Simmer 30 minutes, then add the cabbage, zucchini, and pasta and simmer until the cabbage is tender, about 20 minutes. Remove from the heat; cover and let stand 10 minutes. Serve, sprinkled with the cheese.

Per serving: 197 Calories, 2 g Total Fat, 0 g Saturated Fat, 1 mg Cholesterol, 197 mg Sodium, 32 g Total Carbohydrate, 5 g Dietary Fiber, 14 g Protein, 113 mg Calcium.

POINTS per serving: 3.

Di Giorno   In Liguria, there's a peasant dish called *minestrone fritto*, or "fried minestrone." Leftover soup is thickened with flour, formed into patties, and sautéed in olive oil.

Pasta e Fagioli

Originally a peasant dish from the Veneto, this hearty pasta-and-bean soup is served at even the most sophisticated restaurants throughout Italy. Make it a day ahead; it will thicken and the flavors will blend.

Makes 4 servings

4 teaspoons olive oil

1 onion, chopped

2 celery stalks, chopped

1/2 carrot, sliced

1 slice Canadian bacon, diced

1 (19-ounce) can cannellini beans, rinsed and drained

3 cups low-sodium beef broth

1 (28-ounce) can Italian plum tomatoes (no salt added), chopped

1 cup tubetti or elbow macaroni

1/4 teaspoon salt

Freshly ground pepper, to taste

2 tablespoons grated Parmesan cheese

2 tablespoons minced fresh sage, or 1 teaspoon dried

1. Heat a nonstick saucepan. Swirl in the oil, then add the onion. Sauté until golden, then add the celery, carrot, and bacon. Sauté until the vegetables are softened. Add the beans, broth, and tomatoes; bring to a boil. Reduce the heat and simmer, stirring frequently, until slightly thickened.

2. Transfer 1 cup of the beans with a little of the cooking liquid to a food processor or blender and puree; return to the saucepan. Bring to a low boil. Stir in the tubetti, salt, and pepper; cook, stirring frequently, until the pasta is tender but still firm, about 5 minutes. Cool to room temperature; cover and refrigerate several hours or overnight.

3. Thirty minutes before serving, reheat the soup over low heat, adding 1/2 cup water at a time until the soup reaches the desired consistency. Serve, sprinkled with the cheese and sage.

Per serving: 467 Calories, 9 g Total Fat, 2 g Saturated Fat, 8 mg Cholesterol, 724 mg Sodium, 70 g Total Carbohydrate, 13 g Dietary Fiber, 27 g Protein, 198 mg Calcium.

POINTS *per serving: 7.*

Aromatic White Bean Soup with Vegetables

Though you might associate ginger more with Asian cooking, it is fairly common throughout Italy, having been brought with other spices via the trade routes.

Makes 4 servings

³/₄ cup dried great Northern beans, picked over, rinsed, and drained

2 teaspoons olive oil

2 fennel bulbs, trimmed and chopped

2 onions, chopped

2 celery stalks, chopped

2 garlic cloves, minced

2 tablespoons grated peeled fresh ginger

1 bay leaf

¹/₂ teaspoon crushed red pepper

5 cups water

2 medium all-purpose potatoes, cooked and diced

2 tomatoes, chopped

¹/₄ cup chopped flat-leaf parsley

1 teaspoon salt

¹/₄ teaspoon ground white pepper

2 tablespoons fresh lemon juice

1. Combine the beans with cold water to cover by 2–3 inches; soak overnight. Drain, discarding the liquid.

2. Heat the oil in a nonstick saucepan, then add the fennel, onions, and celery. Sauté until the vegetables soften. Add the garlic and ginger and sauté until aromatic. Add the bay leaf, crushed red pepper, beans, and water; bring to a boil. Reduce the heat and simmer, stirring occasionally, until the beans are tender, about 1 hour. Remove from the heat to cool slightly. Discard the bay leaf.

3. Working in batches if necessary, transfer the soup to a food processor and puree. Return to the saucepan and add the potatoes, tomatoes, parsley, salt, and pepper; heat to serving temperature. Stir in the lemon juice just before serving.

Per serving: 262 Calories, 3 g Total Fat, 0 g Saturated Fat, 0 mg Cholesterol, 635 mg Sodium, 49 g Total Carbohydrate, 20 g Dietary Fiber, 12 g Protein, 138 mg Calcium.

POINTS per serving: 1.

D i   G i o r n o   To soak the beans quickly, put them in a large saucepan and add water to cover. Bring to a boil, then boil for 2 minutes. Remove from the heat, cover, and let stand for 1 hour. Drain off the water before using.

Lentil Soup

This soup tastes great, freezes well, and is low in fat, high in fiber. It's also versatile: Toss in a few cubed potatoes when you add the carrots, or stir in a handful of chopped spinach or escarole 10 or 15 minutes before serving.

Makes 8 servings

2 teaspoons olive oil

2 onions, finely chopped

1 garlic clove, minced

1 (1-pound) bag lentils, picked over, rinsed, and drained

8 cups water

2 carrots, sliced

4 celery stalks, sliced

3 leeks, cleaned and sliced

1 (14¹/₂-ounce) can Italian plum tomatoes (no salt added), finely chopped

2 tablespoons red-wine vinegar

1 tablespoon minced sage

1 bay leaf

¹/₄ teaspoon salt

Freshly ground pepper, to taste

1. Heat a nonstick saucepan. Swirl in the oil, then add the onions and garlic. Sauté until the onions are golden. Add the lentils and water; bring to a boil. Stir in the carrots, celery, and leeks. Cover, reduce the heat and simmer, stirring occasionally, until the lentils and vegetables are tender, about 45 minutes.

2. Stir in the tomatoes, vinegar, sage, bay leaf, salt, and pepper; if the soup looks too thick, add 1–2 cups of water. Cover and simmer 30 minutes longer, stirring frequently. Discard the bay leaf.

Per serving: 253 Calories, 2 g Total Fat, 0 g Saturated Fat, 0 mg Cholesterol, 109 mg Sodium, 44 g Total Carbohydrate, 9 g Dietary Fiber, 17 g Protein, 80 mg Calcium.

POINTS per serving: 3.

D i G i o r n o   Our favorite way to freeze soup: Ladle it into zip-close freezer bags, squeeze out all the air, and seal. Press the bags so they're fairly flat and the soup is evenly distributed, then stack them like tiles. They'll take up much less room in your freezer, and they'll thaw in about 15 minutes in a bowl of warm water.

Zuppa di Verdura

The two types of potatoes in this hearty country soup serve two different purposes: Delicate Yukon gold potatoes fall apart easily and are used as a thickener. Firm red potatoes retain their shape and roast wonderfully. For a more assertive flavor, substitute an equal amount of chopped basil for the parsley, in the style of Veneto.

Makes 8 servings

- 1 cup baby carrots, halved crosswise
- 6 garlic cloves, peeled
- 1 green bell pepper, seeded and cut into chunks
- 2 medium zucchini, cut into chunks
- 2 celery stalks, cut into chunks
- 1 leek, cleaned and cut into chunks
- 1/4 pound green beans, cut into chunks
- 2 medium red potatoes, peeled and cut into chunks
- 5 1/2 cups vegetable broth
- 2 medium Yukon gold potatoes, peeled and grated
- 1 large tomato, peeled, seeded, and cut into chunks
- 1/4 cup packed chopped flat-leaf parsley
- 1/4 teaspoon salt
- 1/4 teaspoon freshly ground pepper

1. Preheat the oven to 400°F. Combine the carrots, garlic, bell pepper, zucchini, celery, leek, green beans, red potatoes, and 1 cup of the broth in a baking dish. Roast until the vegetables are fork-tender, about 30 minutes.

2. Transfer the vegetables and pan juices to a saucepan. Add the Yukon Gold potatoes, the tomato, and the remaining 4 1/2 cups of broth; bring to a boil. Reduce the heat and simmer, covered, until the soup thickens slightly, about 15 minutes. Stir in the parsley, salt, and pepper.

Per serving: 100 Calories, 1 g Total Fat, 0 g Saturated Fat, 0 mg Cholesterol, 791 mg Sodium, 22 g Total Carbohydrate, 4 g Dietary Fiber, 4 g Protein, 44 mg Calcium.

POINTS per serving: 1.

Zuppa di Verdura

Roasted Squash Soup

This soup is thickened much like a *zuppa,* but instead of bread or potato, we use squash, in Piedmontese style. Acorn squash has a strong, rich flavor, so if you prefer a slightly sweeter soup, substitute butternut squash.

Makes 6 servings

1 large acorn squash, halved and seeded

1 large onion, peeled and quartered

1 1/2 cups vegetable broth

1/2 cup fat-free milk

1/2 teaspoon ground allspice

1/2 teaspoon salt

1/4 teaspoon ground white pepper

Fresh grated nutmeg

1. Preheat the oven to 400°F. Combine the squash, onion, and 1/2 cup of the broth in a baking dish. Cover with foil and roast until very tender, about 45 minutes.

2. Scoop the squash pulp into a food processor (discard the skin). Add the onion, pan juices, and the remaining cup of broth and puree, then transfer to a saucepan. Stir in the milk, allspice, salt, and pepper and heat to serving temperature. Serve, topped with freshly grated nutmeg.

Per serving: 52 Calories, 0 g Total Fat, 0 g Saturated Fat, 0 mg Cholesterol, 457 mg Sodium, 12 g Total Carbohydrate, 2 g Dietary Fiber, 2 g Protein, 56 mg Calcium.

POINTS per serving: 1.

Di Giorno   Ground spices are certainly convenient, but it's the rare cook who uses a container before the flavor and fragrance have dissipated (generally in six months to a year). Whole spices, on the other hand, can last for years, and they really aren't so difficult to use. You'll need a special grater for nutmeg, but most other spices can be ground in a clean coffee grinder. (An easy way to clean the mill: Whirl a slice of white bread after each time you grind spices. The bread will absorb the bits of spice as well as the aromatic oils.)

Onion Minestra

This soup reflects the French influence on the cuisine of northern Italy. While the French would caramelize the onion first, the Italians just sauté it lightly to soften. Barley is a popular grain throughout northern Italy, from Friuli in the east to Piedmont in the west.

Makes 8 servings

1/2 tablespoon olive oil

2 large onions, thinly sliced

6 cups beef broth

4 bay leaves

1/8 teaspoon crushed red pepper

1/2 cup quick-cooking barley

8 teaspoons grated pecorino Romano cheese

Heat the oil in a nonstick saucepan, then add the onions. Sauté until soft and translucent, about 10 minutes. Add the broth, bay leaves, and crushed red pepper; bring just to a boil. Stir in the barley, reduce the heat, and simmer, covered, until the barley is tender, 15–20 minutes. Discard the bay leaves. Serve, sprinkled with the cheese.

Per serving: 77 Calories, 1 g Total Fat, 0 g Saturated Fat, 0 mg Cholesterol, 752 mg Sodium, 11 g Total Carbohydrate, 3 g Dietary Fiber, 5 g Protein, 15 mg Calcium.

***POINTS** per serving: 1.*

Fennel and Onion Zuppa

This is a chunky *zuppa*; for a smoother soup, puree it after cooking. Tuscan in origin, fennel in Italy is sometimes called Florence fennel. In American supermarkets, it may be labeled anise. Reserve the fronds when you trim the fennel; it makes a pretty garnish.

Makes 6 servings

2 teaspoons olive oil

1 onion, halved lengthwise, then thinly sliced crosswise

1 large fennel bulb, halved lengthwise, then thinly sliced crosswise (reserve the fronds)

1 medium Yukon gold potato, peeled and grated

4 cups chicken broth

1 teaspoon salt

1/4 teaspoon freshly ground pepper

Heat the oil in a nonstick saucepan, then add the onion. Sauté until translucent, then add the fennel, potato, broth, salt, and pepper. Bring to a simmer and cook, covered, until the soup is very thick and the vegetables are tender, about 45 minutes. Serve, garnished with the reserved fennel fronds.

Per serving: 75 Calories, 4 g Total Fat, 1 g Saturated Fat, 3 mg Cholesterol, 1,076 mg Sodium, 8 g Total Carbohydrate, 2 g Dietary Fiber, 2 g Protein, 25 mg Calcium.

POINTS *per serving: 1.*

Spinach and Rice Soup

If you're familiar with the creamy texture Arborio rice gives to a risotto, you can imagine how it thickens this simple soup.

Makes 4 servings

2 (10-ounce) bags triple-washed spinach, cleaned (do not dry)

2 teaspoons olive oil

1 small onion, chopped

4 cups low-sodium chicken broth

1/2 cup Arborio rice

4 teaspoons grated Parmesan cheese

1. Put the spinach in a nonstick saucepan; cover and cook over low heat until the leaves are just tender, 2–3 minutes. Drain over a bowl, reserving the liquid.

2. Heat the oil in the saucepan, then add the onion. Sauté until softened, about 3 minutes. Add the spinach and cook, stirring constantly, until wilted, about 2 minutes. Add the broth and spinach liquid and bring to a boil. Stir in the rice, reduce the heat, and simmer, stirring occasionally, until the rice is tender, about 30 minutes. Serve, sprinkled with the cheese.

Per serving: 179 Calories, 6 g Total Fat, 2 g Saturated Fat, 1 mg Cholesterol, 287 mg Sodium, 27 g Total Carbohydrate, 4 g Dietary Fiber, 10 g Protein, 183 mg Calcium.

POINTS *per serving 3.*

Tortellini in Brodo

Both Bologna and Modena claim to have invented *tortellini* ("little cakes"—although the inspiration for their shape is said to be Venus' navel); they are now common throughout Italy. In Emilia-Romagna, these are called *cappelletti* ("little caps"). Vary this recipe by using your favorite filled pastas and broths.

Makes 8 servings

8 cups low-sodium vegetable broth

48 Meat-Filled Tortellini (page 52), or 1 (12-ounce) package frozen meat-filled tortellini

4 teaspoons grated Parmesan cheese

Bring the broth to a boil; add the tortellini. When the broth returns to a boil, reduce the heat and simmer until the tortellini are tender but still firm around the edges. Serve, sprinkled with the cheese.

Per serving: 214 Calories, 6 g Total Fat, 2 g Saturated Fat, 91 mg Cholesterol, 296 mg Sodium, 28 g Total Carbohydrate, 1 g Dietary Fiber, 11 g Protein, 87 mg Calcium.

POINTS per serving: 5.

D i G i o r n o   Cooking frozen tortellini in the broth means one less pot to dirty, but you might find the broth gets too starchy. Try cooking the tortellini separately and stirring them in at the last minute.

Orzo in Brodo

Brodos, or clear broths, often have cooked pasta added at the end of cooking (in a *minestra,* the pasta is cooked in the broth; the starch it gives off thickens the soup). In Italian, the word *orzo* refers to what we would call barley. To get one cup of cooked orzo, cook $1/3$ cup raw orzo in boiling salted water until al dente, about 8 minutes.

Makes 4 servings

12 garlic cloves, roasted (page 5) and peeled

$1/4$ teaspoon salt

3 cups chicken broth

1 cup cooked orzo

$1^1/2$ cups arugula, chopped (about $1^1/2$ ounces)

Freshly ground pepper, to taste

Puree the garlic, salt, and $1/4$ cup of the broth in a food processor. Put the remaining $2^3/4$ cups of broth in a saucepan. Stir in the garlic mixture and bring to a simmer. Stir in the orzo, arugula, and pepper and heat to serving temperature.

Per serving: 124 Calories, 3 g Total Fat, 1 g Saturated Fat, 4 mg Cholesterol, 900 mg Sodium, 19 g Total Carbohydrate, 1 g Dietary Fiber, 4 g Protein, 32 mg Calcium.

POINTS per serving: 3.

Di Giorno   Italians use larger, mature arugula leaves in soups. They have a more assertive flavor than the mild baby leaves typically used in salads.

Tuscan Tripe Soup

Tripe, the lining of a cow's stomach, is beloved by many Italians. We call for honeycomb tripe, which is the most tender, has the most delicate flavor, and is the most readily available in supermarkets. When cooked, it has a soft yet crunchy texture. Choose a tripe that is a pale off-white; refrigerate it for no more than one day. Most supermarket meat departments sell fresh tripe, which has actually been cleaned and partially cooked. It is far superior to frozen tripe.

Makes 8 servings

1/2 pound fresh honeycomb tripe

8 cups cold water

1 teaspoon olive oil

1 onion, sliced

1 carrot, sliced

1 celery stalk, sliced

3 garlic cloves, minced

1/8 teaspoon crushed red pepper

1 medium red potato, peeled and chopped

4 cups beef broth

Salt, to taste

Freshly ground pepper, to taste

1 teaspoon Italian seasoning

1/2 cup toasted bread cubes

1. Combine the tripe and water in a nonstick saucepan. Bring to a simmer and cook, uncovered, until the tripe is firm and turns pure white, about 5 minutes. Drain, rinse, and cut into thin strips.

2. Rinse and dry the saucepan. Heat it, swirl in the oil, then add the onion, carrot, celery, garlic, and crushed red pepper. Sauté until the onion turns translucent. Return the tripe to the pot. Add the potato, broth, salt, pepper, and Italian seasoning. Bring to a simmer and cook, covered, until the tripe is fork-tender, about 2 hours. Stir in the bread cubes before serving.

Per serving: 74 Calories, 2 g Total Fat, 1 g Saturated Fat, 27 mg Cholesterol, 822 mg Sodium, 7 g Total Carbohydrate, 1 g Dietary Fiber, 7 g Protein, 16 mg Calcium.

POINTS per serving: 1.

D i G i o r n o   We leave the tripe a bit crunchy, as they would in Italy. If you prefer the soft, meltingly tender tripe as in menudo, simmer the soup for an additional 45 to 60 minutes. You can, of course, buy croutons in any number of flavorings, but we think they're best when freshly made: Cut the bread into 1/2-inch cubes and toast under the broiler for about 3 minutes, shaking the pan midway through.

Learning to Love Something New

As you explore Italian food, you're bound to come across some ingredients you're certain you dislike. Perhaps it's something strongly flavored, like anchovies, capers, or broccoli rabe, or an animal you don't like the looks of—squid (*calamari*), octopus (*polpo*), or whelk (*scungilli*). Maybe it's a food you didn't even know was edible, like tripe (cow's stomach), or an all-time "unfavorite," like liver. There are many wonderful Italian dishes that celebrate these ingredients, and giving them a try might just cure you—or someone you cook for—of neophobia (fear of the new). Consider:

• If you didn't like something in the past, don't assume you'll never like it. Tastes change: You liked baby food once, but would probably find it bland and mushy now.

• You may not have had the food cooked or handled properly. If well made, calamari is tender and delicious; badly made, it's like rubber bands. Remember, too, that there are many ways to prepare any food; anchovies on pizza might be too much to handle, but a little anchovy sauce on a swordfish may knock your socks off (try Broiled Swordfish with Anchovy-Crumb Crust on page 175). Try a new food at your favorite restaurant—chances are, the chef will make it in a way you'll love.

• You may have had a bad experience when you first tried the food; perhaps your mother wouldn't give you dessert until you'd finished your liver, for example. These associations are learned—and can be unlearned, too. To retry a food you disliked, have the food in a pleasant, pressure-free setting. You just might like it.

• Try the food when you've worked up a good appetite. Studies show that hunger can increase the preference for a food.

• Pair a food you think you dislike with something you love—like serving calamari in a rich homemade tomato sauce over your favorite pasta (try our recipe for Linguine with Calamari in Tomato Sauce on page 85), sprinkling capers over a beloved veal dish (try Veal Scallopine with Lemon and Capers, page 211) or combine pungent broccoli rabe with potatoes (see page 242 for Broccoli Rabe with Potatoes), and feel free to cut the amount of greens in half, or even a quarter, just to get yourself started. This association with a taste you already like is called "flavor-flavor learning" by researchers.

• Don't give up. Studies show that children (the rulers of the picky-eater kingdom) need to be exposed to a new food ten times before they'll accept it; you just might, too.

Zuppa di Prosciutto

Prosciutto is an Italian cured ham. Try to find authentic *prosciutto di Parma* (it's available at many supermarket deli counters). Its distinctive flavor really shines in this simple soup.

Makes 6 servings

1 medium red potato, peeled and chopped

4 cups chicken broth

2 garlic cloves, peeled

1/2 cup Italian bread cubes

2 slices (about 1 ounce) prosciutto, chopped

1/8 teaspoon crushed red pepper

Combine the potato and broth in a saucepan; press in the garlic. Cook until the potato is fork-tender, about 15 minutes. Stir in the bread cubes, prosciutto, and crushed red pepper. Cook until the potato and bread fall apart when whisked, about 10 minutes longer.

Per serving: 59 Calories, 4 g Total Fat, 1 g Saturated Fat, 6 mg Cholesterol, 740 mg Sodium, 4 g Total Carbohydrate, 0 g Dietary Fiber, 2 g Protein, 5 mg Calcium.

POINTS per serving: 2.

D i   G i o r n o   *Zuppa* is the Italian word for a soup that is thickened with bread or potato; this recipe uses both. This is a perfect way to use up bread past its prime—in Italy, where fresh bread is acquired daily, *zuppe* are made with the day-old bread.

Zuppa di Pesce

In Apulia, fish *zuppe* usually include chile pepper and a summer squash. Sea scallops are traditional, but if you can find the smaller, sweeter, highly seasonal bay scallops, by all means use them. All this hearty soup needs is a loaf of crusty bread as an accompaniment.

Makes 4 servings

2 teaspoons olive oil

1 medium zucchini, chopped

1/4 teaspoon crushed red pepper

2 cloves garlic, peeled

1 (8-ounce) bottle clam juice

1 cup water

1 (14 1/2-ounce) can diced tomatoes

1 tablespoon plain dried bread crumbs

2 tablespoons minced flat-leaf parsley

2 tablespoons chopped basil

Salt, to taste

Freshly ground pepper, to taste

1/2 pound cleaned calamari, bodies cut into rings

1/2 pound sea scallops, quartered

Heat a nonstick saucepan. Swirl in the oil, then add the zucchini and crushed red pepper. Sauté until the zucchini is browned. Press in the garlic and sauté until fragrant. Stir in the clam juice, water, and tomatoes. Reduce the heat and simmer, covered, 15 minutes. Stir in the bread crumbs, parsley, basil, salt, pepper, calamari, and scallops. Cook until the seafood turns opaque, about 5 minutes longer.

Per serving: 185 Calories, 4 g Total Fat, 1 g Saturated Fat, 151 mg Cholesterol, 673 mg Sodium, 16 g Total Carbohydrate, 2 g Dietary Fiber, 21 g Protein, 62 mg Calcium.

POINTS per serving: 4.

Clam and Leek Minestra

Minestre are soups that include pasta or rice; unlike a *brodo,* where cooked pasta is stirred in at the end so the broth stays clear, the pasta or rice is cooked in the *minestra,* so the soup is thicker. Arborio rice lends a particularly creamy texture to the soup. You can use whole clams, as we did for the soup in the photograph. Simply substitute 3 dozen littleneck or mahogany clams for the canned.

Makes 4 servings

1/2 tablespoon olive oil

1 red finger chile pepper, seeded and chopped

2 medium leeks, cleaned and sliced

3 (6-ounce) cans chopped clams, drained (reserve juice)

2 1/2 cups chicken broth

1/2 cup Arborio rice

2 tablespoons chopped flat-leaf parsley

Heat a nonstick saucepan. Swirl in the oil, then add the chile. Sauté until it begins to sizzle, then add the leek and sauté until it turns golden, 2–3 minutes. Add the clam juice, the broth, and rice; bring just to a boil. Reduce the heat and simmer, covered, until the rice is tender, about 20 minutes, do not let the soup boil. Add the clams, then stir in the parsley.

Per serving: 173 Calories, 3.5 g Total Fat, .5 g Saturated Fat, 44 mg Cholesterol, 389 mg Sodium, 16 g Total Carbohydrate, .5 g Dietary Fiber, 18 g Protein, 73 mg Calcium.

POINTS per serving: 3.5.

D i G i o r n o   The emperor Nero was said to have played the fiddle while Rome burned, but he must have considered himself something of a singer as well. According to legend, he ate leeks often, believing that they would improve his singing voice.

Clam and Leek Minestra

three

pasta

Fresh Pasta Dough

Light and tender, this pasta can be used in just about any recipe. If you're using it for filled pasta, your yield will vary slightly, depending on the thinness and elasticity of the dough. Once rolled and cut, the pasta can be used fresh, dried, or frozen.

Makes 4 servings (about 1 pound fresh pasta dough or 6–8 ounces dried pasta, enough for 48 filled pastas)

1 3/4 cups all-purpose flour

3 eggs, at room temperature

1/4 teaspoon salt

Manual Method:

1. Spoon about $1^{1}/2$ cups of the flour onto a clean, dry countertop, and make a well in the center. Break the eggs into the well and add the salt. With a fork or small whisk, lightly beat eggs, gradually incorporating the flour. When the dough becomes very thick and too difficult to stir, gather it into a ball with your hands; the dough should feel wet and sticky. Set it aside.

2. Scrape up the flour and any bits of dough that are stuck to the counter. Transfer to a sieve and shake the flour back onto the counter; discard any dried pieces of dough. Gradually knead the sifted flour and the remaining $1/4$ cup of flour into the dough until it is smooth, satiny and no longer sticky, 5–7 minutes.

3. Transfer the dough to a roller-type pasta machine and proceed according to the manufacturer's instructions.

Food Processor Method:

1. Fit a food processor with the plastic blade. Put $1^{1}/4$ cups of the flour into the work bowl. Lightly beat the eggs and salt in a separate bowl; add to the flour. Pulse until the dough is blended and crumbly but does not yet hold together in a ball, 4–5 times.

2. Turn the dough onto a clean, dry counter and knead, gradually incorporating the remaining $1/2$ cup of flour, until the dough is smooth, satiny, and no longer sticky, 5–7 minutes.

3. Transfer the dough to a roller-type pasta machine and proceed according to the manufacturer's instructions.

To Dry the Pasta:

Dust the cut pasta lightly with flour and lay it flat on cotton towels, or drape it over drying racks or the backs of chairs. When dry, carefully transfer it to a large bowl or platter. Store, uncovered, in a cool dry place 2–3 days, in the refrigerator 2–3 weeks, or freeze in zip-close bags up to 1 month.

To Cook the Pasta:

Bring 4 quarts of water to a full boil. Add the pasta and stir; when the water returns to a boil, stir again and begin timing. Fresh pasta takes only 10–15 seconds to cook after the water returns to a boil; if it has been dried or frozen, it will take a few minutes longer. Test frequently for doneness. Drain the pasta; do not rinse with cold water.

Per serving: 248 Calories, 4 g Total Fat, 1 g Saturated Fat, 159 mg Cholesterol, 183 mg Sodium, 41 g Total Carbohydrate, 1 g Dietary Fiber, 10 g Protein, 27 mg Calcium.

POINTS *per serving: 5.*

Di Giorno   Eggs can harbor dangerous bacteria and should never be left at room temperature for more than 30 minutes. To warm them safely and rapidly, put them in a bowl of very warm (not hot) water for no more than ten minutes.

Meat-Filled Tortellini

You can use this filling for tortellini, cappelletti, or ravioli. Try it with different sauces or broths to enhance its delicate flavor and texture. However, try it at least once with the classic Tomato-Herb Sauce (page 61) and a light sprinkling of freshly grated Parmesan cheese. Since each tortellini requires only $1/2$ teaspoon of the filling, a little goes a long way. Double or halve the recipe, or freeze any leftovers.

Makes 4 servings

1 teaspoon olive oil

1 ounce ground skinless turkey breast

1 ounce ground skinless chicken breast

$1/4$ teaspoon ground white pepper

1 slice high-quality bologna, chopped

$1/4$ cup part-skim ricotta cheese

2 tablespoons grated Parmesan cheese

1 egg white

$1/4$ teaspoon ground nutmeg

1 pound Fresh Pasta Dough (page 50)

1. Heat the oil in a nonstick skillet, then add the turkey, chicken, and pepper. Brown the meats, breaking them apart with a spoon. With a slotted spoon, transfer to a cutting board. Add the bologna and mince until very fine. Combine the meats with the ricotta, Parmesan, egg white, and nutmeg. Cover and refrigerate until firm, at least 1 hour but no more than 12 hours.

2. Lightly dust a countertop with flour. Put a sheet of wax paper on a baking sheet and lightly spray with nonstick spray. Break off a chunk of pasta dough the size of a lemon; cover the remaining dough. Using a roller-type pasta machine, roll the dough as thin as possible into a roughly 6 × 18-inch rectangle. Set on the floured counter.

3. With a $2^{1}/2$–3-inch biscuit cutter or sharp-rimmed glass, cut the dough into 12 disks. One at a time, put $1/2$ teaspoon of the filling in the center of each disk; fold in half to form a semicircle, then press the edges firmly to seal. Holding the disk gently between your index finger and thumb with curved edge up, wrap it around your index finger until the two ends meet, then fold the curved top down. Pinch the ends firmly to seal. As you finish sealing each tortellini, place it on the wax paper, making sure it doesn't touch any others. Repeat with the remaining dough (incorporate scraps into your next sheets) and filling to make 48 tortellini. Refrigerate, uncovered, until ready to use, up to 2 days, turning them occasionally to dry evenly, or freeze them first on the wax paper–lined baking sheet, then in zip-close plastic bags up to 1 month. (They are easier to handle when frozen.) Do not thaw before cooking.

4. To cook, gently drop the tortellini, a few at a time, into a large pot of boiling water; if fresh, make sure they don't stick to one another. Cook until tender, 7–8 minutes. With a slotted spoon, transfer to a warm serving bowl. Add the sauce of your choice and toss gently to coat.

Per serving: 351 Calories, 11 g Total Fat, 4 g Saturated Fat, 181 mg Cholesterol, 410 mg Sodium, 43 g Total Carbohydrate, 1 g Dietary Fiber, 19 g Protein, 146 mg Calcium.

POINTS per serving: 8.

Pumpkin-Filled Cappelletti

Pumpkin puree makes this pasta stuffing easy; make a double or even triple batch of cappelletti and freeze the filled pasta for holiday dinners (use them within three months of freezing). For the simple yet delicious sauce seen in the photograph, heat a little butter with some crumbled fresh or dried sage. The herb's slightly bitter flavor provides a perfect foil for the sweet filling.

Makes 4 servings

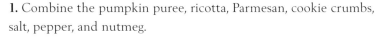

- **¹/₂ cup canned pumpkin puree**
- **1 tablespoon part-skim ricotta cheese**
- **2 tablespoons grated Parmesan cheese**
- **¹/₂ amaretti cookie (1-inch diameter), crushed into fine crumbs**
- **¹/₂ teaspoon salt**
- **¹/₄ teaspoon ground white pepper**
- **¹/₈ teaspoon ground nutmeg**
- **1 pound Fresh Pasta Dough (page 50)**

1. Combine the pumpkin puree, ricotta, Parmesan, cookie crumbs, salt, pepper, and nutmeg.

2. Lightly dust a countertop with flour. Place a sheet of wax paper on a baking sheet and lightly spray with nonstick spray. Break off a chunk of pasta dough the size of a lemon; cover the remaining dough. Using a roller-type pasta machine, roll the dough as thin as possible. Set on the floured counter and trim to form a 6 × 18-inch rectangle.

3. With a sharp knife or pastry cutter, cut the dough into 3-inch squares. One at a time, put ¹/₂ teaspoon of the filling in the center of each square; fold in half to make a triangle. Seal the edges and fold back the peaked edge. Holding gently between your index finger and thumb with the point up, wrap around your index finger and press the ends lightly to seal. As you finish sealing each cappelletti, place it on the wax paper, making sure it doesn't touch any others. Repeat with the remaining dough (incorporate scraps into your next sheets) and filling to make 48 cappelletti. Refrigerate, uncovered, until ready to use, up to 8 hours, or freeze them first on the wax paper–lined baking sheet, then in zip-close plastic bags up to 1 month. (They are easier to handle when frozen.) Do not thaw before cooking.

4. To cook, gently drop the cappelletti, a few at a time, into a large pot of boiling water; if fresh, make sure they don't stick to one another. Cook until tender, 7–8 minutes. With a slotted spoon, transfer to a serving bowl. Add the sauce of your choice and toss gently.

Per serving: 290 Calories, 6 g Total Fat, 2 g Saturated Fat, 165 mg Cholesterol, 423 mg Sodium, 44 g Total Carbohydrate, 1 g Dietary Fiber, 13 g Protein, 117 mg Calcium.

POINTS *per serving: 6.*

Pumpkin-Filled Cappelletti with sage butter

Greens-Filled Ravioli

Swiss chard and spinach, accented with a bit of onion and creamy ricotta cheese, make a delicious pasta filling. Any leftovers can be refrigerated for up to two days, or frozen. Nothing beats a simple tomato sauce to enhance the flavor of this filling.

Makes 4 servings

1 cup cleaned Swiss chard leaves

1 cup cleaned spinach leaves

1 teaspoons olive oil

1 slice prosciutto, finely chopped

2 tablespoons minced onion

1/4 cup part-skim ricotta cheese

2 tablespoons grated Parmesan cheese

1 egg white, lightly beaten

1/4 teaspoon ground nutmeg

1/4 teaspoon ground white pepper

1 pound Fresh Pasta Dough (page 50)

1. Put the chard and spinach in a steamer basket; set in a saucepan over 1 inch of boiling water. Cover tightly and steam until tender, 2–3 minutes. Squeeze out any excess moisture and chop finely.

2. Heat the oil in a nonstick skillet, then add the prosciutto and onion. Sauté until the onion is softened. Add the greens; reduce the heat and stir until thoroughly coated with oil. Stir in the ricotta, Parmesan, egg white, nutmeg, and pepper.

3. Lightly dust a countertop with flour. Put a sheet of wax paper on a baking sheet and lightly spray with nonstick spray. Break off a chunk of pasta dough the size of a lemon; cover the remaining dough. Using a roller-type pasta machine, roll the dough as thin as possible. Set on the floured counter and trim to form a 6 × 17-inch rectangle.

4. Starting 1 inch from the top and side edges, put half-teaspoons of the filling 2 inches apart on the pasta. Break off another lemon-size chunk of dough, incorporating the scraps from the first sheet. Roll out another sheet of dough and trim to form another 6 × 17-inch rectangle. Gently place over the filling. To seal the edges, trace lines between the dots of filling, first lengthwise, then crosswise, with a moistened finger. With a pastry cutter, cut over the lines to make twenty-four 2-inch squares. Carefully lift and transfer to the wax paper, making sure the ravioli don't touch one another. Repeat with the remaining dough (incorporate scraps into your next sheets or freeze) and filling to make 48 ravioli. Refrigerate, uncovered, until ready to use, up to 2 days, or freeze first on the wax paper–lined baking sheet, then in zip-close plastic bags up to 1 month. (They are easier to handle when frozen.) Do not thaw before cooking.

5. To cook, gently drop the ravioli, a few at a time, into a large pot of boiling water; if fresh, make sure they don't stick to one another. Cook until tender, 7–8 minutes. With a slotted spoon, carefully transfer to a warm serving bowl. Add the sauce of your choice and toss gently to coat.

Per serving: 328 Calories, 9 g Total Fat, 3 g Saturated Fat, 171 mg Cholesterol, 425 mg Sodium, 44 g Total Carbohydrate, 2 g Dietary Fiber, 17 g Protein, 163 mg Calcium.

POINTS *per serving: 7.*

D i G i o r n o   Like England's Stilton and France's Camembert, Parmigiano-Reggiano is one of the world's great cheeses. This aged, straw-colored hard cheese has a granular texture and a deep, nutty flavor that becomes buttery in the mouth. Grated over pasta or stirred into a risotto or soup, it awakens other flavors without overwhelming them. It also makes a superb table cheese: For a spectacular finish to a meal, break off small chunks of Parmigiano-Reggiano and serve with fresh fruit (or dip the chunks into fine, aged balsamic vinegar).

Cheese-Filled Ravioli

This filling does not keep well in the refrigerator, so plan either to use it the same day you make it or to freeze it. Thaw in the refrigerator and use within one to two hours of thawing.

Makes 4 servings

1/2 cup part-skim ricotta cheese

2 tablespoons grated Parmesan cheese

2 tablespoons minced flat-leaf parsley

1/2 egg white

1/4 teaspoon ground white pepper

1/8 teaspoon ground nutmeg

1 pound Fresh Pasta Dough (page 50)

1. Combine the cheeses, parsley, egg white, pepper, and nutmeg.

2. Lightly dust a countertop with flour. Put a sheet of wax paper on a baking sheet and lightly spray with nonstick spray. Break off a chunk of pasta dough the size of a lemon; cover the remaining dough. Using a roller-type pasta machine, roll the dough as thin as possible. Set on the floured counter and trim to form a 6 × 17-inch rectangle.

3. Starting 1 inch from the top and side edges, put half-teaspoons of filling 2 inches apart on the pasta. Break off another lemon-size chunk of dough, incorporating the scraps from the first sheet. Roll out another sheet of dough and trim to form another 6 × 17-inch rectangle. Gently place over first layer to cover the filling. To seal the edges, trace lines between the dots of filling with a moistened finger. With a pastry cutter, cut over the lines to make 24 squares. Carefully transfer to the wax paper, making sure the ravioli don't touch one another. Repeat with the remaining dough (incorporate scraps into your next sheets and filling to make 48 ravioli. Refrigerate, uncovered, until ready to use, up to 2 hours or freeze first on the wax paper–lined baking sheet, then in zip-close plastic bags up to 1 month. (They are easier to handle when frozen.) Do not thaw before cooking.

4. To cook, gently drop the ravioli, a few at a time, into a large pot of boiling water; if fresh, make sure they don't stick to each other. Cook until tender, 7–8 minutes. With a slotted spoon, transfer to a warm serving bowl. Add the sauce of your choice and toss gently to coat.

Per serving: 320 Calories, 8 g Total Fat, 4 g Saturated Fat, 173 mg Cholesterol, 328 mg Sodium, 43 g Total Carbohydrate, 2 g Dietary Fiber, 16 g Protein, 187 mg Calcium.

POINTS *per serving: 7.*

Tomato Sauce

Simplicity itself, this sauce is at the heart of many a memorable pasta dish. Double, triple, or even quadruple this recipe and freeze it in $^1/_2$-cup portions so you'll always have some on hand.

Makes 4 servings

4 teaspoons olive oil

12 plum tomatoes, chopped (about 3 cups), or 1 (35-ounce) can best-quality Italian plum tomatoes, drained and chopped

1 garlic clove, minced

$^1/_4$ teaspoon salt

Freshly ground pepper, to taste

Heat the oil in a nonstick saucepan, then add the tomatoes, garlic, salt, and pepper. Cook, stirring frequently, until reduced to about 2 cups, about 15 minutes.

Per serving: 69 Calories, 5 g Total Fat, 1 g Saturated Fat, 0 mg Cholesterol, 147 mg Sodium, 7 g Total Carbohydrate, 2 g Dietary Fiber, 1 g Protein, 9 mg Calcium.

POINTS per serving: 1.

D i   G i o r n o   Don't be a fresh tomato snob! Italian cooks have no qualms about relying on canned tomatoes—of the highest quality—in winter. *Pommarola* refers to the sauce of fresh tomatoes made in summertime, but *sugo scappato* (roughly translated, *scappato* means "loophole"), a sauce made with canned tomatoes, is what you'll find simmering on Italian stoves in the wintertime.

Know Your Tomatoes

Q. What's the best type of tomato for making tomato sauce?

A. Italians favor plum tomatoes because they have more of the pulp that adds body to sauce. Roma is the most common plum tomato on this side of the Atlantic, but the undisputed best variety for sauce is san marzano—particularly those grown in San Marzano, Italy. Compared with other plum tomatoes, san marzanos are meatier, more intensely tomatoey, and less sweet. You can find imported canned san marzanos in gourmet stores and Italian groceries. Read the label to make sure they're actually from San Marzano.

Q. Do plum or cherry tomatoes need to be seeded?

A. Seeding is largely a matter of preference; many cooks don't bother with it, though some claim the seeds make a tomato sauce bitter, especially if cooked for more than a half hour. The seeds in cherry tomatoes—a variety designed to be eaten out of hand—are mild enough to ignore.

Q. Is it true I can make sun-dried tomatoes at home?

A. It is indeed. To make sun-dried tomatoes, buy several pounds of plum tomatoes when they are in season and inexpensive (you'll need five pounds of fresh tomatoes to yield one pound of dried). Cut them in half lengthwise and place, cutside up, on baking sheets. Roast in a 170°F oven until dry but still pliable; start checking them after five or six hours. Do not let the tomatoes become brittle or too dark. If stored in an airtight container, they will last indefinitely.

Q. Do I have to blanch tomatoes in order to peel them?

A. Blanching tomatoes (dropping them briefly in boiling water to loosen their skins, then cooling in ice water) isn't the only way to peel them. If you have a gas stove, you can hold the tomato on a long-handled fork over the burner, turning until the skin splits. Let cool, then peel.

Q. It's winter and the supermarket tomatoes are tasteless. Which canned products can I use instead of fresh?

A. For freshest taste, look for whole or diced tomatoes in juice (not puree, which adds a cooked flavor, nor crushed tomatoes, which have puree added). Buying imports isn't a guarantee of quality; experiment with different brands to find one you like best.

Tomato-Herb Sauce

This sauce enlivens even the plainest fare. Try it with pasta, meat, fowl, fish, or vegetables. It's fast and easy to make on the spur of the moment.

Makes 4 servings

4 teaspoons olive oil

12 plum tomatoes, chopped (about 3 cups), or 1 (35-ounce) can best-quality Italian plum tomatoes, drained and chopped

2 tablespoons minced flat-leaf parsley

2 tablespoons minced fresh basil, or 1 teaspoon dried

1 tablespoon minced fresh oregano, or 1 teaspoon dried

2 teaspoons minced fresh thyme, or 1/2 teaspoon dried

1 garlic clove, minced

1/4 teaspoon salt

Freshly ground pepper, to taste

Heat the oil in a nonstick saucepan, then add the tomatoes, parsley, basil, oregano, thyme, garlic, salt, and pepper. Cook, stirring frequently, until reduced to about 2 cups, about 15 minutes.

Per serving: 72 Calories, 5 g Total Fat, 1 g Saturated Fat, 0 mg Cholesterol, 148 mg Sodium, 7 g Total Carbohydrate, 2 g Dietary Fiber, 1 g Protein, 29 mg Calcium.

POINTS per serving: 1.

D i   G i o r n o   There are those who insist that peeling tomatoes is the easiest thing in the world. If you're not one of them, here's a secret: Freeze the tomatoes. To use them in sauces or soups, simply run them under water and rub off the skins. A warning: Freezing will compromise the texture of the tomatoes (when they thaw, ice crystals damage their cell walls), so while you wouldn't want to use frozen tomatoes that are thawed in a salad, they are perfect in soups, stews, and sauces.

Meat Sauce

Best with a tubular pasta like rigatoni and ziti, or long, thick strands such as tagliatelle and fettuccine, this sauce is a robust staple in any Italian kitchen.

Makes 4 servings

1 (14 1/2-ounce) can whole Italian plum tomatoes (no salt added), with their juice

2 teaspoons olive oil

1 small onion, chopped

1 celery stalk, minced

1/4 cup minced carrot

1 garlic clove, minced

1/4 pound lean ground beef (10% or less fat)

1/4 teaspoon salt

1/4 teaspoon ground white pepper

2 sun-dried tomato halves (not packed in oil), minced

1/4 cup minced flat-leaf parsley

1 bay leaf

1. Pulse the tomatoes and their juice in a food processor until coarsely chopped.

2. Heat the oil in a nonstick saucepan, then add the onion. Sauté until softened. Add the celery, carrot, and garlic; sauté until the vegetables are slightly wilted.

3. Add the beef and brown, breaking apart the meat with a spoon; season with the salt and pepper. Add the wine, reduce the heat, and cook until most of the liquid evaporates, about 4 minutes. Stir in the canned tomatoes, sun-dried tomatoes, parsley, and bay leaf; cook, stirring, until the sauce begins to bubble. Reduce the heat and simmer, stirring occasionally, until thickened, 30 minutes. Discard the bay leaf before serving.

Per serving: 115 Calories, 5 g Total Fat, 1 g Saturated Fat, 18 mg Cholesterol, 182 mg Sodium, 8 g Total Carbohydrate, 2 g Dietary Fiber, 7 g Protein, 45 mg Calcium.

POINTS per serving: 2.

Capellini with Pesto

We love this savory herb paste on long, thin strands of pasta, but it's also delicious with grilled poultry or meat, fresh sliced tomatoes, crusty peasant breads, or scrambled eggs.

Makes 4 servings

2 cups packed basil leaves

1/2 cup packed flat-leaf parsley leaves

2 tablespoons grated Parmesan cheese

1 tablespoon low-sodium chicken broth, heated

1 garlic clove, quartered

Freshly ground pepper, to taste

4 teaspoons olive oil

1/2 pound capellini

1. Put the basil, parsley, cheese, broth, garlic, and pepper in a food processor or blender; pulse until finely chopped, about 5 times. With the machine running, slowly drizzle in the oil and process until the mixture forms a coarse paste, scraping the sides of the bowl if necessary.

2. Cook the capellini according to package directions. Drain and put in a serving bowl. Top with the pesto and toss to coat.

Per serving: 317 Calories, 7 g Total Fat, 1 g Saturated Fat, 2 mg Cholesterol, 76 mg Sodium, 49 g Total Carbohydrate, 2 g Dietary Fiber, 16 g Protein, 465 mg Calcium.

***POINTS** per serving: 7.*

Di Giorno   Refrigerated in a glass jar, pesto will keep for up to two weeks. It also freezes beautifully, so make a lot of it in the summer when basil is abundant. Spoon it into ice cube trays and freeze, then pop the cubes in zip-close freezer bags to use during the next fall and winter.

Penne Rigate with Red Pepper Pesto

Purists might wrinkle their noses at the thought of pesto made with anything but basil, but *pesto* means "pounded" in Italian (and derives from the same word as pestle does); technically it refers to any food mashed in a mortar. A food processor yields smoother results with infinitely less effort.

Makes 4 servings

2 large red bell peppers

2 cups penne rigate

1/4 cup grated Parmesan cheese

2 tablespoons sliced almonds

2 teaspoons tomato paste

1 garlic clove, crushed

1/4 teaspoon salt

2 teaspoons olive oil

1. Preheat the broiler. Line a baking sheet with foil and set the bell peppers on the foil. Broil the peppers 5 inches from the heat, turning frequently with tongs, until the skin is lightly charred on all sides. Fold up the foil to cover the peppers and steam for 10 minutes. Set a strainer over a bowl; peel, seed, and devein the peppers over the strainer. Discard the peels and seeds.

2. Cook the penne according to package directions. Drain, reserving 1/4 cup of the cooking liquid, and transfer to a serving bowl.

3. Meanwhile, put the peppers, cheese, almonds, tomato paste, garlic, and salt in a food processor; puree until thick and creamy but not perfectly smooth. With the machine running, slowly drizzle in the oil and process until it is completely absorbed, about 1 minute. If the mixture is too thick, drizzle in some of the pasta cooking liquid. Pour over the penne and toss to coat.

Per serving: 333 Calories, 8 g Total Fat, 2 g Saturated Fat, 7 mg Cholesterol, 334 mg Sodium, 45 g Total Carbohydrate, 3 g Dietary Fiber, 17 g Protein, 169 mg Calcium.

***POINTS** per serving: 7.*

Di Giorno   You might want to make a double batch of this because it will disappear fast! In addition to a pasta sauce, you can use it to spread on rounds of crusty bread for a speedy crostini. Just refrigerate the pesto in a glass container for up to one week.

Penne with Broccoli

Pasta and broccoli, accented with anchovies and pine nuts, are a popular combination throughout Italy. Pine nuts can be found in small glass jars in the baking section of most supermarkets. They have a very high fat content and can go rancid quickly. Refrigerate them for up to three months, or freeze them for up to nine months.

Makes 4 servings

2 cups penne

1 pound broccoli crowns, cut into florets (about 4 cups)

1 cup low-sodium chicken or vegetable broth

4 teaspoons olive oil

1 onion, chopped

2 garlic cloves, minced

4 teaspoons pine nuts

2 anchovy fillets, rinsed, or 1 teaspoon anchovy paste

1/4 teaspoon crushed red pepper

4 teaspoons grated Parmesan cheese

1. Cook the penne according to package directions. Drain and put in a serving bowl.

2. Meanwhile, put the broccoli in a steamer basket; set in a saucepan over 1 inch of boiling water. Cover tightly and steam until barely tender, about 5 minutes.

3. Bring $1/2$ cup of the broth and the oil to a simmer in a nonstick skillet; add the onion and garlic. Cook, stirring frequently, until the onion is softened. Add the pine nuts, anchovies, and crushed red pepper; cook, stirring constantly, until the anchovies are mashed. Stir in the broccoli and remaining $1/2$ cup of broth; cook, stirring frequently, until the liquid is reduced by half, about 5 minutes. Pour over the penne and toss to coat. Serve, sprinkled with the cheese.

Per serving: 283 Calories, 8 g Total Fat, 2 g Saturated Fat, 3 mg Cholesterol, 175 mg Sodium, 42 g Total Carbohydrate, 6 g Dietary Fiber, 13 g Protein, 108 mg Calcium.

POINTS *per serving: 5.*

Perciatelli alla Boscaiola

Wild mushrooms and tomatoes give this woodman's-style sauce, pronounced *boss-kai-OH-lah*, a rich, earthy flavor. *Perciatelli* (also called *fide bucati* or *bucatini*) is a long hollow pasta; if you can't find it, substitute spaghetti.

Makes 4 servings

1 (1-ounce) package dried porcini mushrooms (about 3/4 cup)

4 teaspoons olive oil

2 ounces well-trimmed prosciutto or lean boiled ham, chopped

2 garlic cloves, minced

4–6 plum tomatoes, chopped

2 cups white mushrooms, thinly sliced

2 cups shiitake mushrooms, thinly sliced

1/4 cup minced flat-leaf parsley

1/4 teaspoon salt

Freshly ground pepper, to taste

6 ounces perciatelli

1. Soak the porcini in warm water to cover until softened, about 30 minutes. Strain the liquid through a coffee filter-lined strainer; reserve the soaking liquid.

2. Heat a nonstick skillet. Swirl in the oil, then add the prosciutto and garlic. Sauté 1 minute, then stir in the porcini and soaking liquid; cook, stirring frequently, until the liquid evaporates, 3–5 minutes. Add the tomatoes, mushrooms, parsley, salt, and pepper. Cook, stirring occasionally, 15 minutes, until thickened.

3. Meanwhile, cook the perciatelli according to package directions. Drain and put in a serving bowl. Add the sauce and toss to coat.

Per serving: 275 Calories, 8 g Total Fat, 1 g Saturated Fat, 12 mg Cholesterol, 411 mg Sodium, 42 g Total Carbohydrate, 4 g Dietary Fiber, 12 g Protein, 26 mg Calcium.

POINTS per serving: 5.

D i G i o r n o   Dried mushrooms are very gritty, so be sure to strain the soaking liquid before using it.

Tagliatelle with Artichoke Hearts and Tomatoes

Elegant enough for company, hearty enough for a family meal, and simple to prepare, this is sure to become part of your regular repertoire.

Makes 4 servings

1 (9-ounce) box frozen artichoke hearts

6 ounces tagliatelle

4 teaspoons olive oil

1 onion, finely chopped

1 garlic clove, minced

8 plum tomatoes, chopped

$^1/_4$ teaspoon salt

Freshly ground pepper, to taste

$^1/_4$ cup minced flat-leaf parsley

4 teaspoons grated Parmesan cheese

1. Cook the artichoke hearts according to package directions. Cut into bite-size pieces and put in a serving bowl.

2. Meanwhile, cook the tagliatelle according to package directions. Drain and add to the bowl with the artichoke hearts.

3. While the artichokes and pasta are cooking, heat the oil in a nonstick skillet, then add the onion and garlic. Sauté until the onion is softened. Add the tomatoes, salt, and pepper and cook, stirring occasionally, until thickened, about 10 minutes. Pour over the pasta and artichokes; toss to coat. Serve, sprinkled with the parsley and cheese.

Per serving: 255 Calories, 6 g Total Fat, 1 g Saturated Fat, 2 mg Cholesterol, 216 mg Sodium, 42 g Total Carbohydrate, 5 g Dietary Fiber, 9 g Protein, 63 mg Calcium.

POINTS *per serving: 5.*

Di Giorno   Tagliatelle and fettuccine are long strands of pasta that are pretty much interchangeable; the former is a mere $^1/_8$-inch wider. According to legend, the shape of tagliatelle was inspired by the long tresses of Lucrezia Borgia, a fifteenth-century Italian duchess.

Farfalle with Lemon and Herbs

This light, refreshing, no-cook sauce is perfect for a summer luncheon. Start the meal with Fresh Tomato Crostini (page 10) and serve Espresso Granita (page 297) and Chocolate-Almond Biscotti (page 314) for dessert.

Makes 4 servings

¹/₄ cup minced flat-leaf parsley

¹/₄ cup minced basil

¹/₄ cup minced mint

Zest of 1 lemon, finely grated

2 tablespoons fresh lemon juice

1 tablespoon olive oil

¹/₄ teaspoon salt

¹/₄ teaspoon ground white pepper

3 cups farfalle

¹/₄ cup low-sodium chicken broth, heated

4 teaspoons grated Parmesan cheese

Fresh herb sprigs

1. Combine the parsley, basil, mint, lemon zest, lemon juice, oil, salt, and pepper in a serving bowl.

2. Meanwhile, cook the farfalle according to package directions. Drain and add to the herbs. Add the broth and cheese; toss lightly to coat. Serve, garnished with fresh herb sprigs.

Per serving: 208 Calories, 5 g Total Fat, 1 g Saturated Fat, 2 mg Cholesterol, 199 mg Sodium, 34 g Total Carbohydrate, 1 g Dietary Fiber, 7 g Protein, 70 mg Calcium.

POINTS per serving: 4.

D i G i o r n o   Cut the zest from the lemon before you juice it. Once you've removed the zest, roll the lemon between your hand and the counter-top to break up the pulp inside (it will yield more juice). Don't throw the halves away after you've juiced the lemon. Toss them into the water when you're washing dishes—they'll impart a lovely fragrance, and they'll help cut through grease.

Penne Arrabiata

This dish, popular in the central regions of Abruzzo, Molise, and Lazio, gets its name from the hot pepper that flavors it (*arrabiata* means "enraged"). Adjust the amount of crushed red pepper to suit your comfort level.

Makes 4 servings

2 cups penne

4 teaspoons olive oil

1 onion, finely chopped

8–10 plum tomatoes, chopped

2 garlic cloves, minced

1/2 teaspoon crushed red pepper, or to taste

1/4 teaspoon salt

Fresh parsley sprigs

1. Cook the penne according to package directions. Drain and put in a serving bowl.

2. Meanwhile, heat the oil in a nonstick skillet, then add the onion. Sauté until softened, then add the tomatoes, garlic, crushed red pepper, and salt. Cook, stirring occasionally, until thickened, about 10 minutes. Pour over the penne and toss to coat. Serve, garnished with parsley.

Per serving: 225 Calories, 5 g Total Fat, 1 g Saturated Fat, 0 mg Cholesterol, 146 mg Sodium, 38 g Total Carbohydrate, 2 g Dietary Fiber, 6 g Protein, 20 mg Calcium.

POINTS per serving: 5.

Spaghettini con Aglio e Olio

Popular as an evening snack with Roman revelers, this humble, easy, and savory dish wins points for being a great standby when the cupboard is bare. A side dish of *giardiniera*, preserved vegetables in vinegar, makes a simple yet satisfying meal.

Makes 4 servings

6 ounces spaghettini

1/4 cup + 2 tablespoons low-sodium chicken broth

4 teaspoons olive oil

2 garlic cloves, minced

1/8 teaspoon crushed red pepper

2 tablespoons minced flat-leaf parsley

1. Cook the spaghettini according to package directions. Drain and put in a serving bowl.

2. Combine the broth, oil, garlic, and crushed red pepper in a nonstick skillet. Cook, stirring constantly, until the garlic becomes fragrant and starts to sizzle. Pour over the spaghettini and sprinkle with the parsley; toss to coat.

Per serving: 203 Calories, 5 g Total Fat, 1 g Saturated Fat, 0 mg Cholesterol, 15 mg Sodium, 33 g Total Carbohydrate, 1 g Dietary Fiber, 6 g Protein, 14 mg Calcium.

POINTS per serving: 4.

D i G i o r n o   There's only one rule with this simple dish: Don't let the garlic burn. It will become bitter and acrid, and will ruin the oil.

Orecchiette with Broccoli Rabe and Cannellini

Orecchiette (pronounced *oh-reh-K'YEH-teh*), or "little ears," are a small round pasta from Apulia, where they are commonly served with turnip greens or broccoli rabe. Cannellini beans are not a traditional ingredient in this dish, but their creamy texture and mellow flavor is a perfect foil for the bitter greens and the hot pepper.

Makes 4 servings

1 bunch broccoli rabe, cleaned and coarsely chopped

4 teaspoons olive oil

1 onion, coarsely chopped

1/2 cup low-sodium vegetable broth

4 garlic cloves, minced

1/4 teaspoon salt

1/4 teaspoon crushed red pepper

1 (16-ounce) can cannellini beans, rinsed and drained

1 teaspoon fresh lemon juice

1 1/2 cups orecchiette

4 teaspoons grated Parmesan cheese

1. Put the broccoli rabe in a steamer basket; set in a saucepan over 1 inch of boiling water. Cover tightly and steam until tender, 5–7 minutes.

2. Heat a nonstick skillet. Swirl in the oil, then add the onion. Sauté until golden. Add the broccoli rabe, broth, garlic, salt, and crushed red pepper; cook, stirring occasionally, until most of the liquid evaporates. Stir in the beans and lemon juice; heat to serving temperature.

3. Meanwhile, cook the orecchiette according to package directions. Drain and put in a serving bowl. Top with the vegetables and toss to combine. Serve, sprinkled with the cheese.

Per serving: 368 Calories, 7 g Total Fat, 1 g Saturated Fat, 2 mg Cholesterol, 443 mg Sodium, 59 g Total Carbohydrate, 10 g Dietary Fiber, 18 g Protein, 119 mg Calcium.

POINTS per serving: 6.

Fettuccine with Vegetables in Salsa Fresca

No fuss—just plenty of fresh tomato flavor. Unless you're able to find perfectly fresh, vine-ripened tomatoes, don't take the time to make this sauce. Serve warm or at room temperature.

Makes 4 servings

1/2 pound fettuccine

2 small zucchini, sliced lengthwise paper thin

2 carrots, sliced lengthwise paper
   thin

2 tomatoes, peeled, seeded, and
   chopped

10 small black olives, pitted and
   quartered

1 tablespoon extra-virgin olive oil

2 teaspoons grated Parmesan
   cheese

1 teaspoon minced pickled hot
   red pepper

1 garlic clove, minced

Freshly ground pepper, to taste

1. Cook the fettuccine according to package directions. After about 8 minutes, add the zucchini and carrots; cook until the pasta is al dente and the vegetables are tender, 2–4 minutes longer.

2. Meanwhile, combine the tomatoes, olives, oil, cheese, red pepper, garlic, and ground pepper in a serving bowl. Drain the pasta and vegetables, then add to the sauce, tossing to coat.

Per serving: 255 Calories, 7 g Total Fat, 1 g Saturated Fat, 41 mg Cholesterol, 124 mg Sodium, 42 g Total Carbohydrate, 4 g Dietary Fiber, 9 g Protein, 62 mg Calcium.

POINTS per serving: 5.

D i G i o r n o   To cut the zucchini and carrots into paper-thin slices, run a vegetable peeler down the length of them.

Fettuccine with Vegetables in Salsa Fresca

Fettuccine Alfredo

Parmesan cheese, mushrooms, and just a bit of cream make this lightened sauce as rich tasting as the original. Because this rendition is still fairly high in fat, save this dish for an occasional splurge.

Makes 4 servings

6 ounces fettuccine

4 teaspoons margarine

Freshly ground pepper, to taste

1/4 cup heavy cream

2 tablespoons grated Parmesan cheese

1 large white mushroom, cut into paper-thin slices

1. Spray a large nonstick skillet with nonstick spray.

2. Cook the fettuccine according to package directions. Drain and put in the skillet, then set the skillet over medium heat. Add the margarine and pepper and toss gently. Add the cream and toss gently until it is heated through and most of it is absorbed. Add the cheese and mushrooms; toss gently until the pasta is evenly coated with melted cheese, 2–3 minutes.

Per serving: 265 Calories, 13 g Total Fat, 5 g Saturated Fat, 65 mg Cholesterol, 142 mg Sodium, 31 g Total Carbohydrate, 1 g Dietary Fiber, 9 g Protein, 97 mg Calcium.

POINTS per serving: 6.

Farfalle with Asparagus

The arrival of butterflies is a sure sign of spring, and what better way to celebrate the season than with this dish—farfalle, or butterfly-shaped pasta, and asparagus, tossed with a light, creamy sauce. Pair with an entrée like Salmon in Green Sauce (page 177) and you'll be well on your way to a healthful case of spring fever.

Makes 4 servings

4 cups farfalle

4 teaspoons olive oil

3 shallots, minced

1/4 cup low-sodium chicken broth

1/4 cup light cream

1/4 teaspoon salt

Freshly ground pepper, to taste

24 asparagus spears, trimmed, cut diagonally into 1-inch lengths, and steamed

4 teaspoons grated Parmesan cheese

1. Cook the farfalle according to package directions. Drain and put in a serving bowl.

2. Meanwhile, heat the oil in a nonstick skillet, then add the shallots. Sauté until softened. Reduce the heat, add the broth and cream, and cook, stirring constantly, until reduced by half, about 10 minutes; do not boil. Pour over the farfalle, sprinkle with the salt and pepper, and toss to coat. Top with the asparagus and cheese and serve at once.

Per serving: 271 Calories, 10 g Total Fat, 3 g Saturated Fat, 12 mg Cholesterol, 249 mg Sodium, 37 g Total Carbohydrate, 2 g Dietary Fiber, 10 g Protein, 74 mg Calcium.

POINTS *per serving: 6.*

Spinach-Stuffed Shells

Although small- or medium-size pasta shells are more common in many parts of Italy, here, the jumbo ones are easier to handle when you stuff them in this Florentine-inspired recipe.

Makes 4 servings

6 ounces jumbo pasta shells

1 (10-ounce) box frozen chopped spinach, thawed and squeezed dry

1 1/3 cups nonfat ricotta cheese

1/4 pound extra-lean ham, diced

1/4 teaspoon salt

1/8 teaspoon ground nutmeg

Freshly ground pepper, to taste

1 1/2 cups tomato sauce (no salt added)

2 tablespoons grated Parmesan cheese

1. Preheat the oven to 400°F. Spray a 9 × 13-inch baking dish with nonstick spray.

2. Cook the pasta shells according to package directions. Drain and rinse under cold water.

3. Meanwhile, combine the spinach, ricotta, and ham. Stir in the salt, nutmeg, and pepper. Spoon the filling into the shells and put them in the baking dish. Cover with the tomato sauce, then sprinkle with the Parmesan. Bake until the sauce is bubbling and the filling is lightly browned, about 25 minutes. Let stand a few minutes before serving.

Per serving: 354 Calories, 5 g Total Fat, 2 g Saturated Fat, 22 mg Cholesterol, 840 mg Sodium, 46 g Total Carbohydrate, 5 g Dietary Fiber, 30 g Protein, 593 mg Calcium.

POINTS *per serving: 6.*

D i G i o r n o   If you prefer, use fresh spinach. After you've cleaned the leaves, put them in a large strainer. When the pasta water comes to a boil but before you add the shells, set the strainer into the boiling water until the spinach wilts. Rinse it under cold water, squeeze out all the excess water, and chop.

Spinach-Stuffed Shells

Ziti with Cabbage and Onions

Cabbage makes frequent appearances on tables throughout northern Italy. This sweet-and-sour pasta dish is a nice complement to a simple pork roast or plain grilled chops.

Makes 4 servings

4 teaspoons olive oil

2 red onions, chopped

2 pounds green cabbage, shredded (about 8 cups)

1 cup low-sodium chicken broth

2 garlic cloves, minced

1 tablespoon balsamic vinegar

2 teaspoons fennel seeds

1/4 teaspoon salt

Freshly ground pepper, to taste

2 cups ziti

1. Heat a nonstick saucepan. Swirl in the oil, then add the onions. Sauté until browned. Add the cabbage, broth, and garlic and sauté until the cabbage wilts, about 5 minutes. Stir in the vinegar, fennel seeds, salt, and pepper. Reduce the heat and simmer, covered, until the cabbage is tender, about 20 minutes. Uncover, raise the heat slightly, and cook until the liquid evaporates, about 5 minutes longer.

2. Meanwhile, cook the ziti according to package directions. Drain and put in a serving bowl. Top with the cabbage and toss to combine.

Per serving: 260 Calories, 6 g Total Fat, 1 g Saturated Fat, 0 mg Cholesterol, 198 mg Sodium, 45 g Total Carbohydrate, 5 g Dietary Fiber, 9 g Protein, 105 mg Calcium.

POINTS per serving: 5.

Vegetarian Penne "Bolognese"

When you see *bolognese* on a menu, you know the sauce is tomato-based, chunky with meat and vegetables, and enriched with red wine and cream. This clever twist on the classic uses richly flavored sun-dried tomatoes rather than beef. Long, slow simmering makes it wonderful; it's worth taking the time to make it right.

Makes 4 servings

16 sun-dried tomato halves
   (not packed in oil)

2 teaspoons olive oil

2 teaspoons margarine

2 thin carrots, thinly sliced

2 celery stalks, thinly sliced

1 onion, finely chopped

1 cup canned diced tomatoes (no
   salt added)

¹/₂ cup dry red wine

1 cup low-sodium vegetable broth

1 cup evaporated fat-free milk

Pinch ground nutmeg

1 cup thawed frozen peas

¹/₄ cup water

2 cups penne

4 teaspoons grated Parmesan
   cheese

1. Soak the sun-dried tomatoes in warm water to cover until soft, about 15 minutes. Drain and pat dry with paper towels, then chop them.

2. Heat the oil and margarine in a nonstick saucepan, then add the carrots, celery, and onion. Sauté until the onion is translucent, then add the sun-dried tomatoes, canned tomatoes, and wine; cook, stirring frequently, until the liquid evaporates. Stir in the broth, milk, and nutmeg and bring to a boil. Reduce the heat and simmer, stirring occasionally, until the vegetables are soft, 15–20 minutes; add a little water if the liquid evaporates too quickly. Stir in the peas and water; simmer until the peas are heated through.

3. Meanwhile, cook the penne according to package directions. Drain and put in a serving bowl. Top with the sauce and toss to coat. Serve, sprinkled with the cheese.

Per serving: 384 Calories, 6 g Total Fat, 1 g Saturated Fat, 4 mg Cholesterol, 251 mg Sodium, 62 g Total Carbohydrate, 7 g Dietary Fiber, 17 g Protein, 275 mg Calcium.

POINTS per serving: 7.

Di Giorno   Pour leftover evaporated milk into a glass jar and refrigerate. Its thick consistency makes it a great stand-in for half-and-half in your morning coffee, or you can thin it with an equal amount of water and use as you would regular milk.

Penne with Vodka Cream Sauce

Sauced with cream, tomato, and vodka, this lightened version of a real restaurant favorite is thought by many Americans to be an invention of nouvelle cuisine. The Italians, however, claim that they've been enjoying it for years. Stewed Artichokes (page 251) or Sautéed Broccoli with Garlic and Lemon (page 236) makes a nice accompaniment.

Makes 4 servings

2 cups penne

4 teaspoons olive oil

3 shallots, minced

1/4 cup low-sodium chicken broth

1 tablespoon tomato paste (no salt added)

1/4 teaspoon crushed red pepper

1/4 cup heavy cream

2 tablespoons vodka

2 tablespoons minced flat-leaf parsley

4 teaspoons grated Parmesan cheese

1. Cook the penne according to package directions. Drain and put in a serving bowl.

2. Meanwhile, heat the oil in a nonstick skillet, then add the shallots. Sauté until softened. Stir in the broth, tomato paste, and crushed red pepper. Reduce the heat to low, then add the cream and vodka. Cook, stirring constantly, until heated through; do not boil. Pour the sauce over the penne and toss to coat. Serve, sprinkled with the parsley and cheese.

Per serving: 295 Calories, 12 g Total Fat, 5 g Saturated Fat, 22 mg Cholesterol, 115 mg Sodium, 35 g Total Carbohydrate, 1 g Dietary Fiber, 7 g Protein, 54 mg Calcium.

POINTS per serving: 7.

Di Giorno   If you know you'll be tempted by leftover heavy cream in your fridge, freeze it for up to six months. Pour the cream into ice cube trays or a muffin tin (measure the volume first, since their sizes can vary significantly) and freeze. When solid, transfer to a zip-close freezer bag and freeze. Thaw in the refrigerator, and shake well before using.

Penne with Vodka Cream Sauce and
Stewed Artichokes (page 251)

Perciatelli with Peperonata

The thick hollow strands of perciatelli go well with this traditional green pepper sauce. If you can't find it, try spaghetti, linguine, or fettuccine instead.

2 large green bell peppers, seeded and cut into thin strips

1 large tomato, peeled, seeded, and diced

1 small onion, thinly sliced

4 teaspoons olive oil

Pinch salt

1 teaspoon olive paste (olivada)

¹/₄ teaspoon dried oregano

6 ounces perciatelli

2 tablespoons grated pecorino Romano cheese

Freshly ground pepper, to taste

1. Layer the peppers, tomato, and onion in a nonstick saucepan. Drizzle with the oil and sprinkle with the salt. Cover and cook over low heat, stirring occasionally, until the vegetables are softened, about 20 minutes. If the mixture looks dry, add a tablespoon or so of warm water. Stir in the olive paste and oregano. Remove from the heat and let stand a few minutes.

2. Meanwhile, cook the perciatelli according to package directions. Drain and add to the saucepan. Sprinkle with the cheese and pepper, then toss to coat.

Per serving: 265 Calories, 7 g Total Fat, 2 g Saturated Fat, 5 mg Cholesterol, 155 mg Sodium, 42 g Total Carbohydrate, 4 g Dietary Fiber, 8 g Protein, 68 mg Calcium.

POINTS per serving: 5.

D i G i o r n o   There are two types of olive paste: Tapenade is the Provençal specialty that includes capers and anchovies; it is served as a dip or spread. Olivada, the Italian olive paste, is a puree of black olives, olive oil, and sometimes freshly ground pepper; as in this recipe, it's used as a seasoning. Olive paste comes in tubes and will last indefinitely in the refrigerator, but it's easy to make your own. Chop 6 pitted kalamata olives in a mini food processor, then drizzle in ¹/2–1 teaspoon of olive oil; the paste should be thick. Refrigerate in a glass jar for no more than 1 week.

Capellini with Seafood

Nearly every port in Italy has some version of pasta with seafood. This version, with its emphasis on light, fresh herbs and subtle flavors, is probably from the north.

Makes 4 servings

12 medium clams, scrubbed

12 medium mussels, scrubbed and debearded

1/4 cup dry white wine

2 garlic cloves, minced

2 teaspoons olive oil

1/2 pound bay scallops, rinsed, drained, and patted dry

5 ounces medium shrimp, peeled and deveined

2 tablespoons minced parsley

1 tablespoon thyme leaves

1 tablespoon minced oregano

6 ounces capellini

Freshly ground pepper, to taste

1. Combine the clams, mussels, wine, and garlic in a large saucepan. Cover and cook over medium heat until the shellfish open, 4–5 minutes. Discard any clams or mussels that don't open. Set aside with the cooking liquid.

2. Heat the oil in a nonstick skillet, then add the scallops, shrimp, parsley, thyme, and oregano. Sauté until the shrimp are pink and the scallops are opaque. Remove from the heat and add the shellfish.

3. Meanwhile, cook the capellini according to package directions. Drain and put in a serving bowl. Add the seafood and sprinkle with pepper; toss to combine.

Per serving: 318 Calories, 5 g Total Fat, 1 g Saturated Fat, 80 mg Cholesterol, 236 mg Sodium, 36 g Total Carbohydrate, 1 g Dietary Fiber, 28 g Protein, 73 mg Calcium.

POINTS per serving: 7.

Pasta Shells with Clams and Broccoli

Who would guess that two such unlikely ingredients could form such a magnificent partnership? Onion, garlic, and just a hint of lemon make it work. If you can't find tiny pasta shells, any small pasta will do.

Makes 4 servings

1 1/4 cups tiny pasta shells

1 pound broccoli crowns, cut into florets (about 4 cups)

24 medium clams, scrubbed

2 onions, chopped

1/2 cup dry white wine

4 teaspoons olive oil

2 garlic cloves, minced

1/2 teaspoon crushed red pepper

1 tablespoon fresh lemon juice

1. Cook the pasta shells according to package directions. Drain and put in a serving bowl.

2. Put the broccoli in a steamer basket; set in a saucepan over 1 inch of boiling water. Cover tightly and steam until barely tender but still bright green, 5–7 minutes. Add to the shells.

3. Meanwhile, combine the clams, onions, wine, oil, garlic, and crushed red pepper in a large saucepan. Cover and cook over medium heat until the clams open, 4–5 minutes. Discard any clams that don't open. When cool enough to handle, remove the clams from their shells, and coarsely chop them. Add the clams, their cooking liquid, and the lemon juice to the shells and broccoli; toss to combine.

Per serving: 319 Calories, 6 g Total Fat, 1 g Saturated Fat, 19 mg Cholesterol, 69 mg Sodium, 45 g Total Carbohydrate, 6 g Dietary Fiber, 18 g Protein, 104 mg Calcium.

POINTS per serving: 6.

Di Giorno   It's preferable to undercook the broccoli slightly. It will continue to cook after you've removed it from the heat.

Linguine with Calamari in Tomato Sauce

If your only experience with calamari is the heavily breaded, deep-fried appetizer, this flavorful, hearty sauce will come as a revelation. Do take care not to cook the calamari over too high a flame. It will become unpleasantly tough and chewy.

Makes 16 servings

1 tablespoon olive oil

1 onion, finely chopped

3 garlic cloves, minced

2 tablespoons tomato paste (no salt added)

2 (28-ounce) cans peeled Italian tomatoes, pureed

2 (8-ounce) cans tomato sauce (no salt added)

1 tablespoon minced fresh basil, or 1 teaspoon dried

Freshly ground pepper, to taste

2 1/2 pounds cleaned calamari, bodies cut into rings

1 1/2 pounds linguine

1. Heat the oil in a large nonstick saucepan, then add the onion and garlic. Sauté until softened, about 5 minutes. Add the tomato paste and cook, stirring constantly, 3–4 minutes. Stir in the pureed tomatoes, tomato sauce, basil, and pepper; bring to a boil. Cook, stirring occasionally, 10 minutes. Partially cover, reduce the heat and simmer, stirring occasionally, 45 minutes.

2. Add the calamari and continue to simmer the sauce until the calamari is tender and the sauce is very thick, $1^1/2$–2 hours. Do not let the sauce come to a boil or the calamari will toughen.

3. Cook the linguine according to package directions. Drain and put in a serving bowl. Top with the sauce and toss to coat.

Per serving: 266 Calories, 3 g Total Fat, 0 g Saturated Fat, 165 mg Cholesterol, 56 mg Sodium, 42 g Total Carbohydrate, 2 g Dietary Fiber, 18 g Protein, 62 mg Calcium.

POINTS per serving: 5.

Gnocchi Pasta with Shrimp and Broccoli Rabe

Loosely translated, broccoli rabe means "turnip flowers" (*broccolo* meaning "sprout," *rapa* meaning "turnip"), but do not confuse them with turnip greens (which the Italians call *cime di rape*). The vegetable has a pungent, bitter flavor that stands up nicely to the peperoncino and garlic. Discard the leaves, which can be very bitter, and any thick stalks. Peel the thinner stalks before chopping them, if you like. You can find gnocchi pasta in the dried pasta aisle; it has a hollow, curled shape that works well with chunky accompaniments, such as those in this dish.

Makes 4 servings

- **4 cups chopped cleaned broccoli rabe**
- **2 cups gnocchi-shaped pasta**
- **1/2 pound medium shrimp, peeled and deveined**
- **1 tomato, seeded and cubed**
- **4 teaspoons olive oil**
- **1 garlic clove, halved**
- **1/2 peperoncino (small Italian pickled pepper)**
- **1/4 teaspoon salt**
- **Freshly ground pepper, to taste**

1. Preheat the oven to 475°F.

2. Cook the broccoli rabe in a large pot of boiling water until slightly softened, 2–3 minutes. With a slotted spoon, transfer it to a colander and drain. Rinse it under cold water and drain again.

3. Cook the pasta in the boiling water according to package directions. Drain and put in a 9 × 13-inch baking dish. Add the broccoli rabe, shrimp, tomato, oil, garlic, peperoncino, salt, and pepper, and toss together. Cover with foil and bake until the shrimp are cooked through, about 10 minutes. Discard the garlic and peperoncino before serving.

Per serving: 285 Calories, 6 g Total Fat, 1 g Saturated Fat, 86 mg Cholesterol, 270 mg Sodium, 38 g Total Carbohydrate, 3 g Dietary Fiber, 10 g Protein, 90 mg Calcium.

POINTS *per serving: 6.*

D i G i o r n o   Resist the urge to top this, or any, fish-and-pasta dish with cheese. It's just not done in Italy; the flavors clash.

Gnocchi Pasta with Shrimp and Broccoli Rabe

Fettuccine al Limone

In this unusual sauce, the sweetness of slow-cooked onion and the saltiness of anchovies are offset by the tartness of lemon. When you cook anchovies, they dissolve and their flavor mellows considerably. In fact, even if you're sure you hate them, try this recipe.

Makes 4 servings

1 lemon

1/2 pound fettuccine

2 teaspoons olive oil

1 small onion, finely chopped

2 anchovy fillets, rinsed and minced

1/2 cup fat-free milk

1 teaspoon cornstarch, dissolved in 2 teaspoons water

2 teaspoons unsalted butter

1. Grate the zest from the lemon and reserve, then cut the lemon in half. Squeeze the juice from one half, then discard the rind. Cut the remaining half into thick slices, discarding the stem.

2. Cook the fettuccine according to package directions, adding the lemon slices to the water. Drain and put in a serving bowl; discard the lemon slices.

3. Meanwhile, heat a nonstick skillet. Swirl in the oil, then add the onion. Sauté until deep gold, about 15 minutes. Stir in the anchovies and cook, stirring gently, until they soften to a paste, 2–3 minutes. Stir in the lemon zest and juice and cook, stirring, until the liquid evaporates. Add the milk and dissolved cornstarch, then bring to a boil and cook until thickened. Add the butter and stir until it melts. Pour over the pasta and toss to coat.

Per serving: 223 Calories, 6 g Total Fat, 2 g Saturated Fat, 8 mg Cholesterol, 192 mg Sodium, 38 g Total Carbohydrates, 3 g Dietary Fiber, 8 g Protein, 52 mg Calcium.

POINTS per serving: 4.

Spaghetti alla "Puttanesca"

Traditionally, puttanesca does not include tuna, but its meaty texture and robust flavor seem a natural combination with the earthy flavors of this sauce.

Makes 4 servings

6 ounces spaghetti

1 tablespoon olive oil

10 ounces tuna steak, cut into chunks

4 plum tomatoes, chopped

6 large black olives, pitted and chopped

1 tablespoon capers, drained

2 garlic cloves, minced

2 anchovy fillets, rinsed and minced, or 1 teaspoon anchovy paste

$1/4$ teaspoon crushed red pepper

$1/4$ cup minced flat-leaf parsley

1. Cook the spaghetti according to package directions. Drain and put in a serving bowl.

2. Meanwhile, heat a nonstick skillet. Swirl in the oil, then add the tuna. Sauté until golden brown. Add the tomatoes, olives, capers, garlic, anchovies, and crushed red pepper. Cook, stirring frequently, until thickened. Pour over the spaghetti and sprinkle with the parsley; toss to combine.

Per serving: 317 Calories, 9 g Total Fat, 2 g Saturated Fat, 28 mg Cholesterol, 227 mg Sodium, 35 g Total Carbohydrate, 2 g Dietary Fiber, 23 g Protein, 29 mg Calcium.

POINTS *per serving: 7.*

Farfalle with Grilled Swordfish and Vegetables

This is a perfect meal for a sultry summer evening. After marinating, grill the fish and vegetables out-doors; cook the farfalle ahead of time and serve the whole dish at room temperature.

Makes 4 servings

1/2 cup dry white wine

1/4 cup fresh lemon juice

1/4 cup low-sodium tomato juice

1/4 cup minced flat-leaf parsley

4 teaspoons olive oil

1 tablespoon minced basil

1 tablespoon minced oregano

1 tablespoon thyme leaves

1/4 teaspoon salt

Freshly ground pepper, to taste

10 ounces swordfish, cut into cubes

1 green bell pepper, seeded and cut into 1-inch pieces

1 red bell pepper, seeded and cut into 1-inch pieces

8 plum tomatoes, halved

4 cups farfalle

1. Combine the wine, lemon juice, tomato juice, parsley, oil, basil, oregano, thyme, salt, and pepper. Pour half into a large zip-close plastic bag; add the swordfish, both bell peppers, and the tomatoes. Squeeze out the air and seal the bag; turn to coat the food. Refrigerate, turning the bag occasionally, at least 2 hours or overnight. Cover and refrigerate the remaining marinade.

2. If you are using bamboo skewers, soak three 12-inch sticks in water for 30 minutes. Bring the refrigerated marinade to room temperature. Spray the broiler or grill rack with nonstick spray. Preheat the broiler, or prepare the grill.

3. Drain the fish and vegetables and discard the marinade. Thread the fish, peppers, and tomatoes on separate skewers. Broil or grill the fish and vegetables, turning once, until the pepper and tomato skins are charred and the fish is golden brown and cooked through, about 10 minutes. Remove from the skewers and put in a serving bowl. Add the remaining wine mixture and toss to coat.

4. Meanwhile, cook the farfalle according to package directions. Drain and add to the vegetables and fish; toss to combine. Serve hot or at room temperature.

Per serving: 337 Calories, 8 g Total Fat, 1 g Saturated Fat, 28 mg Cholesterol, 212 mg Sodium, 40 g Total Carbohydrate, 3 g Dietary Fiber, 21 g Protein, 44 mg Calcium.

***POINTS** per serving: 7.*

Di Giorno   Finding fresh herbs at supermarkets can be a hit-or-miss proposition. If your market is out of one of these herbs, substitute a dried variety, but remember the rule: Use one third as much dried herb as fresh (in this recipe, use one teaspoon dried). If your dried herbs lack fragrance and punch, crumbling them between your fingers helps to release their aromatic oils.

Linguine with Red Clam Sauce

This is the classic *linguine alle vongole*, the Neapolitan clam sauce with tomatoes.

Makes 4 servings

12 medium clams, scrubbed

1/4 cup dry white wine

1 tablespoon thyme leaves

1 tablespoon minced oregano

2 large garlic cloves, minced

1/4 teaspoon crushed red pepper

6 ounces linguine

4 teaspoons olive oil

8 plum tomatoes, chopped

1 Italian frying pepper (see Di Giorno, p. 137), seeded and chopped

1/4 cup minced flat-leaf parsley

1/4 teaspoon salt

Freshly ground pepper, to taste

1. Combine the clams, wine, thyme, oregano, garlic, and crushed red pepper in a large saucepan. Cover and cook over medium heat until the clams open, 4–5 minutes. Discard any clams that don't open. When cool enough to handle, remove the clams from their shells and coarsely chop them. Reserve the shells for garnish, if desired; reserve the cooking liquid separately.

2. Cook the linguine according to package directions. Drain and put in a serving bowl.

3. Meanwhile, heat the oil in a nonstick skillet, then add the tomatoes, frying pepper, parsley, salt, and pepper. Sauté until the vegetables soften, then add the clam liquid. Reduce the heat and simmer until thickened, 5–10 minutes. Stir the clams into the sauce and heat to serving temperature. Pour over the linguine and toss to coat. Garnish with the clam shells, if desired.

Per serving: 264 Calories, 6 g Total Fat, 1 g Saturated Fat, 10 mg Cholesterol, 167 mg Sodium, 40 g Total Carbohydrate, 3 g Dietary Fiber, 11 g Protein, 49 mg Calcium.

POINTS per serving: 5.

Di Giorno   If your clams feel particularly heavy for their size, it could be a sign that they contain a lot of grit, which they'll release into the cooking liquid as soon as their shells open. You can soak them in a mixture of 2 quarts water and 2 1/2 tablespoons salt (refrigerate them in this brine for no more than one hour; drain the clams before using). If the cooking liquid looks sandy, pour it very carefully into the vegetable mixture, leaving the last tablespoon or so and any grit in the saucepan.

Linguine with White Clam Sauce

If you lack the time or inclination to use fresh clams, skip Step 1, and substitute a 10-ounce can of whole baby clams.

Makes 4 servings

18 medium clams, scrubbed

$1/2$ cup dry white wine

6 ounces linguine

4 teaspoons olive oil

4 garlic cloves, minced

$1/4$ cup minced flat-leaf parsley

$1/2$ teaspoon crushed red pepper

1. Combine the clams and wine in a large saucepan. Cover and cook over medium heat until the clams open, 4–5 minutes. Discard any clams that don't open. When cool enough to handle, remove the clams from their shells and coarsely chop them. Reserve the shells for garnish, if desired; reserve the cooking liquid separately.

2. Cook the linguine according to package directions. Drain and put in a serving bowl.

3. Meanwhile, heat the oil in a nonstick skillet, then add the garlic, parsley, crushed red pepper, and reserved liquid. Cook, stirring frequently, until the liquid is reduced by half, about 7 minutes. Add the clams and heat to serving temperature. Pour over the linguine and toss to coat. Garnish with the clam shells, if desired.

Per serving: 257 Calories, 6 g Total Fat, 1 g Saturated Fat, 14 mg Cholesterol, 32 mg Sodium, 35 g Total Carbohydrate, 1 g Dietary Fiber, 11 g Protein, 45 mg Calcium.

***POINTS** per serving: 5.*

Spaghettini with Mussels Marinara

Marinara means "in the style of the mariner." The story goes that fishermen's wives would whip up a fast sauce of tomatoes, herbs, olive oil, and garlic when their husbands returned home with the day's catch, which would be added to the sauce. It's traditionally served over long pasta strands.

Makes 4 servings

6 ounces spaghettini

4 teaspoons olive oil

1 (14 1/2-ounce) can Italian plum tomatoes (no salt added), drained and chopped

3 garlic cloves, minced

1/2 teaspoon crushed red pepper

24 medium mussels, scrubbed and debearded

1/3 cup minced flat-leaf parsley

1. Cook the spaghettini according to package directions. Drain and put in a serving bowl.

2. Meanwhile, heat the oil in a saucepan, then add the tomatoes, garlic, and crushed red pepper. Sauté about 2 minutes, then add the mussels. Cover and cook until the mussels open, 4–5 minutes. Discard any mussels that don't open. With a slotted spoon, transfer the mussels to a bowl.

3. Stir the parsley into the tomato sauce and cook until the liquid is reduced by half, about 5 minutes longer. Return the mussels to the sauce and heat to serving temperature. Pour the sauce over the spaghettini and toss to combine.

Per serving: 252 Calories, 6 g Total Fat, 1 g Saturated Fat, 12 mg Cholesterol, 135 mg Sodium, 37 g Total Carbohydrate, 2 g Dietary Fiber, 11 g Protein, 45 mg Calcium.

POINTS per serving: 5.

D i G i o r n o   Look for farm-raised mussels, which are almost always devoid of grit and sand; they don't have barnacles to scrape off, either. Whether cultivated or wild, you'll need to scrub the mussels under cool running water, then pull off the beards with your fingers. Don't do this in advance, though—mussels need to be cooked soon after they are debearded.

Spaghettini with Mussels, Garlic, and Wine

Easy, quick, inexpensive, attractive, flavorful, and filling—few dishes can boast so many attributes!

Makes 4 servings

6 ounces spaghettini

1/2 cup dry white wine

2 teaspoons olive oil

1/4 cup minced flat-leaf parsley

1 tablespoon fresh thyme leaves, or 1 teaspoon dried leaves, crumbled

4 garlic cloves, minced

1/4 teaspoon crushed red pepper

24 medium mussels, scrubbed and debearded

1. Cook the spaghettini according to package directions. Drain and put in a serving bowl.

2. Meanwhile, combine the wine, oil, parsley, thyme, garlic, and crushed red pepper in a saucepan. Cook, stirring constantly, until the garlic becomes fragrant. Add the mussels; cover and cook until the mussels open, 4–5 minutes. Discard any mussels that don't open. Pour the sauce over the spaghettini and toss to combine.

Per serving: 243 Calories, 4 g Total Fat, 1 g Saturated Fat, 12 mg Cholesterol, 130 mg Sodium, 35 g Total Carbohydrate, 1 g Dietary Fiber, 11 g Protein, 43 mg Calcium.

***POINTS** per serving: 5.*

Spaghettini with Mussels, Garlic, and Wine

Linguine with Sun-Dried Tomatoes and Goat Cheese

A winning trio of flavors makes this no-cook sauce a summertime favorite. Round out the meal with a basic arugula salad drizzled with good-quality balsamic vinegar.

Makes 4 servings

1 1/2 cups packed basil leaves

4 teaspoons pine nuts

1 tablespoon olive oil

2 garlic cloves, minced

1/4 teaspoon salt

Freshly ground pepper, to taste

16 sun-dried tomato halves (not packed in oil)

6 ounces linguine

2 ounces herbed or plain goat cheese, crumbled

1. Puree the basil, pine nuts, oil, garlic, salt, and pepper in a food processor or blender.

2. Soak the tomatoes in warm water to cover until softened, about 15 minutes. Drain, discarding the liquid, and chop the tomatoes.

3. Meanwhile, cook the linguine according to package directions. Drain and put in a serving bowl. Add the pesto, tomatoes, and goat cheese; toss to coat.

Per serving: 303 Calories, 10 g Total Fat, 4 g Saturated Fat, 13 mg Cholesterol, 232 mg Sodium, 42 g Total Carbohydrate, 3 g Dietary Fiber, 12 g Protein, 148 mg Calcium.

POINTS *per serving: 6.*

Rigatoni with Three Cheeses

Mozzarella, Parmesan, and fontina bring macaroni and cheese into a sophisticated—but still familiar—realm. To round out the meal and keep cleanup to a minimum, pop a vegetable casserole such as Ciambotta (page 250) in the oven, too.

Makes 4 servings

3 cups rigatoni

$1/2$ cup fat-free milk

$1/3$ cup shredded skim-milk mozzarella cheese

$1^1/2$ ounces fontina cheese, grated (about $1/4$ cup)

$1/4$ cup minced flat-leaf parsley

1 tablespoon fresh thyme leaves, or 1 teaspoon dried leaves, crumbled

$1/4$ teaspoon ground white pepper

2 tablespoons grated Parmesan cheese

1. Preheat the oven to 425°F. Spray a 1-quart baking dish with non-stick spray.

2. Cook the rigatoni according to package directions. Drain and return to the pot. Stir in the milk, mozzarella, fontina, parsley, thyme, and pepper. Spoon into the baking dish and sprinkle with the Parmesan. Bake until golden and bubbling, 15–18 minutes. Let stand 5 minutes before serving.

Per serving: 253 Calories, 6 g Total Fat, 3 g Saturated Fat, 18 mg Cholesterol, 283 mg Sodium, 35 g Total Carbohydrate, 1 g Dietary Fiber, 15 g Protein, 264 mg Calcium.

POINTS per serving: 5.

SAY "FORMAGGIO": AN ITALIAN CHEESE PRIMER

Type	Characteristics	How to Use It	Buying Notes
Asiago	This pale yellow cheese is sold fresh, medium, or aged. When fresh, it has a mild, piquant flavor and soft texture; as it ages, it becomes granular and the flavor develops to a nutty, cheddarlike sharpness.	Aged Asiago can be grated into soups, risottos, salads and pastas; younger versions can be sliced into sandwiches or served as part of a cheese course.	The wax covering indicates age: clear or white (fresh), brown (medium), or black (aged). Domestic Asiago, produced in Wisconsin, is superb; no need to buy pricey imports.
Gorgonzola	A soft, ivory-colored cheese with streaks of blue. Its earthy flavor sharpens with aging.	Intensely flavored, a little Gorgonzola goes a long way. Slice some into a roasted vegetable sandwich, or crumble into creamy salad dressings or dips. It goes particularly well with pears, and a thin slice over hot polenta is an exquisite combination.	Italian Gorgonzola is superb, but domestic varieties are worth trying.
Mozzarella	A soft, fresh cheese with mild, buttery flavor; mozzarella becomes magically elastic when melted. Though it's most commonly made with cow's milk, water buffalo-milk mozzarella is prized in Italy.	Mozzarella's indispensible in classic cheese-topped dishes like pizza and eggplant parmigiana, but it's also fine in a sandwich. Or, toss cubed mozzarella with tomato chunks, basil leaves, and a little vinaigrette dressing. Fat-free mozzarella doesn't melt well; use it only in fillings.	Part-skim is good for all-around use, but freshly-made whole-milk mozzarella—available in Italian groceries—is a divine treat.
Ricotta	A mild, fresh cheese with a soft, slightly grainy texture and sweet, milky taste.	Toss with hot pasta and herbs for an instant creamy "sauce," layer it in casseroles like lasagna, or stuff it into pastas or pastries.	For a splurge, seek out freshly-made ricotta in Italian groceries. It's miles away from the grainy supermarket stuff.
Romano (Pecorino Romano)	A sharp, ivory-colored hard cheese made from sheep's milk (*pecorino* is Italian for "sheep"). It has a salty, pungent flavor.	Romano is strictly a grating cheese, used in strongly flavored pasta sauces, as a topping for hearty soups, or to add punch to a pesto (in combination with Parmesan cheese). Don't use it interchangeably with Parmesan cheese; the flavors are quite different.	Domestic Romano, made from cow's milk, doesn't have the pungency of its Italian counterpart. Don't buy it pregrated; it loses flavor in the process.

Lasagne with Tomatoes and Cheese

One of the most popular of Italian foods, this Neapolitan classic is an indispensable part of any festive meal. Make a double batch and freeze one (for up to 2 months) for your next special occasion. Giardinetto al Forno (page 232) or Drunken Escarole (page 254) is a natural side dish.

Makes 8 servings

1 cup part-skim ricotta cheese

¹/₄ cup grated Parmesan cheese

1 egg white

Freshly ground pepper, to taste

9 lasagna noodles

2 cups Tomato Sauce (page 59)

³/₄ cup shredded skim-milk moz-zarella cheese

1. Combine the ricotta, Parmesan, egg white, and pepper.

2. Cook the lasagna noodles according to package directions. Drain and place the noodles in a single layer on sheets of foil or wax paper.

3. Preheat the oven to 400°F. Spray a 9 × 13-inch baking dish with nonstick spray. Spread ¹/₂ cup of the tomato sauce over the bottom of the baking dish. Top with 3 lasagna noodles, then spread with one third of the cheese mixture. Drizzle with another ¹/₂ cup of the tomato sauce then sprinkle with ¹/₄ cup of the mozzarella. Top with 3 more lasagna noodles and repeat the layers, ending with the mozzarella. Cover with foil and bake 25 minutes; uncover and bake until bubbling and slightly crispy on top, about 10 minutes longer. Let stand 5 minutes before serving.

Per serving: 237 Calories, 7 g Total Fat, 3 g Saturated Fat, 15 mg Cholesterol, 299 mg Sodium, 29 g Total Carbohydrate, 2 g Dietary Fiber, 14 g Protein, 242 mg Calcium.

***POINTS** per serving: 5.*

D i G i o r n o   If you use no-boil lasagna noodles, you can omit Step 2.

Spaghetti with Meatballs

Perhaps the most popular Italian-American dish, this dynamic duo brings back many a childhood memory. Make a double batch of the sauce and freeze half for busy evenings.

Makes 8 servings

4 teaspoons olive oil

1 onion, finely chopped

1 (35-ounce) can Italian plum tomatoes, drained and chopped (reserve the juice)

1 garlic clove, minced

$^1/_2$ pound lean ground beef (10% or less fat)

$^1/_4$ pound lean ground veal

$^1/_4$ cup grated Parmesan cheese

3 tablespoons plain dried bread crumbs

3 egg whites

$^3/_4$ cup minced flat-leaf parsley

1 tablespoon minced fresh basil, or 1 teaspoon dried

2 teaspoons minced fresh oregano, or $^1/_2$ teaspoon dried

1 teaspoon minced fresh thyme, or $^1/_4$ teaspoon dried

$^1/_4$ teaspoon salt

Freshly ground pepper, to taste

12 ounces spaghetti

Additional grated Parmesan cheese (optional)

1. Heat the oil in a large saucepan, then add the onion. Sauté until softened. Stir in the tomatoes and garlic; reduce the heat and simmer, stirring occasionally.

2. Meanwhile, thoroughly combine the beef, veal, cheese, bread crumbs, egg whites, $^1/_4$ cup of the parsley, the basil, oregano, thyme, salt, and pepper. With moistened hands, shape into 24 walnut-size balls. Drop the meatballs gently into the sauce. Reduce the heat and simmer, without stirring, until the meatballs are cooked through, about 25 minutes. Stir in the remaining $^1/_2$ cup of parsley. Continue to cook, adding the reserved tomato juice, $^1/_4$ cup at a time, if the sauce thickens too quickly, until the meatballs are tender and the sauce thickens, 30–45 minutes longer.

3. Cook the spaghetti according to package directions. Drain and put in a serving bowl. Top with the sauce and meatballs. Serve, topped with additional cheese (if using).

Per serving: 317 Calories, 8 g Total Fat, 3 g Saturated Fat, 35 mg Cholesterol, 264 mg Sodium, 41 g Total Carbohydrate, 3 g Dietary Fiber, 19 g Protein, 139 mg Calcium.

POINTS *per serving: 6.*

Spaghetti alla Carbonara

Egg substitute and Canadian bacon fill in for traditional eggs and pancetta (the delicate and very fatty Italian bacon)—but all the great taste is still here. Either Cannellini-Stuffed Peppers (page 244) or Sweet-and-Sour Onions (page 235) would be a great *contorno*, or side dish.

Makes 4 servings

6 ounces spaghetti

2 slices Canadian bacon, julienned

3 shallots, finely chopped

1 tablespoon olive oil

2 garlic cloves, bruised and peeled

2/3 cup fat-free egg substitute

1/4 cup grated Parmesan cheese

1 tablespoon minced flat-leaf parsley

Freshly ground pepper, to taste

1. Cook the spaghetti according to package directions.

2. Meanwhile, combine the bacon, shallots, oil, and garlic in a nonstick skillet. Sauté until the bacon is browned and the garlic is golden on all sides, then discard the garlic. If the spaghetti is not yet done, remove the skillet from the heat.

3. Drain the spaghetti and add to the bacon; set the skillet over low heat. Add the egg substitute and cheese; toss to coat. Serve, sprinkled with the parsley and pepper.

Per serving: 290 Calories, 8 g Total Fat, 3 g Saturated Fat, 15 mg Cholesterol, 484 mg Sodium, 35 g Total Carbohydrate, 1 g Dietary Fiber, 17 g Protein, 176 mg Calcium.

POINTS per serving: 6.

Di Giorno   There's some debate over where the name for this Roman specialty comes from. Some say it's called "charcoal style" because it was originally made with squid ink pasta, or because the bits of pancetta look like small pieces of charcoal. Others say it was named for the nineteenth-century radical group *I Carbonari*, or after the coal miners in the mountains outside of Rome.

Pappardelle with Savory Meat Sauce

The Tuscans serve these wide-ribbon noodles with a sauce of wild game. Dark turkey meat is a delicious substitute and makes a splendid counterpoint to the other savory ingredients; just be sure to leave enough time to marinate the turkey. Wilted Swiss Chard and Spinach Salad (page 151) is the perfect side dish.

Makes 4 servings

³/₄ pound skinless boneless turkey thighs, cut into chunks

¹/₂ cup dry red wine

1 rosemary sprig

4 teaspoons olive oil

¹/₂ onion, chopped

1 celery stalk, sliced

1 small carrot, sliced

2 sun-dried tomato halves (not packed in oil), minced

1 garlic clove, minced

1 bay leaf

¹/₄ teaspoon salt

Freshly ground pepper, to taste

1 cup hot water

1 tablespoon tomato paste (no salt added)

6 ounces pappardelle or other wide-ribbon noodles

4 teaspoons grated Parmesan cheese

1. Combine the turkey, wine, and rosemary in a large zip-close plastic bag. Squeeze out the air and seal the bag; turn to coat the turkey. Refrigerate, turning the bag occasionally, at least 2 hours or overnight.

2. Drain the turkey; reserve the wine, but discard the rosemary sprig. Heat the oil in a nonstick saucepan, then add the turkey. Reduce the heat and cook, stirring frequently, until lightly browned. Stir in the onion, celery, carrot, tomatoes, garlic, bay leaf, salt, and pepper; cook, stirring constantly, until the onion is golden.

3. Stir in the hot water, the reserved wine, and the tomato paste. Simmer, adding more hot water if the sauce thickens too quickly, until the turkey is tender, about 30 minutes. Discard the bay leaf. Transfer the sauce to a food processor and pulse a few times to shred the meat.

4. Meanwhile, cook the pappardelle according to package directions. Drain and put in a serving bowl. Top with the sauce and cheese; toss to combine.

Per serving: 337 Calories, 10 g Total Fat, 2 g Saturated Fat, 95 mg Total Cholesterol, 253 mg Sodium, 35 g Total Carbohydrate, 2 g Dietary Fiber, 22 g Protein, 71 mg Calcium.

POINTS *per serving: 7.*

Pappardelle with Savory Meat Sauce

Perciatelli all'Amatriciana

In the central Italian town of Amatrice, this sauce is made with *guanciale*, the salted, cured, and dried pig's cheeks that are used much as pancetta is elsewhere. Canadian bacon is a more readily available substitute. If you can't find perciatelli, which is a long hollow pasta that's sometimes called bucatini, spaghetti is also traditional.

Makes 4 servings

4 teaspoons olive oil

1 onion, finely chopped

2 slices Canadian bacon, diced

1 (14 1/2-ounce) can Italian plum tomatoes (no salt added), drained and chopped

1/4 teaspoon crushed red pepper

1/4 teaspoon salt

6 ounces perciatelli

4 teaspoons grated Parmesan cheese

1. Heat a nonstick skillet. Swirl in the oil, then add the onion and bacon. Sauté until the onion is golden and the bacon is lightly browned. Stir in the tomatoes, crushed red pepper, and salt. Reduce the heat and simmer, stirring frequently, until the sauce thickens, about 15 minutes.

2. Meanwhile, cook the perciatelli according to package directions. Drain and put in a serving bowl. Top with the sauce and cheese; toss to combine.

Per serving: 261 Calories, 7 g Total Fat, 1 g Saturated Fat, 9 mg Cholesterol, 392 mg Sodium, 39 g Total Carbohydrate, 2 g Dietary Fiber, 11 g Protein, 73 mg Calcium.

POINTS per serving: 5.

Ziti with Sausage and Peppers

Here's a robust family-pleaser that's chock-full of flavor and texture. Italian-style turkey sausage is widely available in supermarkets; it's every bit as savory as—but much less fatty than—the pork-based version. Depending on your taste, use the sweet or hot version.

Makes 4 servings

4 teaspoons olive oil

2 onions, coarsely chopped

4 Italian frying peppers (see Di Giorno, p. 137), seeded and cut into 1-inch pieces

1 cup low-sodium tomato juice

2 garlic cloves, minced

2 links Italian-style turkey sausage (about $^1/_4$ pound), casings removed

$^1/_2$ cup diced canned tomatoes (no salt added)

1 tablespoon minced fresh oregano, or 1 teaspoon dried

$^1/_4$ teaspoon salt

Freshly ground pepper, to taste

2 cups ziti

4 teaspoons grated Parmesan cheese

1. Heat the oil in a nonstick skillet, then add the onions. Sauté until softened. Add the frying peppers and $^1/2$ cup of the tomato juice; cook, stirring frequently, until the peppers start to soften. Add the garlic and sausage and brown, breaking apart the meat with a wooden spoon.

2. Add the tomatoes, the remaining $^1/2$ cup of tomato juice, the oregano, salt, and pepper. Reduce the heat and cook, stirring frequently, until the vegetables are tender and the sauce thickens.

3. Meanwhile, cook the ziti according to package directions. Drain and put in a serving bowl. Top with the sauce and cheese; toss to combine.

Per serving: 323 Calories, 9 g Total Fat, 1 g Saturated Fat, 25 mg Cholesterol, 347 mg Sodium, 48 g Total Carbohydrate, 3 g Dietary Fiber, 14 g Protein, 82 mg Calcium.

POINTS *per serving: 7.*

Rigatoni with Sausage and Fennel

Spicy sausage and sweet fennel are balanced by the tomato in this dish. We like it with rigatoni, but any sturdy pasta shape is suitable.

Makes 4 servings

4 teaspoons olive oil

2 onions, chopped

1 fennel bulb, trimmed and chopped

1 garlic clove, minced

2 links Italian-style turkey sausage (about $^1/_4$ pound), casings removed

4–6 plum tomatoes, chopped

$^1/_2$ teaspoon fennel seeds

$^1/_4$ teaspoon salt

Freshly ground pepper, to taste

3 cups rigatoni

2 teaspoons grated Parmesan cheese

1. Heat the oil in a nonstick skillet, then add the onion, fennel, and garlic. Sauté until the vegetables begin to soften. Add the sausage and brown, breaking apart the meat with a spoon. Stir in the tomatoes, fennel seeds, salt, and pepper; cook, stirring frequently, until the vegetables are tender and the sauce thickens.

2. Meanwhile, cook the rigatoni according to package directions. Drain and put in a serving bowl. Add the sauce and cheese; toss to combine.

Per serving: 291 Calories, 9 g Total Fat, 1 g Saturated Fat, 24 mg Cholesterol, 394 mg Sodium, 41 g Total Carbohydrate, 3 g Dietary Fiber, 12 g Protein, 75 mg Calcium.

POINTS per serving: 6.

Sausage and Pepper "Lasagne"

Until the mid-twentieth century, lasagne was considered a luxurious dish and was only eaten by the wealthy because most Italian homes didn't have baking ovens. For a different presentation, we roll the noodles with the cheese, before covering with the tomato sauce, rather than layer the noodles with the tomato sauce and cheese.

Makes 6 servings

2 links Italian-style turkey sausage (about $^1/_4$ pound), casings removed

$^1/_2$ cup chopped seeded red bell pepper

$^1/_2$ cup chopped seeded green bell pepper

1 small onion, chopped

1 teaspoon dried oregano

$^1/_4$ teaspoon fennel seeds, crushed

1 (14 $^1/_2$-ounce) can crushed tomatoes

6 lasagna noodles

1 cup part-skim ricotta cheese

$^1/_3$ cup shredded part-skim mozzarella cheese

1 egg

2 tablespoons grated Parmesan cheese

$^1/_8$ teaspoon crushed red pepper

1. Spray a nonstick saucepan with nonstick spray and set over medium-high heat. Add the sausage, both bell peppers, the onion, $^1/_2$ teaspoon of the oregano, and the fennel seeds. Sauté, breaking apart the sausage with a spoon, until it is browned and the vegetables are tender. Add the tomatoes and bring to a boil. Reduce the heat and simmer, stirring occasionally, until thickened, about 20 minutes.

2. Cook the lasagna noodles according to package directions. Drain and lay flat on a sheet of foil or wax paper. Preheat the oven to 350°F.

3. Combine the ricotta, mozzarella, egg, Parmesan, crushed red pepper, and the remaining oregano. Spread about 3 tablespoons over each lasagna noodle, then roll them up. Spread $^1/_2$ cup of the sauce in an 8-inch square baking dish. Put the lasagna rolls, seam-side down, in the baking dish, then spoon the rest of the sauce over them. Cover with foil and bake until the sauce is bubbling, about 30 minutes. Let stand 10 minutes before serving.

Per serving: 246 Calories, 9 g Total Fat, 5 g Saturated Fat, 67 mg Cholesterol, 319 mg Sodium, 25 g Total Carbohydrate, 2 g Dietary Fiber, 16 g Protein, 243 mg Calcium.

POINTS per serving: 5.

risottos, gnocchi, and polenta

Risotto alla Milanese

Saffron and lemon zest give this classic risotto its regal quality and lovely color. If you stir constantly after each addition of liquid, you will be rewarded with decadently creamy risotto. This dish is traditionally paired with the braised veal shank dish Osso Buco (page 208).

Makes 4 servings

3 1/2 cups low-sodium chicken broth

1/4 teaspoon saffron threads

1 tablespoon olive oil

1 onion, chopped

1 cup Arborio rice

1/2 cup dry white wine

2 tablespoons grated Parmesan cheese

1 teaspoon margarine

2 teaspoons grated lemon zest

Freshly ground pepper, to taste

1. Bring the broth to a boil. Reduce the heat and keep at a simmer.

2. In a small bowl, dissolve the saffron in 1 cup of the broth.

3. Heat the oil in a nonstick saucepan, then add the onion. Sauté until softened. Add the rice and cook, stirring, until the outer shell is translucent, about 1 minute.

4. Add the wine and 1/2 cup of the simmering broth and stir until they are absorbed. Continue to add broth, alternating between the saffron broth and the simmering broth, 1/2 cup at a time, stirring until it is absorbed before adding more, until the rice is just tender. The cooking time should be about 20 minutes from the first addition of broth. Stir in the cheese, margarine, lemon zest, and pepper; serve at once.

Per serving: 294 Calories, 9 g Total Fat, 2 g Saturated Fat, 4 mg Cholesterol, 216 mg Sodium, 43 g Total Carbohydrate, 1 g Dietary Fiber, 9 g Protein, 97 mg Calcium.

POINTS per serving: 6.

Risotto with Swiss Chard and Tomatoes

One secret to successful risotto is to use *superfino* rice, a short-grained Italian rice with a very high starch content. We call for Arborio because it's commonly available in North America, but if you find Carnaroli, or a *semifino* such as Vialone Nano, feel free to use one of them instead.

Makes 4 servings

3 1/2 cups low-sodium vegetable broth

4 cups coarsely chopped cleaned Swiss chard leaves

4 teaspoons olive oil

1 onion, finely chopped

4 plum tomatoes, chopped

1 cup Arborio rice

1 cup dry white wine

4 teaspoons grated Parmesan cheese

Freshly ground pepper, to taste

1. Bring the broth to a boil. Reduce the heat and keep at a simmer.

2. Put the chard in a steamer basket; set in a saucepan over 1 inch of boiling water. Cover tightly and steam until barely tender, about 5 minutes.

3. Heat the oil in a nonstick saucepan, then add the onion. Sauté until softened, then add the tomatoes and cook until they begin to break down, about 2 minutes. Add the rice and cook, stirring, until the outer shell is translucent, about 1 minute.

4. Add the wine and 1/2 cup of the broth and stir until they are absorbed. Stir in the chard. Continue to add broth, 1/2 cup at a time, stirring until it is absorbed before adding more, until the rice is just tender. The cooking time should be 18–20 minutes from the first addition of broth. Stir in the cheese and pepper; serve at once.

Per serving: 322 Calories, 6 g Total Fat, 1 g Saturated Fat, 2 mg Cholesterol, 186 mg Sodium, 51 g Total Carbohydrate, 2 g Dietary Fiber, 6 g Protein, 60 mg Calcium.

POINTS *per serving: 7.*

Risotto with Spinach and Gorgonzola Cheese

Sharp Gorgonzola and slightly bitter spinach contrast wonderfully with the creamy texture of this elegant risotto. If you can't find Gorgonzola, substitute Roquefort, Stilton, Maytag, or another blue cheese.

Makes 4 servings

1 (10-ounce) box frozen chopped spinach, thawed

$1/2$ cup water

3 cups low-sodium chicken broth

4 teaspoons olive oil

2 onions, chopped

1 cup Arborio rice

1 cup dry white wine

$1 1/2$ ounces Gorgonzola cheese, crumbled (about $1/3$ cup)

Freshly ground pepper, to taste

1. Cook the spinach in the water according to package directions. Cover and set aside.

2. Bring the broth to a boil. Reduce the heat and keep at a simmer.

3. Heat the oil in a nonstick saucepan, then add the onions. Sauté until softened. Add the rice and cook, stirring, until the outer shell is translucent, about 1 minute.

4. Add the wine and $1/2$ cup of the broth and stir until they are absorbed. Stir in the spinach and its liquid. Continue to add broth, $1/2$ cup at a time, stirring until it is absorbed before adding more, until the rice is just tender. The cooking time should be about 20 minutes from the first addition of broth. Stir in the cheese and pepper; serve at once.

Per serving: 346 Calories, 10 g Total Fat, 4 g Saturated Fat, 9 mg Cholesterol, 289 mg Sodium, 47 g Total Carbohydrate, 3 g Dietary Fiber, 11 g Protein, 162 mg Calcium.

POINTS per serving: 7.

Risotto alla Contadina

This "peasant-style" risotto is robustly flavored and hearty enough to be a meal in itself. Pair it with Sautéed Endive (page 241) or Arugula-Gorgonzola Salad (page 156) and a glass of Pinot Grigio.

Makes 4 servings

5 cups chicken broth

¹/₂ tablespoon olive oil

2 large scallions, sliced

4 large cloves garlic, minced

1¹/₂ cups Arborio rice

1 (10-ounce) package frozen baby peas, thawed

7 ounces smoked turkey sausage, chopped

Freshly ground pepper, to taste

1¹/₂ tablespoons grated Parmesan cheese

1. Bring the broth to a boil. Reduce the heat and keep at a simmer.

2. Heat the oil in a nonstick saucepan, then add the scallions and garlic. Sauté until the scallion is softened. Add the rice and cook, stirring, until it is lightly toasted, about 3 minutes.

3. Add 1 cup of the broth and stir until it is absorbed. Continue to add broth, ¹/₂ cup at a time, stirring until it is absorbed before adding more, until the rice is just tender; add the peas and sausage with the last addition of broth. The cooking time should be about 30 minutes from the first addition of broth. Stir in the pepper and cheese; serve at once.

Per serving: 519 Calories, 9 g Total Fat, 3 g Saturated Fat, 37 mg Cholesterol, 807 mg Sodium, 83 g Total Carbohydrate, 5 g Dietary Fiber, 22 g Protein, 121 mg Calcium.

POINTS per serving: 10.

Di Giorno   Every household in the north of Italy has its own preferred risotto pot. Whether or not your household has a dedicated risotto pot, the one you use should have a heavy bottom and straight sides and be wider than it is high.

Risotto Verde with Tomatoes

This substantial risotto can easily serve four as a main course; it could also be served as a side dish for six to accompany most poultry and seafood. Don't add the basil until the last minute, because you want it to remain bright green and very fragrant (if you add it too early, the acid from the wine will turn the basil black, and cooking it longer will mute its flavor and aroma).

Makes 4 servings

4 cups chicken broth

2 teaspoons olive oil

2 scallions, sliced

1¹/₄ cups Arborio rice

1 (10-ounce) box frozen chopped
    spinach, thawed and
    squeezed dry

¹/₄ cup dry white wine

2 tablespoons chopped basil

1 tomato, seeded and chopped

¹/₂ teaspoon salt

¹/₂ teaspoon freshly ground
    pepper

¹/₄ teaspoon ground nutmeg

2 tablespoons grated Parmesan
    cheese

1. Bring the broth to a boil. Reduce the heat and keep at a simmer.

2. Heat the oil in a nonstick saucepan, then add the scallions. Sauté until softened. Add the rice and cook, stirring, until it is lightly toasted, about 3 minutes.

3. Add 1 cup of the broth and stir until it is absorbed. Continue to add broth, ¹/₂ cup at a time, stirring until it is absorbed before adding more, until the rice is just tender; add the spinach and wine with the last addition of broth. The cooking time should be 15–20 minutes from the first addition of broth. Stir in the basil, tomato, salt, pepper, nutmeg, and cheese; serve at once.

Per serving: 335 Calories, 8 g Total Fat, 2 g Saturated Fat, 7 mg Cholesterol, 1,405 mg Sodium, 55 g Total Carbohydrate, 3 g Dietary Fiber, 9 g Protein, 131 mg Calcium.

***POINTS** per serving: 7.*

Risotto Verde with Tomatoes

Pumpkin Risotto

This slightly sweet, pale orange risotto is an excellent partner for poultry, especially roast turkey or duck, or pork. For a special touch, hollow out small pumpkins and serve it in the shells, garnished with fresh sage.

Makes 4 servings

3 1/2 cups low-sodium chicken broth

4 teaspoons olive oil

2 onions, chopped

1 garlic clove, minced

1 cup Arborio rice

1 cup dry white wine

1 cup canned pumpkin puree

1/4 cup grated Parmesan cheese

1/4 teaspoon salt

Ground white pepper, to taste

1/8 teaspoon ground nutmeg

1. Bring the broth to a boil. Reduce the heat and keep at a simmer.

2. Heat the oil in a nonstick saucepan, then add the onions and garlic. Sauté until softened. Add the rice and cook, stirring, until the outer shell is translucent, about 1 minute.

3. Add the wine and 1/2 cup of the broth and stir until they are absorbed. Continue to add broth, 1/2 cup at a time, stirring until it is absorbed before adding more, until the rice is just tender. The cooking time should be about 20 minutes from the first addition of broth. Stir in the pumpkin, cheese, salt, and pepper; heat to serving temperature. Serve at once, sprinkled with the nutmeg.

Per serving: 357 Calories, 10 g Total Fat, 3 g Saturated Fat, 8 mg Cholesterol, 439 mg Sodium, 48 g Total Carbohydrate, 1 g Dietary Fiber, 11 g Protein, 187 mg Calcium.

POINTS *per serving: 8.*

Di Giorno   When you buy the pumpkin puree, be sure to purchase unsweetened, unseasoned, 100 percent pumpkin, and not pumpkin pie filling. To make pumpkin puree, chop 1/4 pound of peeled pumpkin (butternut squash works well, too) into 1-inch chunks. Boil in 1 cup of water until it can be pierced with a fork easily, then puree the pumpkin chunks with about 1/2 cup of the cooking liquid in a food processor or blender.

Ruby Risotto

Seek out mild, creamy pecorino Toscano; it complements the beets better than do Parmesan or the more assertive pecorino Romano. This vibrant red side dish goes nicely with Stuffed Roast Pork Loin (page 220) or Roasted Basil Chicken (page 186).

Makes 6 servings

2 red or golden beets, trimmed

4 1/2 cups chicken broth

2 teaspoons olive oil

1 small onion, finely chopped

1 1/2 cups Arborio rice

1/2 cup dry white wine

Freshly ground pepper, to taste

2 tablespoons chopped flat-leaf parsley

2 tablespoons grated pecorino Toscano cheese

1. Preheat the oven to 400°F. Wrap the beets in foil and roast until fork-tender, about 45 minutes. Let cool about 10 minutes, then peel and chop them.

2. Bring the broth to a boil. Reduce the heat and keep at a simmer.

3. Heat the oil in a nonstick saucepan, then add the onion. Sauté until softened. Add the rice and cook, stirring, until it is lightly toasted, about 3 minutes.

4. Add the wine and 1/2 cup of the broth and stir until they are absorbed. Add another cup of the broth and stir until it is absorbed. Continue to add broth, 1/2 cup at a time, stirring until it is absorbed before adding more, until the rice is just tender; add the beets with the last addition of broth. The cooking time should be about 20 minutes from the first addition of broth. Stir in the pepper, parsley, and cheese; serve at once.

Per serving: 264 Calories, 5 g Total Fat, 1 g Saturated Fat, 5 mg Cholesterol, 812 mg Sodium, 44 g Total Carbohydrate, 3 g Dietary Fiber, 6 g Protein, 42 mg Calcium.

POINTS *per serving: 5.*

D i   G i o r n o   Here's an easy way to peel the roasted beets: Run them under cold water and rub off the skins.

Risotto with Radicchio

Radicchio, the deep maroon, pleasantly bitter chicory from the Veneto, is delicious cooked. In this dish, it melts into the rice and takes on a pretty magenta color as it mellows in flavor—a fascinating and delectable transformation.

Makes 4 servings

3 1/2 cups low-sodium beef broth

4 teaspoons olive oil

1 onion, chopped

1 cup Arborio rice

1 head radicchio, trimmed and cut into thin strips

1 cup dry red wine

2 tablespoons grated Parmesan cheese

Freshly ground pepper, to taste

1. Bring the broth to a boil. Reduce the heat and keep at a simmer.

2. Heat the oil in a nonstick saucepan, then add the onion. Sauté until golden. Add the rice and cook, stirring, until the outer shell is translucent, about 1 minute.

3. Stir in the radicchio, wine, and 1/2 cup of the broth and stir until the liquid is absorbed. Continue to add broth, 1/2 cup at a time, stirring until it is absorbed before adding more, until the rice is just tender. The cooking time should be about 20 minutes from the first addition of broth. Stir in the cheese and pepper; serve at once.

Per serving: 321 Calories, 6 g Total Fat, 2 g Saturated Fat, 4 mg Cholesterol, 169 mg Sodium, 45 g Total Carbohydrate, 2 g Dietary Fiber, 11 g Protein, 105 mg Calcium.

POINTS per serving: 7.

D i   G i o r n o   If you shy away from radicchio because its price per pound is high, take heart: The average head is so light that you'll spend much less than you think. Choose a head with a firm base and well-colored, tightly packed leaves (avoid heads with any brown on the leaves). Store it in a perforated plastic bag in the refrigerator for up to a week.

Risotto with Fresh Herbs

Whether your herb garden is a few pots on the windowsill or a dedicated plot of land, this risotto is a perfect showcase for your green thumb. Experiment with different herbs and their flavors, but don't use any dried herbs—the taste just won't be the same.

Makes 4 servings

4 1/2 cups low-sodium vegetable or chicken broth

4 teaspoons olive oil

3 shallots, minced

2 scallions, thinly sliced

1 cup Arborio rice

1/2 cup minced flat-leaf parsley

1/4 cup minced mint

1/4 cup minced chives

1/4 cup minced basil

4 teaspoons grated Parmesan cheese

1/4 teaspoon ground white pepper

1. Bring the broth to a boil. Reduce the heat and keep at a simmer.

2. Heat the oil in a nonstick saucepan, then add the shallots and scallions. Sauté until softened. Add the rice and cook, stirring, until the outer shell is translucent, about 1 minute.

3. Add 1 1/2 cups of the broth and stir until it is absorbed. Continue to add broth, 1/2 cup at a time, stirring until it is absorbed before adding more, until the rice is just tender. The cooking time should be about 20 minutes from the first addition of broth. Stir in the parsley, mint, chives, basil, cheese, and pepper; serve at once.

Per serving: 298 Calories, 7 g Total Fat, 1 g Saturated Fat, 2 mg Cholesterol, 184 mg Sodium, 53 g Total Carbohydrate, 1 g Dietary Fiber, 6 g Protein, 86 mg Calcium.

POINTS per serving: 6.

Di Giorno   Feel free to vary the herbs as you like, or try the following combinations: equal parts of basil and parsley, with just a bit of rosemary,or equal parts of basil, marjoram, and oregano. Using only rosemary is the classic version; all basil, Genoese-style; and using all parsley would make this a great first course before a fish stew.

Risotto with Zucchini and Peppers

Begin testing the risotto for doneness about 18 minutes after the first addition of broth. It will continue to cook after you remove it from the heat.

Makes 4 servings

4 1/2 cups low-sodium vegetable broth

4 teaspoons olive oil

2 onions, chopped

1 garlic clove, minced

1 cup Arborio rice

4 small zucchini, diced

1 red bell pepper, seeded and diced

2 tablespoons minced basil

2 tablespoons minced oregano

4 teaspoons grated Parmesan cheese

Freshly ground pepper, to taste

1. Bring the broth to a boil. Reduce the heat and keep at a simmer.

2. Heat the oil in a nonstick saucepan, then add the onions and garlic. Sauté until softened. Add the rice and cook, stirring, until the outer shell is translucent, about 1 minute.

3. Add $1^{1}/2$ cups of the broth, the zucchini and bell pepper and stir until the broth is absorbed. Continue to add broth, $1/2$ cup at a time, stirring until it is absorbed before adding more, until the rice and vegetables are just tender. The cooking time should be about 20 minutes from the first addition of broth. Stir in the basil, oregano, cheese, and pepper; serve at once.

Per serving: 314 Calories, 6 g Total Fat, 1 g Saturated Fat, 2 mg Cholesterol, 126 mg Sodium, 58 g Total Carbohydrate, 2 g Dietary Fiber, 8 g Protein, 87 mg Calcium.

POINTS *per serving: 6.*

Di Giorno   The traditional way to eat risotto is to mound it on a plate, then flatten just the section that you're eating. That way it doesn't cool too rapidly.

Risotto with Mushrooms

Mushrooms impart an earthy quality to this classic northern Italian dish. Wild mushrooms like cremini, porcini, or shiitake make it even better—perfect with a roast or hearty meat dish.

Makes 4 servings

3 1/2 cups low-sodium beef broth

4 teaspoons olive oil

1 onion, chopped

3 shallots, minced

2 cups thinly sliced white mushrooms

2 cups thinly sliced wild mushrooms

1 cup Arborio rice

1 cup dry white wine

1/4 cup minced flat-leaf parsley

4 teaspoons grated Parmesan cheese

Freshly ground pepper, to taste

1. Bring the broth to a boil. Reduce the heat and keep at a simmer.

2. Heat the oil in a nonstick saucepan, then add the onion and shallots. Sauté until softened. Add the mushrooms and sauté until they release some of their liquid. Add the rice and cook, stirring, until the outer shell is translucent, about 1 minute.

3. Add the wine and 1/2 cup of the broth and stir until they are absorbed. Continue to add broth, 1/2 cup at a time, stirring until it is absorbed before adding more, until the rice and mushrooms are tender. The cooking time should be about 20 minutes from the first addition of broth. Stir in the parsley, cheese, and pepper; serve at once.

Per serving: 326 Calories, 6 g Total Fat, 1 g Saturated Fat, 2 mg Cholesterol, 110 mg Sodium, 49 g Total Carbohydrate, 2 g Dietary Fiber, 11 g Protein, 55 mg Calcium.

POINTS per serving: 7.

Di Giorno   Shallots are one of the milder-tasting members of the onion, or allium, family. They have deep ochre, papery skins like common yellow onions, but when you peel them you'll find they grow in cloves, similar to garlic, which also needs to be peeled. Although garlic is the allium of choice in Italian cooking, we like how the shallots' delicate flavor enhances but doesn't interfere with the mushrooms' earthy flavor.

Risotto with Leeks and Fennel

The delicate licorice-like flavor of the fennel and the earthy flavor of the leeks combine deliciously to make this a superb risotto. It goes beautifully with meat (especially lamb), fish, or fowl, but is also hearty enough to stand by itself.

Makes 4 servings

3 ¹/₂ cups low-sodium vegetable broth

4 teaspoons olive oil

3 leeks, cleaned and thinly sliced

2 fennel bulbs, trimmed and chopped

1 cup Arborio rice

1 cup dry white wine

2 tablespoons grated Parmesan cheese

Freshly ground pepper, to taste

1. Bring the broth to a boil. Reduce the heat and keep at a simmer.

2. Heat 2 teaspoons of the oil in a nonstick saucepan, then add the leeks and fennel. Sauté until softened. Add the rice and stir until the outer shell is translucent, about 1 minute.

3. Add the wine and ¹/₂ cup of the broth and cook, stirring, until they are absorbed. Continue to add the broth, ¹/₂ cup at a time, stirring until it is absorbed before adding more, until the rice and vegetables are tender. The cooking time should be about 20 minutes from the first addition of broth. Stir in the remaining oil, the cheese, and pepper; serve at once.

Per serving: 367 Calories, 8 g Total Fat, 2 g Saturated Fat, 4 mg Cholesterol, 334 mg Sodium, 56 g Total Carbohydrate, 2 g Dietary Fiber, 8 g Protein, 161 mg Calcium.

POINTS *per serving: 8.*

Risotto with Shrimp and Scallops

This is a truly elegant risotto—serve it with Asparagus Gratinata (page 248) in the spring.

Makes 4 servings

3 1/2 cups low-sodium chicken broth

4 teaspoons olive oil

1 onion, chopped

1 cup Arborio rice

1 cup dry white wine

3/4 pound medium shrimp, peeled and deveined

1/2 pound bay scallops, rinsed and drained

4 teaspoons grated Parmesan cheese

1 tablespoon fresh thyme, or 1 teaspoon dried, crumbled

Freshly ground pepper, to taste

1. Bring the broth to a boil. Reduce the heat and keep at a simmer.

2. Heat the oil in a nonstick saucepan, then add the onion. Sauté until softened. Add the rice and cook, stirring, until the outer shell is translucent, about 1 minute.

3. Add the wine and $1/2$ cup of the broth and stir until they are absorbed. Continue to add broth, $1/2$ cup at a time, stirring until it is absorbed before adding more, until all but about 1 cup of the broth has been used. Add the remaining broth and the shrimp and scallops; cook, stirring, until all the liquid is absorbed, the shrimp are pink, the scallops are just opaque, and the mixture is creamy, 6–8 minutes longer. The cooking time from the first addition of broth should be about 20 minutes. Stir in the cheese, thyme, and pepper; serve at once.

Per serving: 420 Calories, 9 g Total Fat, 2 g Saturated Fat, 112 mg Cholesterol, 341 mg Sodium, 45 g Total Carbohydrate, 1 g Dietary Fiber, 31 g Protein, 107 mg Calcium.

POINTS per serving: 9.

Di Giorno   Bay scallops are small (about $1/2$- to $3/4$-inch diameter) and have a wonderfully sweet flavor. Their price is equally dear—you'll rarely find them for less than ten dollars per pound. The larger, somewhat less tender sea scallops can be used if you prefer, but cut them in half or into quarters, depending on how large they are (they frequently measure two inches in diameter). Avoid the tiny calico scallops; they tend to become rubbery.

Crispy Risotto Balls

If you hate to see anything go to waste, try this dish—it's an excellent use of leftover risotto. Serve it as a side dish, an antipasto, or as a *spuntino*, or snack. You may find yourself making extra risotto on purpose! This works best with a fairly simple risotto, rather than one with lots of mix-ins or strong flavors (for the nutrition analysis, we used Risotto alla Milanese, but try it with Risotto with Mushrooms or Risotto with Fresh Herbs on pages 121 and 119).

Makes 8 servings

2 ounces fresh mozzarella cheese, chopped (about ¹/2 cup)

2 slices prosciutto (about 1 ounce), chopped

2 cups Risotto alla Milanese (page 110), chilled

¹/4 cup plain dried bread crumbs

1. Put a nonstick baking sheet into the oven and preheat it to 475°F.

2. Mix the cheese and prosciutto in a small bowl. With moistened hands, form 2 tablespoons of the risotto into a patty. Place 1 tablespoon of the cheese mixture on the risotto and top with 2 more tablespoons of the risotto. Form into a ball and roll to coat in the bread crumbs. Repeat the process to make 8 filled risotto balls.

3. Spray the baking sheet with nonstick spray. Place the risotto balls on the sheet and spray them. Bake until crisp and golden all over, about 10 minutes, turning them after 5 minutes.

Per serving: 127 Calories, 5 g Total Fat, 2 g Saturated Fat, 9 g Cholesterol, 357 mg Sodium, 15 g Total Carbohydrate, 0 g Dietary Fiber, 4 g Protein, 64 mg Calcium.

POINTS *per serving: 3.*

D i G i o r n o   Be sure your hands remain moistened as you handle the risotto, otherwise it will stick.

Crispy Risotto Balls

Gnocchi

These featherweight potato dumplings are great with any light, not-too-chunky sauce. Try them with Tomato Sauce (page 59), Tomato-Herb Sauce (page 61), or basil pesto (see Capellini with Pesto, page 63), as well as with pumpkin sauce (page 130).

Makes 4 servings, or 72 gnocchi

1 pound baking potatoes, scrubbed

¹/₂ cup all-purpose flour

¹/₄ teaspoon salt

1. Preheat the oven to 400°F. Poke a few holes in the potatoes with a fork. Bake until tender, about 1 hour. Let cool slightly, then peel. Press the pulp through a ricer or food mill; there should be about 1 ¹/₂ cups potato pulp. While the pulp is still hot, stir in the flour and the salt.

2. Lightly dust a countertop with flour. Put a sheet of wax paper on a baking sheet. Turn out the potato dough and knead until smooth but slightly sticky. Break off a chunk of dough the size of a lemon; keep the remaining dough covered. Roll the dough into a 1-inch thick rope. Cut into 1-inch pieces, then roll each piece against the tines of a fork to make decorative grooves; set aside on the wax paper, making sure the gnocchi don't touch one another. Repeat with the remaining dough. Refrigerate, lightly covered, up to 2 days or freeze first on the wax paper-lined baking sheet, then in zip-close plastic bags up to 1 month.

3. Cook the gnocchi in a large pot of boiling water in batches without crowding, until they float to the surface, about 30–45 seconds. With a slotted spoon, transfer to a serving bowl. Repeat until all gnocchi are cooked. Toss lightly with the sauce of your choice.

Per serving: 150 Calories, 0 g Total Fat, 0 g Saturated Fat, 0 mg Cholesterol, 140 mg Sodium, 33 g Total Carbohydrate, 2 g Dietary Fiber, 4 g Protein, 8 mg Calcium.

***POINTS** per serving: 3.*

D i   G i o r n o   Gnocchi can be tricky to make, but here are two tips: First, bake the potatoes in the oven. If you cook them in a microwave, they'll get too mealy. Second, use the ricer or food mill we call for to puree the pulp; using one of them will provide the proper texture.

Basil Gnocchi

In Liguria, they serve potato gnocchi topped with basil pesto, but these little dumplings are also delectable with the herb mixed in.

Makes 4 servings

1 pound baking potatoes, scrubbed

³/4 cup all-purpose flour

¹/4 cup + 2 tablespoons minced basil

¹/4 teaspoon salt

2 cups Tomato-Herb Sauce (page 61), heated

4 teaspoons freshly grated Parmesan cheese

1. Preheat the oven to 400°F. Poke a few holes in the potatoes with a fork. Bake until tender, about 1 hour. Let cool slightly, then peel. Press the pulp through a ricer or food mill into a large bowl. While the pulp is still hot, stir in the flour, ¹/4 cup of the basil, and the salt.

2. Lightly dust a countertop with flour. Put a sheet of wax paper on a baking sheet. Turn out the potato dough and knead until smooth but slightly sticky. Break off a chunk of dough the size of a lemon; keep the remaining dough covered. Roll the dough into a 1-inch thick rope. Cut into 1-inch pieces, then roll each piece against the tines of a fork to make decorative grooves; set aside on the wax paper, making sure the gnocchi don't touch one another. Repeat with the remaining dough. Refrigerate, lightly covered, up to 2 days or freeze first on the wax paper–lined baking sheet, then in zip-close plastic bags up to 1 month.

3. Place ¹/4 cup of the tomato sauce in a large serving bowl.

4. Cook the gnocchi in a large pot of boiling water in batches, without crowding, until they float to the surface, 30–45 seconds. With a slotted spoon, transfer immediately to the serving bowl, alternating layers of sauce and gnocchi. Serve at once, sprinkled with the remaining 2 tablespoons of basil and the cheese.

Per serving: 272 Calories, 6 g Total Fat, 1 g Saturated Fat, 2 mg Cholesterol, 327 mg Sodium, 49 g Total Carbohydrate, 4 g Dietary Fiber, 7 g Protein, 102 mg Calcium.

POINTS *per serving: 5.*

Sweet Potato Gnocchi with Gorgonzola Sauce

Using sweet potato rather than white potato adds an interesting flavor and visual dimension to this gnocchi. The sweetness and vivid color of the potato provides an elegant foil for the sharpness and paleness of the Gorgonzola. As a variation, skip making the sauce, as we did for the dish in the photograph. Instead, drizzle the gnocchi with olive oil, some crumbled gorgonzola, and a sprinkling of parsley.

Makes 4 servings

1 pound sweet potato (about 1 large potato), scrubbed

³/₄ cup all-purpose flour

¹/₂ teaspoon salt

³/₄ cup nonfat ricotta cheese

¹/₄ cup Gorgonzola cheese

3 tablespoons fat-free milk

1¹/₂ tablespoons chopped flat-leaf parsley

1. Preheat the oven to 400°F. Poke a few holes in the potato with a fork. Bake until tender when pierced with a knife, about 1 hour. Let cool slightly, then peel. Press the pulp through a ricer or food mill into a large bowl. While the pulp is still hot, mix in the flour and salt with lightly floured hands.

2. Lightly dust a countertop with flour. Put a sheet of wax paper on a baking sheet. Turn out the potato dough and knead until smooth but slightly sticky. Break off a chunk of dough the size of a lemon; keep the remaining dough covered. Roll the dough into 1-inch thick ropes. Cut into 1-inch pieces, then roll each piece against the tines of a fork to make decorative grooves. Set aside on wax paper, making sure the gnocchi don't touch one another. Repeat with the remaining dough.

3. To make the sauce, mix the ricotta, Gorgonzola, and milk in a blender until well combined. Transfer to a large bowl.

4. Cook the gnocchi in a large pot of boiling water in batches until they float to the surface, 1–2 minutes. With a slotted spoon, transfer to the bowl with the sauce and toss to coat. Repeat until all the gnocchi are cooked. Serve at once.

Per serving: 272 Calories, 3 g Total Fat, 1 g Saturated Fat, 7 mg Cholesterol, 460 mg Sodium, 48 g Total Carbohydrate, 4 g Dietary Fiber, 14 g Protein, 140 mg Calcium.

POINTS *per serving: 5.*

D i G i o r n o   Putting the sweet potato through a ricer rather than mashing it yields a lighter consistency; it will blend more easily with the flour.

Sweet Potato Gnocchi with Gorgonzola Sauce

Gnocchi with Pumpkin Sauce

This dish, with its intriguing sauce, is a favorite in Lombardy and the Veneto. Refrigerate or freeze any extra sauce for another meal.

Makes 4 servings

4 teaspoons olive oil

One 2-pound pumpkin or butternut squash, peeled, halved, seeded, and diced

3 shallots, minced

1 garlic clove, minced

2 cups low-sodium chicken broth

1 tablespoon fresh thyme, or 1 teaspoon dried leaves, crumbled

1 tablespoon minced fresh sage, or 1 teaspoon dried, crumbled

1/4 teaspoon ground white pepper

72 potato gnocchi (page 128)

4 teaspoons grated Parmesan cheese

1 tablespoon packed brown sugar

1/4 teaspoon cinnamon

1/4 teaspoon ground nutmeg

Fresh sage leaves

1. Heat the oil in a nonstick skillet, then add the pumpkin, shallots, and garlic. Sauté until the shallots begin to turn golden. Add the broth, thyme, sage, and pepper; cook, stirring frequently, until the pumpkin is softened and the liquid is reduced by two-thirds, 15–20 minutes longer.

2. Transfer the sauce into a food processor or blender and puree. If it is too thick, add water, 1 tablespoon at a time, until it reaches the desired consistency.

3. Meanwhile, cook the gnocchi in a large pot of boiling water in batches without crowding, until they float to the surface, about 30–45 seconds. With a slotted spoon, transfer to a serving bowl. Repeat until all the gnocchi are cooked. Pour the sauce over the gnocchi; then sprinkle with the cheese, brown sugar, cinnamon, and nutmeg. Serve, garnished with sage leaves.

Per serving: 276 Calories, 7 g Total Fat, 1 g Saturated Fat, 1 mg Cholesterol, 233 mg Sodium, 50 g Total Carbohydrate, 2 g Dietary Fiber, 8 g Protein, 93 mg Calcium.

POINTS per serving: 6.

D i   G i o r n o   If you prefer, use 1 cup of canned pumpkin puree instead of the whole pumpkin. Cook the pumpkin mixture until the flavors blend, and don't puree.

Polenta

Variations on this staple transcend cultures and time: cornmeal mush in Colonial America, grits in the South in the United States, mamaliga in Romania, tamales in Mexico. Polenta is every bit as important in northern Italy as pasta is in the southern part of the country.

Makes 4 servings, about 4 cups

3 1/2 cups water

1/4 teaspoon salt

1 cup coarse-ground yellow cornmeal

1. Bring the water to boil in a heavy pot. Add the salt; reduce the heat so the water is barely simmering. Stirring constantly, slowly add the cornmeal in a thin, steady stream (pick up a handful and sift it through your fist). Reduce the heat and cook, stirring constantly, until the polenta pulls away from the sides of the pot, 10–15 minutes.

2. If serving immediately, pour the polenta onto a large warm platter. If using in further preparation, pour onto a large wooden block or cutting board and let cool slightly before slicing.

Per serving: 126 Calories, 1 g Total Fat, 0 g Saturated Fat, 0 mg Cholesterol, 136 mg Sodium, 27 g Total Carbohydrate, 2 g Dietary Fiber, 3 g Protein, 3 mg Calcium.

POINTS per serving: 2.

D i   G i o r n o   Cheap and filling, polenta has a long history as a peasant food. What have helped to elevate it to chic and trendy tables are the toppings. Polenta's inherent blandness is the perfect foil for sauces of exotic mushrooms or rich cheeses. Served right away, polenta has a soft consistency, much like a hot cereal. If you make it ahead and let it sit, it thickens to a consistency not unlike refrigerated cookie dough.

Polenta with Mushroom "Ragù"

Meaty cremini mushrooms replace the more typical ration of meat in this healthful but hearty ragù. You may also want to try a flavorful assortment of mushrooms, such as cremini, shitake, and white mushrooms, as we did in the dish for the photograph. Make the polenta while the sauce simmers. Besides serving this over mounds of soft polenta, this versatile sauce is tasty over grilled polenta slices, tossed with penne, or stirred into cooked risotto.

Makes 6 servings

1/2 tablespoon olive oil

1 white onion, chopped

2 garlic cloves, chopped

1 pound cremini mushrooms, cleaned, stemmed, and chopped

1 tablespoon dried oregano

1 teaspoon dried basil

1/2 cup dry white wine

1 (28-ounce) can diced tomatoes

1/2 teaspoon salt

Pinch crushed red pepper

4 cups Polenta (page 131)

Heat the oil in a straight-sided nonstick skillet, then add the onion and garlic. Sauté until the onion is translucent, about 1 minute. Add the mushrooms, oregano, basil, and 1/4 cup of the wine. Cook, covered, 2 minutes. Stir in the tomatoes, salt, crushed red pepper, and the remaining 1/4 cup wine; bring just to a boil. Reduce the heat and simmer, uncovered, to form a thick stew, about 20 minutes. Serve over the polenta.

Per serving: 223 Calories, 3 g Total Fat, 0 g Saturated Fat, 0 mg Cholesterol, 541 mg Sodium, 42 g Total Carbohydrate, 6 g Dietary Fiber, 7 g Protein, 75 mg Calcium.

POINTS per serving: 4.

D i   G i o r n o   *Ragù*, from the French *ragoût* (both words come from the Latin *gustus*, which means "taste") typically refers to a thick, hearty long-simmered meat sauce. Here, all the chopped mushrooms need is a brief simmering to blend with the other ingredients, so this sauce is a great fake.

Polenta with Mushroom "Ragù"

Polenta "Gnocchi" alla Romana

Gnocchi alla Romana, traditionally made by cooking semolina in milk, is such a classic dish that it can be traced back to the ancient Romans. Substituting polenta makes this version less labor-intensive.

Makes 4 servings

3 cups Polenta (page 131)

¹/₄ cup grated Parmesan cheese

2 teaspoons olive oil

1. Preheat the oven to 350°F. Spray a 9-inch pie plate with nonstick spray.

2. Prepare the polenta through step 1 and scrape onto a large cutting board. With a knife or spatula dipped in cold water, spread evenly to a ¹/4-inch thickness. Dip a 2-inch biscuit cutter into cold water; cut the polenta into 16 disks, dipping the biscuit cutter in cold water after each cut. Reserve any scraps for another use.

3. Arrange the disks in the pie plate, overlapping as necessary. Sprinkle with the cheese and drizzle with the oil. Bake until crisp and golden, 40–50 minutes. Divide evenly among 4 plates and serve at once.

Per serving: 200 Calories, 7 g Total Fat, 3 g Saturated Fat, 8 mg Cholesterol, 362 mg Sodium, 27 g Total Carbohydrate, 2 g Dietary Fiber, 7 g Protein, 149 mg Calcium.

***POINTS** per serving: 4.*

five

frittatas

Frittata with Leftover Spaghetti

Whether it's a French omelet, Spanish tortilla, Italian frittata, or any other nation's dish, scrambled eggs are often the base for leftovers. Add a salad or vegetable and you've got a meal.

Makes 4 servings

2 cups fat-free egg substitute

3 cups cooked spaghetti

1 1/2 cups Tomato Sauce (page 59)

2 tablespoons grated Parmesan cheese

Freshly ground pepper, to taste

1. Preheat the broiler. Spray a nonstick skillet with a heatproof handle with nonstick spray and set over medium heat.

2. Beat the egg substitute until frothy. Pour it into the skillet, tilting to cover the pan. Top with the spaghetti and tomato sauce. Reduce the heat and cook until the underside is set, about 10 minutes. Broil the frittata 5 inches from the heat until the top is set and just slightly crusty, 1–1 1/2 minutes. Slide the frittata onto a plate and cut into wedges. Serve, sprinkled with the cheese and pepper.

Per serving: 284 Calories, 6 g Total Fat, 2 g Saturated Fat, 4 mg Cholesterol, 411 mg Sodium, 37 g Total Carbohydrate, 3 g Dietary Fiber, 20 g Protein, 127 mg Calcium.

POINTS *per serving: 6.*

Frittata with Peppers and Potatoes

Peppers and eggs have a natural affinity for each other, and adding potatoes just makes a good thing better. For a real treat, top this with a few spoonfuls of Tomato-Herb Sauce (page 61).

Makes 4 servings

4 teaspoons olive oil

4 Italian frying peppers, seeded and chopped

2 medium all-purpose potatoes, diced

1 cup hot water

2 cups fat-free egg substitute

1 tablespoon minced fresh oregano, or 1/2 teaspoon dried

1/4 teaspoon salt

Freshly ground pepper, to taste

2 teaspoons grated Parmesan cheese

1. Preheat the broiler. Heat the oil in a nonstick skillet with a heat-proof handle, then add the frying peppers, potatoes, and water. Cover and cook, stirring frequently and adding 1/2 cup water if the water evaporates too quickly, until the vegetables are tender and the liquid evaporates, about 15 minutes. Transfer to a bowl.

2. Wipe out the skillet with a paper towel, then spray it with non-stick spray and set over medium heat. Beat the egg substitute, oregano, salt, and pepper until frothy. Pour it into the skillet, tilting to cover the pan. Top with the vegetables. Reduce the heat and cook until the underside is set, about 10 minutes. Broil the frittata 5 inches from the heat, until the top is set and slightly crusty, 1–1 1/2 minutes. Slide the frittata onto a plate and cut into wedges. Serve, sprinkled with the cheese.

Per serving: 187 Calories, 5 g Total Fat, 1 g Saturated Fat, 1 mg Cholesterol, 364 mg Sodium, 21 g Total Carbohydrate, 2 g Dietary Fiber, 15 g Protein, 80 mg Calcium.

***POINTS** per serving: 4.*

D i G i o r n o   Italian frying peppers have a pale green skin, thin flesh, and very sweet flavor. Italians call them *peperoni a corno*, which means "horn-shaped peppers," and they are indeed rather long and pointed. If you cannot find them, substitute yellow or red bell peppers (either of which is much sweeter than the green variety).

Frittata with Potatoes and Onions

Frittatas are often eaten at room temperature, which makes them ideal make-aheads for weekend brunches or weekday lunches. (As with any food, though, don't keep a frittata at room temperature for more than two hours.) When they taste as good as this version, you'll find entertaining is a snap. For a milder flavor, replace the onions with two leeks.

Makes 4 servings

4 teaspoons olive oil

2 medium all-purpose potatoes, diced

2 onions, chopped

1 cup hot water

2 cups fat-free egg substitute

1/4 cup minced flat-leaf parsley

4 teaspoons grated Parmesan cheese

1/4 teaspoon salt

Freshly ground pepper, to taste

1. Preheat the broiler. Heat the oil in a nonstick skillet with a heat-proof handle, then add the potatoes, onions, and water. Cook, stirring frequently and adding 1/2 cup water if the water evaporates too quickly, until the potatoes are golden, the onions are tender, and the liquid evaporates, about 15 minutes. Transfer to a bowl.

2. Wipe out the skillet with a paper towel, then spray it with non-stick spray and set over medium heat. Beat the egg substitute, parsley, cheese, salt, and pepper until frothy. Pour it into the skillet, tilting to cover the pan. Top with the vegetables. Reduce the heat and cook until the underside is set, about 10 minutes. Broil the frittata 5 inches from the heat until the top is set and slightly crusty, 1–1 1/2 minutes. Slide the frittata onto a plate and cut into wedges.

Per serving: 186 Calories, 6 g Total Fat, 1 g Saturated Fat, 2 mg Cholesterol, 437 mg Sodium, 18 g Total Carbohydrate, 2 g Dietary Fiber, 15 g Protein, 91 mg Calcium.

POINTS *per serving: 4.*

Frittata with Artichoke Hearts and Mushrooms

Artichoke hearts and mushrooms star in this frittata, which makes a wonderful dish for a spring brunch or luncheon. If you happen to have leftover asparagus on hand, cut into bite-size lengths if necessary, then add to the vegetables in the bowl.

Makes 4 servings

1 (10-ounce) box frozen artichoke hearts

4 teaspoons olive oil

3 shallots, minced

1 garlic clove, minced

2 cups sliced mushrooms

2 cups fat-free egg substitute

1/4 cup minced flat-leaf parsley

2 tablespoons grated Parmesan cheese

1/4 teaspoon salt

Freshly ground pepper, to taste

1. Preheat the broiler. Cook the artichoke hearts according to package directions, until tender. Cut into bite-size pieces. Transfer to a bowl.

2. Heat the oil in a nonstick skillet with a heatproof handle, then add the shallots and garlic. Sauté until the shallots are softened. Stir in the mushrooms and sauté until the mushrooms are tender and the shallots are golden. Add to the artichokes.

3. Wipe out the skillet with a paper towel, then spray it with nonstick spray and set over medium heat. Beat the egg substitute until frothy. Pour it into the skillet, tilting to cover the pan. Top with the vegetables. Reduce the heat and cook until the underside is set, about 10 minutes. Sprinkle with the parsley, cheese, salt, and pepper. Broil the frittata 5 inches from the heat until the top is set and slightly crusty, 1–1 1/2 minutes. Slide the frittata onto a plate and cut into wedges.

Per serving: 179 Calories, 7 g Total Fat, 2 g Saturated Fat, 4 mg Cholesterol, 473 mg Sodium, 13 g Total Carbohydrate, 4 g Dietary Fiber, 17 g Protein, 143 mg Calcium.

POINTS per serving: 3.

Di Giorno   You'll probably find two different types of parsley at your supermarket (though there are more than 30 varieties). Curly parsley has pretty, frilly leaves but not much flavor; it's best as a garnish. Choose flat-leaf (sometimes called Italian) parsley for cooking; its flavor is fresh and sprightly. Flat-leaf parsley and cilantro look almost the same. To tell them apart, gently rub a leaf between your thumb and fingertip. The pressure will release the fragrance, and you'll be able to smell cilantro's distinctive aroma on your fingers.

A Mushroom Primer

From Veal Marsala to Risotto with Mushrooms, the flavor of *funghi* is an integral part of Italian cuisine. Although most cooks rely on the common white mushroom, there are thousands of varieties to add excitement to any dish. Check out the following to know what to choose:

Type	The Look	The Taste/How to Use
Agaricus (White)	Cap ranges in size from $1/2$ to 3 inches in diameter; color ranges from white to pale tan.	Mild, earthy flavor. All-purpose use: raw in salads and vegetable platters; cooked in stuffings and soups.
Cremino	Dark brown, firmer variation of the white mushroom with a cap that ranges from $1/2$ to 2 inches in diameter.	Deeper, denser, earthier flavor than *Agaricus*. Excellent addition to beef, game, and vegetable dishes.
Chanterelle	Trumpet-shaped, ranging in color from bright yellow to orange.	Delicate, nutty flavor; chewy texture. Cooked as side dish or added to other foods; often in cream-based dishes.
Morel	Spongy honey-combed, cone-shaped cap, ranging in size from 2 to 4 inches high; deep tan to extremely dark brown color.	Smoky, earthy, nutty flavor. Marries well with light sauces and meats like chicken, Cornish hen, veal, and rabbit; excellent sautéed in butter.
Oyster	Fan-shaped with smooth, deep-gilled caps; pale gray to dark brownish-gray color.	Robust, peppery flavor when raw; delicate, mild flavor when cooked; melting texture. Good substituted for or combined with the common white mushroom; fleeting flavor best suited to simple dishes and small amounts of fats and oils.
Porcino	Pale brown with a creamy white flesh inside; weight ranging from a couple ounces to a pound; caps size ranges from 1 to 10 inches in diameter.	Meaty, silken texture; pungent, woodsy flavor. Simple preparation is best; lightly cooked in olive oil, added to soups, stuffings, and stews.
Portobello	The fully matured form of the cremino; large dark brown with an open, flat cap.	Dense, meaty texture. Ideal for grilling; cut into thick slices in salads or entrées.

Frittata with Zucchini, Peppers, and Onions

The indirect heat of the oven lessens the risk of your frittata's bottom burning before the eggs are set. Never put a skillet with a plastic handle in the oven, though, or the handle will melt.

Makes 4 servings

4 teaspoons olive oil

2 onions, chopped

2 cups hot water

2 small zucchini, diced

1 red or green bell pepper, seeded and diced

2 cups fat-free egg substitute

1/4 cup minced fresh basil, or 2 teaspoons dried

1/4 teaspoon salt

Freshly ground pepper, to taste

2 tablespoons grated Parmesan cheese

1. Preheat the broiler. Heat the oil in a nonstick skillet with a heat-proof handle, then add the onions. Sauté until softened. Add the water, zucchini, and bell pepper. Reduce the heat, cover, and simmer, stirring frequently, until the vegetables are tender, about 8 minutes. Uncover and cook until the liquid evaporates. Transfer the vegetables to a bowl.

2. Wipe out the skillet with a paper towel, then spray it with non-stick spray and set over medium heat. Beat the egg substitute, basil, salt, and pepper until frothy. Pour it into the skillet, tilting to cover the pan. Top with the vegetables. Reduce the heat and cook until the underside is set, about 10 minutes. Broil the frittata 5 inches from the heat until the top is set and slightly crusty, 1–1 1/2 minutes. Slide the frittata onto a plate and cut into wedges. Serve, sprinkled with the cheese.

Per serving: 160 Calories, 6 g Total Fat, 2 g Saturated Fat, 4 mg Cholesterol, 439 mg Sodium, 10 g Total Carbohydrate, 1 g Dietary Fiber, 16 g Protein, 153 mg Calcium.

POINTS *per serving: 4.*

Frittata with Mozzarella and Tomato Sauce

This looks just like a pizza and it tastes just as good—maybe even better. With Broccoflower and Onion Sauté (page 237) or Sautéed Peppers (page 240), you've got a meal in minutes.

Makes 4 servings

2 cups fat-free egg substitute

3/4 cup Tomato-Herb Sauce (page 61)

3 ounces skim-milk mozzarella cheese, shredded (about 3/4 cup)

Freshly ground pepper, to taste

1. Preheat the broiler. Spray a nonstick skillet with a heatproof handle with nonstick spray and set over medium heat.

2. Beat the egg substitute until frothy. Pour the egg substitute into the skillet, tilting to cover the pan. Dot the surface with the tomato sauce; spread gently, but do not stir. Reduce the heat and cook until the underside is set, about 10 minutes. Sprinkle with the cheese and pepper. Broil the frittata until the top is set and the cheese melts, 1–1 1/2 minutes. Slide the frittata onto a plate and cut into wedges.

Per serving: 119 Calories, 2 g Total Fat, 0 g Saturated Fat, 2 mg Cholesterol, 413 mg Sodium, 5 g Total Carbohydrate, 1 g Dietary Fiber, 19 g Protein, 201 mg Calcium.

POINTS *per serving: 2.*

salads

Orange and Fennel Salad

Fennel and endive are winter vegetables, so this salad is perfect to make when other greens and veggies aren't at their best.

Makes 4 servings

2 fennel bulbs, trimmed and thinly sliced

3 heads Belgian endive, cleaned and separated into leaves

2 small navel oranges, peeled and sectioned

10 small black olives, pitted and halved

¹/₄ teaspoon salt

¹/₄ teaspoon freshly ground pepper

4 teaspoons extra-virgin olive oil

Combine the fennel, endive, oranges, and olives in a salad bowl. Sprinkle with the salt and pepper, then drizzle with the oil and toss to coat. Let stand a few minutes so the flavors can blend.

Per serving: 104 Calories, 6 g Total Fat, 1 g Saturated Fat, 0 mg Cholesterol, 303 mg Sodium, 13 g Total Carbohydrate, 4 g Dietary Fiber, 2 g Protein, 85 mg Calcium.

POINTS per serving: 2.

Broccoli, Raisin, and Pine Nut Salad

Despite its poverty, Sicily has one of the richest culinary traditions—certainly the most diverse—in all of Italy. For more than two thousand years, this Mediterranean island was occupied, and often became the seat of the conquerors, who brought their own foods and culinary traditions. On the west coast of Sicily, which is less than 150 miles from Tunisia, sweet-and-sour flavors, as well as ingredients like pine nuts and raisins, are especially common.

Makes 4 servings

2 tablespoons reduced-calorie mayonnaise

2 tablespoons nonfat sour cream

1 tablespoon packed dark brown sugar

1 tablespoon white-wine vinegar

3 tablespoons pine nuts, toasted

1 pound broccoli crowns, cut into small florets (about 4 cups)

2 tablespoons raisins

2 scallions, thinly sliced

3 slices bacon, crisp-cooked and crumbled

2 cups shredded red cabbage

1. Blend the mayonnaise, sour cream, brown sugar, and vinegar in a small bowl until smooth.

2. Toss the pine nuts, broccoli, raisins, scallions, and bacon in a salad bowl. Drizzle with the dressing and toss to coat. Cover and refrigerate up to 1 day to blend the flavors.

3. Serve the salad over the cabbage.

Per serving: 162 Calories, 8 g Total Fat, 2 g Saturated Fat, 7 mg Cholesterol, 153 mg Sodium, 18 g Total Carbohydrate, 5 g Dietary Fiber, 8 g Protein, 82 mg Calcium.

POINTS *per serving: 3.*

Cauliflower, Caper, and Olive Salad

A version of this recipe is traditionally served on Christmas in Naples, often with slices of eel left over from Christmas Eve. Neapolitans call it *insalata di rinforzo alla napoletana*, or "invigorating salad from Naples."

Makes 4 servings

1 1/2 pounds cauliflower, cut into florets (about 6 cups)

2 celery stalks, chopped

10 small green olives, pitted

10 small black olives, pitted

1/2 cup chopped pickled sweet red peppers

1 tablespoon capers, drained

4 teaspoons extra-virgin olive oil

1 tablespoon cider vinegar

2 tablespoons low-sodium vegetable broth

1/4 teaspoon salt

Freshly ground pepper, to taste

2 tablespoons minced parsley

1. Put the cauliflower in a steamer basket; set in a saucepan over 1 inch boiling water. Cover tightly and steam until barely tender, 5–7 minutes. Rinse under cold water, then drain.

2. Combine the celery, the olives, red peppers, capers, oil, vinegar, broth, salt, and pepper. Mix in the cauliflower. Cover and refrigerate 6–8 hours or overnight to blend the flavors.

3. Bring the salad to room temperature; stir gently. Serve, sprinkled with the parsley.

Per serving: 102 Calories, 7 g Total Fat, 1 g Saturated Fat, 0 mg Cholesterol, 496 mg Sodium, 10 g Total Carbohydrate, 4 g Dietary Fiber, 3 g Protein, 61 mg Calcium.

POINTS per serving: 2.

Cauliflower, Caper, and Olive Salad

Tricolor Salad

A refreshing mixture of tangy and bitter greens, this salad makes a colorful addition to any menu. Shave in a bit of Parmesan or add some mozzarella to make a light lunch.

Makes 4 servings

1 head radicchio, cleaned

1 head Belgian endive, cleaned

1 bunch arugula, cleaned and torn

1/4 cup Oil and Vinegar Salad Dressing (page 161)

1. Set aside 8 of the largest radicchio leaves; tear the rest into bite-size pieces. Set aside 12 of the largest Belgian endive leaves; cut the rest into 1-inch slices.

2. On each of 4 salad plates, arrange 2 of the radicchio leaves and 3 of the endive leaves in a petal pattern. In a large bowl, toss the remaining radicchio and endive, and the arugula with the dressing. Place one-fourth of the salad in the center of each plate; serve at once.

Per serving: 69 Calories, 5 g Total Fat, 1 g Saturated Fat, 0 mg Cholesterol, 159 mg Sodium, 4 g Total Carbohydrate, 2 g Dietary Fiber, 2 g Protein, 77 mg Calcium.

POINTS *per serving: 1.*

Arugula and Radicchio Salad with Parmesan

This salad is proof that the simple things in life can be the best. Balsamic vinegar enhances the flavor of this salad, and cheese provides a tasty complement.

Makes 4 servings

1 head radicchio, cleaned

1 bunch arugula, cleaned

2 tablespoons balsamic vinegar

2 teaspoons extra-virgin olive oil

1 1/2 ounces Parmesan cheese, crumbled

Freshly ground pepper, to taste

Divide the radicchio among 4 salad plates and pile the arugula on top. Drizzle with the vinegar, then the oil. Sprinkle with the cheese, then the pepper.

Per serving: 79 Calories, 6 g Total Fat, 2 g Saturated Fat, 8 mg Cholesterol, 218 mg Sodium, 2 g Total Carbohydrate, 1 g Dietary Fiber, 6 g Protein, 217 mg Calcium.

POINTS *per serving: 2.*

D i G i o r n o   You'll need to buy a wedge of Parmesan cheese in order to crumble it. Seek out authentic Parmigiano-Reggiano cheese; you'll know it by the pale brown rind that has "Parmigiano-Reggiano" stenciled on it. If you have a set of cheese knives, by all means use the knife meant for Parmesan to crumble it (it's the very squat one with the sturdy, slightly almond-shaped, pointed blade). Otherwise, bring the cheese to room temperature, then insert a sturdy knife in it and twist gently.

Arugula and Potato Salad

This salad of new potatoes in a light vinaigrette, served atop peppery arugula, is a far cry from American mayonnaise-based potato salad. Watercress is a fine substitute for arugula, or toss in cubed ham or cooked pancetta. This salad is also outstanding dressed with Creamy Italian Salad Dressing (page 163).

Makes 4 servings

1 1/2 pounds new potatoes

4 scallions, sliced

2 tablespoons dry white wine

4 teaspoons extra-virgin olive oil

1 tablespoon white-wine vinegar

1 garlic clove, bruised

1/4 teaspoon salt

Freshly ground pepper, to taste

1 bunch arugula, cleaned

1. Bring the potatoes and water to cover to a boil. Reduce the heat and simmer, covered, until tender, about 10 minutes. Drain and let cool slightly. Slice the potatoes 1/4 to 1/2-inch thick while still warm.

2. Whisk the scallions, wine, oil, vinegar, garlic, salt, and pepper in a large bowl. Add the potatoes and toss to coat.

3. Just before serving, divide the arugula among 4 salad plates, arranging it around the edges. Remove the garlic from the potato salad; mound the salad in the middle of the plates. Serve warm or at room temperature, but not cold.

Per serving: 168 Calories, 5 g Total Fat, 1 g Saturated Fat, 0 mg Cholesterol, 165 mg Sodium, 27 g Total Carbohydrate, 4 g Dietary Fiber, 4 g Protein, 59 mg Calcium.

POINTS per serving: 3.

D i G i o r n o   Cold temperatures mute flavors—think of the difference between just-from-the-freezer ice cream and that which is slightly softened, or how much less pungent an ice cold beer is than one served just a bit warmer. Serving this salad slightly warmed intensifies its flavors.

Wilted Swiss Chard and Spinach Salad

Italian cooks know how to coax the flavor out of the simplest foods. Dressed with olive oil and lemon juice, cooked greens are particularly welcome with most meat-, fish-, and cheese-based dishes. Try this with other greens too, but remember to adjust the cooking times.

Makes 4 servings

1 small bunch Swiss chard, cleaned and coarsely chopped (keep the stems and leaves separate)

1 (10-ounce) bag triple-washed spinach, cleaned and coarsely chopped

1 tablespoon fresh lemon juice

2 teaspoons extra-virgin olive oil

$^1/_4$ teaspoon salt

Freshly ground pepper, to taste

1. Cut the thin chard stems into 1-inch pieces; discard the thick, tough stems.

2. Cook the chard and spinach in a saucepan over medium-low heat, stirring occasionally and adding water, 1 tablespoon at a time, as needed, until the leaves are wilted and the stems are tender, about 5 minutes. Drain and squeeze out any excess moisture; put in a serving bowl. While still warm, drizzle with the lemon juice, oil, salt, and pepper.

Per serving: 40 Calories, 3 g Total Fat, 0 g Saturated Fat, 0 mg Cholesterol, 256 mg Sodium, 4 g Total Carbohydrate, 2 g Dietary Fiber, 2 g Protein, 75 mg Calcium.

POINTS per serving: 1.

Di Giorno Don't dry the greens after you've washed them. The water that clings to the leaves helps them to wilt and keeps them from scorching when you cook them.

Panzanella

The Tuscans are equally proud of their crusty bread and their thrift. This savory bread-and-tomato salad showcases both; it's perfect for days when the garden is brimming and the bread is a little hard. For best results, use only ripe, in-season tomatoes and crusty peasant bread.

Makes 4 servings

4 tomatoes, peeled and chopped

4 celery stalks, thinly sliced

1 red onion, chopped

1/2 cup minced flat-leaf parsley

2 tablespoons red-wine vinegar

4 teaspoons extra-virgin olive oil

1 garlic clove, minced

1/4 teaspoon salt

Freshly ground pepper, to taste

1 (8-ounce) loaf 1- or 2-day-old Italian bread, coarsely chopped

1/4 cup minced basil

1. Combine the tomatoes, celery, onion, parsley, vinegar, oil, garlic, salt, and pepper. Let stand until the tomatoes have released some of their juice, at least 30 minutes.

2. Soak the bread in water to cover until it just starts to soften, about 3 minutes. Drain and squeeze dry. Put the bread back in the bowl; with a fork, break it into small pieces. Stir it into the tomato mixture, then sprinkle with the basil.

Per serving: 257 Calories, 7 g Total Fat, 1 g Saturated Fat, 0 mg Cholesterol, 514 mg Sodium, 43 g Total Carbohydrate, 5 g Dietary Fiber, 8 g Protein, 114 mg Calcium.

POINTS per serving: 5.

D i G i o r n o   To be sure the bread will have the proper texture, be sure to use a loaf made without preservatives and flavor enhancers. (If you have time, make Italian Loaf on page 260.)

White Bean and Sage Salad

You won't go far in Tuscany without encountering this combination. This salad is delicious as is, or mix in some chopped red onion, flaked tuna, or both. Serve it in hollowed out tomatoes for a pretty summertime presentation.

Makes 4 servings

**2 tablespoons minced fresh sage,
   or 2 teaspoons dried**

4 teaspoons extra-virgin olive oil

1 tablespoon dry white wine

1 tablespoon white-wine vinegar

1 garlic clove, minced

1/4 teaspoon salt

Freshly ground pepper, to taste

**1 (16-ounce) can cannellini
   beans, rinsed and drained**

Whisk the sage, oil, wine, vinegar, garlic, salt, and pepper in a large bowl. Mix in the beans. Cover and let stand 1–2 hours to blend the flavors. Stir gently before serving.

Per serving: 190 Calories, 5 g Total Fat, 1 g Saturated Fat, 0 mg Cholesterol, 138 mg Sodium, 27 g Total Carbohydrate, 4 g Dietary Fiber, 10 g Protein, 41 mg Calcium.

POINTS per serving: 3.

D i   G i o r n o   Since this salad needs to stand at room temperature for up to two hours, it's perfect to bring to a picnic.

Lentil and Radicchio Salad

Although Italians can choose from several varieties of this red to purple-leaf chicory, the most common variety found in the United States is *radicchio di Chioggia*, which is round and red and white-veined. Select a larger head of radicchio, as small heads may actually be past their prime. Mild-tasting lentils make a good foil for bitter radicchio. Take care not to overcook the lentils, as you want them to retain some crunch.

Makes 6 servings

2 1/2 cups water

2 chicken bouillon cubes

2 bay leaves

1 garlic clove, peeled

1 cup lentils, picked over, rinsed, and drained

2 tablespoons low-fat mayonnaise

1 tablespoon Dijon mustard

1 tablespoon white-wine vinegar

1/2 teaspoon salt

1/4 teaspoon freshly ground pepper

1 head radicchio, torn into pieces

1 large scallion, sliced

1. Bring the water, bouillon cubes, bay leaves, and garlic to a boil, then stir in the lentils. Reduce the heat and simmer, covered, until the lentils are barely tender, about 15 minutes. Drain the lentils, discarding the garlic and bay leaves.

2. Meanwhile, thoroughly blend the mayonnaise, mustard, vinegar, salt, and pepper.

3. Combine the lentils, radicchio, and scallion in a serving bowl. Add the dressing and toss to coat. Cover and refrigerate 2–3 hours to blend the flavors.

Per serving: 154 Calories, 2 g Total Fat, 1 g Saturated Fat, 2 mg Cholesterol, 671 mg Sodium, 25 g Total Carbohydrate, 11 g Dietary Fiber, 11 g Protein, 50 mg Calcium.

POINTS per serving: 1.

D i   G i o r n o   Italians often use bouillon cubes in their cooking. Look for brands imported from Italy, which are superior to domestic bouillon cubes.

Chickpea and Rosemary Salad

The rich texture of the chickpeas cuts through the piney, astringent taste of rosemary in this refreshing salad.

Makes 4 servings

Makes 4 servings

**2 plum tomatoes, seeded and
finely chopped**

**3 tablespoons minced fresh rose-
mary, or 1 1/2 teaspoon dried**

4 teaspoons extra-virgin olive oil

4 teaspoons white-wine vinegar

1 garlic clove, minced

1/4 teaspoon salt

Freshly ground pepper, to taste

**1 (16-ounce) can chickpeas,
rinsed and drained**

Combine the tomatoes, rosemary, oil, vinegar, garlic, salt, and pepper. Let stand so the flavors can blend, about 30 minutes. Stir in the chickpeas. Let stand until the chickpeas have absorbed the flavors, about 30 minutes longer.

Per serving: 235 Calories, 8 g Total Fat, 1 g Saturated Fat, 0 mg Cholesterol, 146 mg Sodium, 33 g Total Carbohydrate, 4 g Dietary Fiber, 10 g Protein, 64 mg Calcium.

POINTS per serving: 5.

Arugula-Gorgonzola Salad

Peppery arugula, long popular in Italy, is gaining in popularity in the United States. It can be very gritty; rinse thoroughly in a sink filled with cold water as you would spinach, and dry with paper towels or in a salad spinner. Store it in the refrigerator for up to two days, sealed tightly in a plastic bag.

Makes 4 servings

3 tablespoons honey

1/2 tablespoon Dijon mustard

1 1/2 tablespoons balsamic vinegar

1 bunch arugula, cleaned and torn

1/2 cup crumbled Gorgonzola cheese (about 2 ounces)

Whisk together the honey and mustard, then whisk in the vinegar. Divide the arugula among 4 salad plates. Sprinkle with the cheese, then drizzle with the dressing.

Per serving: 111 Calories, 5 g Total Fat, 3 g Saturated Fat, 12 mg Cholesterol, 307 mg Sodium, 14 g Total Carbohydrate, 0 g Dietary Fiber, 4 g Protein, 88 mg Calcium.

POINTS per serving: 3.

Di Giorno   Most of the balsamic vinegar in North American supermarkets is imitation: strongly flavored wine vinegar blended with sweet, concentrated grape juice. Although they're much less expensive, they're also much less complex. If you decide to splurge on an authentic balsamic vinegar, use it alone as a condiment: Drizzle it over a filet of beef or a bowl of strawberries.

Insalata alla Caprese

On the island of Capri, a sauce of lightly cooked tomatoes, seasoned with fresh basil, olive oil, and mozzarella is served with pasta, meat, and fish. This very simple salad, which for many is the essence of simplicity, demands the highest quality ingredients—no hothouse tomatoes need apply!

Makes 4 servings

2 tomatoes, cut crosswise into 4 slices each

4 ounces mozzarella cheese, cut into 4 slices

4 teaspoons chopped basil

4 teaspoons balsamic vinegar

Salt, to taste

Freshly ground pepper, to taste

On each of 4 salad plates, fan a tomato slice, a slice of cheese, and a second tomato slice. Sprinkle with the basil, drizzle with the vinegar, and sprinkle with salt and pepper.

Per serving: 108 Calories, 7 g Total Fat, 5 g Saturated Fat, 20 mg Cholesterol, 189 mg Sodium, 4 g Total Carbohydrate, 1 g Dietary Fiber, 7 g Protein, 158 mg Calcium.

POINTS per serving: 3.

Di Giorno It has been said that there could not possibly be enough water buffalo in the world to supply the amount of milk necessary for all the *mozzarella di bufala.* Most American mozzarella is made from cow's milk. Choose a tender, fresh baby mozzarella, usually found packed in water at the supermarket deli counter. The rubbery plastic-wrapped variety found in the dairy case is best used on pizza.

Roasted Pear and Prosciutto Salad

The time it will take to roast the pears can vary greatly—from 10 to 20 minutes—depending upon their ripeness; the riper the pear, the less time required. Pears and baby arugula are a classic duo in Friuli, but the more mature arugula common in American supermarkets can overpower the delicate flavor of the pears. Dandelion greens can be somewhat milder, or try frisée (sometimes called curly endive).

Makes 4 servings

2 Bosc pears, peeled, halved, and cored

2 tablespoons crumbled Gorgonzola cheese

1/4 cup nonfat ricotta cheese

2 tablespoons fat-free milk

1 teaspoon white-wine vinegar

1 pound dandelion greens or frisée, cleaned and chopped

2 slices prosciutto (about 1 ounce), chopped

1. Preheat the oven to 400°F. Place the pears, cut-side down, in a baking dish. Roast until easily pierced with a knife, 10–20 minutes.

2. Meanwhile, puree the Gorgonzola, ricotta, milk, and vinegar in a food processor.

3. Divide the greens among 4 salad plates. Dice the pear and scatter over the greens. Sprinkle the prosciutto on top and drizzle with the dressing.

Per serving: 165 Calories, 5 g Total Fat, 2 g Saturated Fat, 10 mg Cholesterol, 320 mg Sodium, 24 g Total Carbohydrate, 6 g Dietary Fiber, 10 g Protein, 292 mg Calcium.

***POINTS** per serving: 3.*

D i   G i o r n o   We call for Bosc pears in this recipe, which tend to hold their shape while roasting. It's easy to core pears with a grapefruit spoon or a melon baller. If you like, reserve some or all of the Gorgonzola to sprinkle over the salad.

Roasted Pear and Prosciutto Salad

Apple and Feta Salad

Fat-free feta cheese can be found in good supermarkets in a variety of flavors; it's a handy alternative to high-fat goat cheese. Although feta cheese, like goat cheese, was first made from goat's milk, most commercially produced fetas are made from cow's or sheep's milk these days. If you don't see Fuji apples in your produce department, use any sweet apple, such as Gala or Golden Delicious.

Makes 4 servings

2 tablespoons white-wine vinegar

2 tablespoons honey

3 cups arugula, cleaned and torn (about 3 ounces)

1 Fuji apple, cored and cut into chunks

3/4 cup crumbed fat-free feta cheese with herbs

Whisk together the vinegar and honey. Combine the arugula, apple, and cheese in a salad bowl. Add the dressing and toss to coat; serve at once.

Per serving: 106 Calories, 0 g Total Fat, 0 g Saturated Fat, 17 mg Cholesterol, 214 mg Sodium, 15 g Total Carbohydrate, 1 g Dietary Fiber, 3 g Protein, 120 mg Calcium.

POINTS per serving: 2.

D i G i o r n o   Look for a white-wine vinegar that is dark amber in color, which indicates that it has been aged in an oak barrel (cheaper varieties are aged in plastic or glass). Better white-wine vinegars are imported from Italy or France.

Oil and Vinegar Salad Dressing

This light and fresh dressing perks up even the most ordinary green salad. Experiment by adding different herbs and spices, fruit juices, minced sun-dried tomatoes or olives, grated cheeses, and mustards.

Makes 4 servings

3 tablespoons dry white or red wine

4 teaspoons extra-virgin olive oil

2 teaspoons balsamic vinegar

2 teaspoons white- or red-wine vinegar

1 garlic clove, bruised and peeled

1 teaspoon minced oregano or marjoram

¹/₄ teaspoon salt

Freshly ground pepper, to taste

In a small jar with a tight-fitting lid or a small bowl, combine the wine, oil, both vinegars, the garlic, oregano, salt and pepper; cover and shake well or whisk until thoroughly blended. Let stand so the flavors can blend, 20–30 minutes; discard the garlic before serving. If refrigerating, bring to room temperature before using.

Per serving (4 teaspoons): 49 Calories, 4 g Total Fat, 1 g Saturated Fat, 0 mg Cholesterol, 136 mg Sodium, 1 g Total Carbohydrate, 0 g Dietary Fiber, 0 g Protein, 5 mg Calcium.

POINTS per serving: 1.

D i G i o r n o   Like wine and olive oil, balsamic vinegar comes in a dizzying array of choices and prices. Look for the words *aceto balsamico tradizionale* on the label. By law, any balsamic vinegar labeled *tradizionale* must be slowly fermented and aged in wooden casks for 12 to more than 100 years. Older balsamic vinegars are sweet, dense, and complex in flavor, with an almost syrupy consistency; in Italy, it's not unheard of to sip them straight! They can sell for as much as $200 a bottle, but vinegars that have been aged for fewer than 12 years are still delicious and can be had for $20.

The Essential Oil

*E*ver since the Greek goddess Athena won the right to control Athens by giving the city an olive tree, the tree, its fruit, and the luxurious oil it produces have been revered throughout the Mediterranean. Though the legend's basis in fact is debatable, the importance of olive oil in Italian cuisine is nothing short of legendary. Here, some terms to know when selecting an olive oil:

Extra-Virgin

The result of the first pressing of olives, extra-virgin olive oil has the lowest acidity, as well as superior taste, color, and aroma. It is considered the best and has a high price to match its reputation. It's also the most delicate: Heat breaks it down, so save it for uncooked or lightly cooked dishes.

Fino

Fino, which means "fine," olive oil is a blend of both extra-virgin and virgin olive oils.

Virgin

The next classification of olive oil, virgin olive oil has a slightly higher acidity than extra-virgin, but is also a first-press oil.

Light

In connection with olive oil, "light" should not be misinterpreted as reduced in calories or fat. Light, here, refers to both the lighter color and fragrance achieved through a special filtration process. Light olive oil has a higher smoke point (see definition below) that results from this process and makes this class of olive oil ideal for frying, baking and cooking.

Pure

Also simply called olive oil, pure olive oil is a combination of refined olive oil and virgin or extra-virgin oil.

Cold-pressed

Olive oils that are cold-pressed are considered the finest. The oil is extracted by pressure—no heat or chemicals are used—and thus have a naturally low level of acidity. By law, virgin olive oils must be cold-pressed.

Smoke Point

An important characteristic of any oil, the smoke point is the stage at which heated fat begins to smoke and emit acrid odors, imparting an unpleasant flavor to foods cooked in it. Olive oil has a relatively low smoke point compared with oils like safflower or peanut, rendering the finest olive oil inferior when used for cooking at high temperatures. For this reason, some cooks suggest having at least two olive oils in your pantry—an extra-virgin for salad dressings or floating onto soups, and a less expensive variety, such as pure or light, for sautéing and cooking at high temperature.

Creamy Italian Salad Dressing

This classic creamy dressing works especially well on potato salads. You could also use it to dress rice or pasta salads, or a green salad. It will keep in a tightly sealed glass jar for up to three days in the refrigerator.

Makes 4 servings

1/2 cup low-fat (1%) buttermilk

1/2 tablespoon light corn syrup

1 tablespoon white-wine vinegar

1/2 teaspoon Italian seasoning

1/2 teaspoon salt

Pinch crushed red pepper

1 garlic clove, peeled

Combine the buttermilk, corn syrup, vinegar, Italian seasoning, salt, and crushed red pepper in a food processor or blender. Press in the garlic and puree.

Per serving (2 tablespoons): 22 Calories, 0 g Total Fat, 0 g Saturated Fat, 2 mg Cholesterol, 327 mg Sodium, 4 g Total Carbohydrate, 0 g Dietary Fiber, 1 g Protein, 36 mg Calcium.

POINTS per serving: 0.

Chive and Parsley Salad Dressing

Think of this dressing when you're looking for an easy yet flavorsome pasta salad: Toss cooked fusilli or shells with quartered cherry tomatoes, then drizzle with this easy vinaigrette.

Makes 6 servings

1/2 cup plain nonfat yogurt

1/2 tablespoon white-wine vinegar

1/2 tablespoon Dijon mustard

1/2 tablespoon chopped flat-leaf parsley

1 teaspoon chopped chives

1/4 teaspoon salt

1/8 teaspoon freshly ground pepper

Whisk together the yogurt, vinegar, mustard, parsley, chives, salt, and pepper in a bowl. Let stand a few minutes so the flavors can blend.

Per serving (4 teaspoons): 10 Calories, 0 g Total Fat, 0 g Saturated Fat, 0 mg Cholesterol, 140 mg Sodium, 2 g Total Carbohydrate, 0 g Dietary Fiber, 1 g Protein, 28 mg Calcium.

POINTS per serving: 0.

Di Giorno Make this dressing as needed; it doesn't last long. Use the dressing within a few hours, then discard. Keep refrigerated when not in use.

Anchovy-Parmesan-Mustard Salad Dressing

Our low-fat rendition of classic Caesar dressing neatly sidesteps the fat and food safety issues of lots of oil and raw egg. Low-fat mayonnaise provides body and we simply omit the egg. Although we use anchovy paste, you could also mash two rinsed and dried anchovy fillets, if you prefer.

Makes 6 servings

1 teaspoon anchovy paste

¹/₂ cup low-fat mayonnaise

3 tablespoons white-wine vinegar

4 teaspoons Dijon mustard

2 garlic cloves, minced

¹/₂ teaspoon salt

¹/₄ teaspoon freshly ground pepper

1 tablespoon grated Parmesan cheese

Whisk together the anchovy paste, mayonnaise, vinegar, mustard, garlic, salt, pepper, and cheese in a bowl. Store in the refrigerator up to 2 days.

Per serving (2 tablespoons): 45 Calories, 3 g Total Fat, 2 g Saturated Fat, 9 mg Cholesterol, 374 mg Sodium, 2 g Total Carbohydrate, 0 g Dietary Fiber, 1 g Protein, 22 mg Calcium.

POINTS *per serving: 1.*

seven

fish
and
shellfish

Pesce al Forno

Because so much of Italy is coastline, nearly every region has some variation on oven-roasted fish, and many areas add potatoes to the roasting pan. What make each region's dish distinctive are the fish that's cooked and the herbs used to season it. This version is inspired by a similar recipe from Tuscany.

Makes 4 servings

1¹/4 pounds all-purpose potatoes, peeled and thinly sliced

2 onions, sliced

1¹/4 pounds pompano, bass, or grouper fillets

2 teaspoons minced rosemary

4 sage leaves, minced

1 teaspoon dried thyme leaves, crumbled

¹/2 teaspoon salt

Freshly ground pepper, to taste

2 teaspoons olive oil

¹/4 cup dry white wine

1. Preheat the oven to 350°F. Spray a 9 × 13-inch baking dish with nonstick spray. Cover the bottom of the dish with the potatoes and onions, arranging the vegetables in alternating rows. Put the fish on top and sprinkle with the rosemary, sage, thyme, salt, and pepper, then drizzle with the oil.

2. Cover with foil and bake, basting occasionally with the pan juices, until the potatoes are tender and the fish is opaque in the center, 50–55 minutes. Pour the wine over the fish and bake, uncovered, 3–5 minutes longer. Serve at once.

Per serving: 307 Calories, 11 g Total Fat, 2 g Saturated Fat, 37 mg Cholesterol, 322 mg Sodium, 30 g Total Carbohydrate, 3 g Dietary Fiber, 20 g Protein, 31 mg Calcium.

POINTS per serving: 6.

Flounder with Lemon, Parsley, and Bread Crumbs

If your fish market is out of flounder or sole, other good choices include red snapper, catfish, and trout.

Makes 4 servings

4 (1/4-pound) flounder or sole
    fillets

4 tablespoons fresh lemon juice

4 teaspoons olive oil

1/4 cup plain dried bread crumbs

1/4 teaspoon salt

1/4 teaspoon ground white
    pepper

1/2 cup minced flat-leaf parsley

Lemon wedges and flat-leaf
    parsley sprigs

1. Preheat the oven to 350°F. Spray a 9 × 13-inch baking dish with nonstick spray. Place the fillets, skin-side down, in the baking dish. Sprinkle each with 1 tablespoon of lemon juice, then brush each fillet with 1 teaspoon of oil.

2. Mix the bread crumbs, salt, and pepper; sprinkle over the fillets. Bake until the fillets are just opaque in the center, 10–12 minutes. Serve, sprinkled with the minced parsley and garnished with lemon wedges and parsley sprigs.

Per serving: 170 Calories, 6 g Total Fat, 1 g Saturated Fat, 51 mg Cholesterol, 278 mg Sodium, 6 g Total Carbohydrate, 1 g Dietary Fiber, 21 g Protein, 45 mg Calcium.

POINTS per serving: 4.

D i G i o r n o   To be sure you're buying impeccably fresh fish, look to see that the fillets are uniform in color and texture. Avoid fillets that have pinkish, brown or grey, or dried-out patches; that have gaps in the flesh; or whose flesh isn't smooth and glistening. Watch carefully when the counter person handles the fish: The flesh should spring back, not remain indented where fingers touched it. If you have any doubts at all, ask to smell the fish. It should smell sweet, or of the sea. If you catch even the faintest scent of ammonia or fishiness, insist on a different fillet.

Baked Striped Bass with Shrimp and Clams

All the tastes of the deep blue sea come together in this elegant, easy, and attractive dish. Although we like striped bass, any firm, non-oily fillet will do; try grouper, blackfish, monkfish, or mahi-mahi.

Makes 4 servings

1 pound striped bass fillet

1/4 pound medium shrimp, peeled and deveined

12 cherrystone clams, scrubbed

1/4 cup dry white wine

2 tablespoons minced flat-leaf parsley

2 tablespoons fresh lemon juice

2 teaspoons olive oil

1/4 teaspoon salt

Freshly ground pepper, to taste

1 lemon, cut into 8 slices

4 sprigs thyme

1. Preheat the oven to 400°F. Spray a 9 × 13-inch baking dish with nonstick spray. Put the fish, shrimp, and clams in the baking dish.

2. Combine the wine, parsley, lemon juice, oil, salt, and pepper; drizzle over the fish and shellfish. Top with the lemon slices and thyme sprigs. Cover with foil and bake until the fish is just opaque in the center, the shrimp are pink, and the clams open, 15–20 minutes. Discard any clams that don't open. Serve at once.

Per serving: 194 Calories, 6 g Total Fat, 1 g Saturated Fat, 138 mg Cholesterol, 269 mg Sodium, 5 g Total Carbohydrate, 0 g Dietary Fiber, 29 g Protein, 50 mg Calcium.

POINTS per serving: 4.

Di Giorno   The easiest way to ensure getting the best fish is to develop a relationship with the counter person in the fish department. Ask questions—about what looks good, what's fresh, and especially when the fish came in (the answer you're looking for is "This morning").

Roasted Cod and Potatoes

Roasted cod and potatoes are a classical Italian combination, but roasting them together inevitably yields less than crisp potatoes, since the cod gives off liquid. Roasting the cod and pan-frying the potatoes overcomes this problem. Round out the meal with Sautéed Broccoli with Garlic and Lemon (page 236) or Wilted Swiss Chard and Spinach Salad (page 151).

Makes 4 servings

4 (5-ounce) cod fillets

4 teaspoons chopped rosemary

Salt, to taste

Freshly ground pepper, to taste

1/2 tablespoon olive oil

6 small red potatoes, thinly sliced

1 medium leek, cleaned and thinly sliced

1. Preheat the oven to 450°F. Put the cod in a baking dish in a single layer. Sprinkle each fillet with 1/2 teaspoon of the rosemary, salt, and pepper. Roast until the cod is opaque in the center, about 15 minutes.

2. Meanwhile, heat the oil in a nonstick skillet, then add the potatoes, leek, the remaining 2 teaspoons of rosemary, and salt and pepper to taste. Cook, stirring occasionally, until well browned, about 10 minutes. Serve the cod, with the potatoes on the side.

Per serving: 256 Calories, 3 g Total Fat, 1 g Saturated Fat, 52 mg Cholesterol, 114 mg Sodium, 28 g Total Carbohydrate, 3 g Dietary Fiber, 29 g Protein, 40 mg Calcium.

***POINTS** per serving: 5.*

Whole Roasted Fish in Balsamic Sauce

Whole fish makes a dramatic presentation for a dinner party, but if you've never prepared one before it can seem a bit daunting. Simplify preparations by purchasing a whole fish that has been gutted and scaled, and that has had its fins removed. When scoring the top of the fish, do not penetrate deep enough to touch any bones, which would make boning more difficult.

Makes 4 servings

1/2 lemon, cut into thin wedges

1 (1 1/4–1 1/2 pound) red snapper or silver bass, cleaned

1 1/2 teaspoons olive oil

1 large garlic clove, chopped

1/2 cup fish stock or chicken broth

1 1/2 tablespoons chopped basil

2 tablespoons balsamic vinegar

1/4 teaspoon salt

1/8 teaspoon freshly ground pepper

1. Preheat the oven to 425°F. Line a baking dish with foil.

2. Stuff the lemon wedges into the cavity of the fish and place it in the baking dish. Score the top in a crosshatch pattern and drizzle with 1/2 teaspoon of the oil. Roast until the fish is opaque at the bone, about 20 minutes.

3. Meanwhile, heat a small nonstick saucepan. Swirl in the remaining 1 teaspoon oil, then add the garlic. Sauté until it starts to turn golden. Add the fish stock, basil, and vinegar. Bring to a boil and boil until reduced by about one third, 3–4 minutes. Stir in the salt and pepper.

4. Bone the fish and serve the sauce on the side.

Per serving: 113 Calories, 3 g Total Fat, 1 g Saturated Fat, 31 mg Cholesterol, 296 mg Sodium, 2 g Total Carbohydrate, 0 g Dietary Fiber, 18 g Protein, 44 mg Calcium.

POINTS *per serving: 3.*

D i   G i o r n o   To estimate the cooking time for a whole fish, use the Canadian rule: Lay the fish flat and measure at the thickest point; cook about ten minutes for each inch of thickness. (The actual time required may vary depending on the density of the fish, not just its height, and the time needed to heat the pan.)

Broiled Tuna with Fennel-Crumb Crust

The fresh taste of fennel will perk up this or any fish. Use the remaining fennel bulb in another recipe, and don't throw away the pretty fronds. Chop them finely and sprinkle them over any dish that features fennel bulb, or use them in place of fresh dill.

Makes 4 servings

4 (1/4-pound) tuna steaks

3 tablespoons plain dried bread crumbs

2 tablespoons minced fennel bulb

1 tablespoon fresh lemon juice

1 tablespoon minced parsley

2 teaspoons olive oil

1 teaspoon fennel seeds, crushed

1/4 teaspoon salt

1/4 teaspoon ground white pepper

1. Spray the broiler rack with nonstick spray; preheat the broiler. Broil the tuna 5 inches from the heat, 4 minutes; turn and broil 2 minutes longer.

2. Meanwhile, combine the bread crumbs, fennel, lemon juice, parsley, oil, fennel seeds, salt, and pepper. Spread over the tuna; broil until the fish is just opaque in the center and the crust is a deep gold, 3–4 minutes. Serve at once.

Per serving: 207 Calories, 8 g Total Fat, 2 g Saturated Fat, 43 mg Cholesterol, 227 mg Sodium, 4 g Total Carbohydrate, 0 g Dietary Fiber, 27 g Protein, 22 mg Calcium.

POINTS per serving: 5.

Grilled Red Snapper with Herb Pesto

Marinating and grilling really bring out the flavors of fish, and a concentrated herb pesto enhances it even more. If you can't find red snapper, try trout, flounder, sole, or any non-oily fish fillet. You can also adapt this recipe for a whole fish; we used a 2-pound red snapper for the dish in the photograph. Cut 2 slits in the cavity and stuff with 1 or 2 sprigs of the herbs and lemon slices. Score the fish, taking care not to cut too deeply. Mix the marinade as directed in a very large zip-close bag or in a glass baking dish. Grill for 10 minutes on each side.

Makes 4 servings

¹/₄ cup fresh lemon juice

¹/₄ cup dry white wine

2 anchovy fillets, rinsed and chopped, or 1 teaspoon anchovy paste

1 pound red snapper fillets

1 cup packed basil leaves

¹/₂ cup packed parsley leaves

¹/₂ cup packed mint leaves

4 teaspoons olive oil

2 garlic cloves

¹/₄ teaspoon salt

Freshly ground pepper, to taste

1. Combine the lemon juice, wine, and anchovies in a zip-close plastic bag; add the fish. Squeeze out the air and seal the bag; turn to coat the fish. Refrigerate, turning the bag occasionally, 1–2 hours.

2. Spray the grill rack with nonstick spray; prepare the grill.

3. Meanwhile, puree the basil, parsley, mint, oil, garlic, salt, and pepper in a food processor or blender.

4. Grill the fish 5 inches from the heat 8 minutes. Spread some of the herb pesto over the fish; cook until the fish is just opaque in the center and the pesto is heated through, about 2 minutes longer. Serve at once, with the remaining pesto on the side.

Per serving: 189 Calories, 6 g Total Fat, 1 g Saturated Fat, 40 mg Cholesterol, 284 mg Sodium, 7 g Total Carbohydrate, 1 g Dietary Fiber, 24 g Protein, 210 mg Calcium.

POINTS per serving: 4.

Di Giorno   Because fish is more delicate than meat or poultry, marinate it for a shorter time, otherwise the fibers will toughen.

Grilled Red Snapper
with Herb Pesto

Grilled Swordfish and Vegetable Spiedini

A *spiedo* is a kitchen spit; *spiedini* are skewered foods that are grilled over a fire. Get everything ready ahead of time and then grill at the last minute.

Makes 4 servings

1 cup dry white wine

$1/4$ cup fresh lemon juice

2 tablespoons minced fresh rosemary, or 1 teaspoon dried

2 tablespoons minced fresh oregano, or 1 teaspoon dried

1 tablespoon minced fresh thyme, or $1/2$ teaspoon dried

2 teaspoons olive oil

2 garlic cloves, minced

2 anchovy fillets, rinsed and chopped, or 1 teaspoon anchovy paste

Freshly ground pepper, to taste

$1^1/4$ pounds swordfish steak, cut into 1-inch cubes

1 green bell pepper, seeded and cut into 1-inch squares

1 red or yellow bell pepper, seeded and cut into 1-inch squares

8 plum tomatoes, halved and seeded

2 small zucchini, cut into 1-inch slices

1 onion, cut into 8 wedges

1. Combine the wine, lemon juice, rosemary, oregano, thyme, oil, garlic, anchovies, and pepper in a zip-close plastic bag; add the fish, bell peppers, tomatoes, zucchini, and onion. Squeeze out the air and seal the bag; turn to coat the food. Refrigerate, turning the bag occasionally, 1–2 hours.

2. Spray the grill rack with nonstick spray; prepare the grill. Spray eight 18-inch metal skewers with nonstick spray.

3. Pour the marinade into a small saucepan and boil, stirring constantly, 3 minutes.

4. Thread the fish and vegetables onto the skewers, alternating them. Put the skewers on the grill rack and brush with half the marinade. Grill 5 minutes, then turn and brush with the remaining marinade. Grill until the fish is just opaque in the center and the vegetables are slightly charred, 3–5 minutes longer.

Per serving: 307 Calories, 9 g Total Fat, 2 g Saturated Fat, 56 mg Cholesterol, 219 mg Sodium, 17 g Total Carbohydrate, 3 g Dietary Fiber, 32 g Protein, 63 mg Calcium.

POINTS per serving: 6.

D i G i o r n o   Raw meat, fish, and poultry can harbor harmful bacteria. Any time a marinade is used as a basting sauce, it's very important to bring it to a rolling boil for three minutes to kill bacteria. A rolling boil is one that you can't "stir down," so if the marinade continues to boil vigorously while you're stirring, you know the temperature is high enough.

Broiled Swordfish with Anchovy-Crumb Crust

Anchovies are often used in Italian cooking. Here they pair up with bread crumbs and capers to form a savory topping for swordfish. This crust is great on mako and tuna, too.

Makes 4 servings

1 pound swordfish steak (1-inch thick)

¹/₄ cup + 2 tablespoons plain dried bread crumbs

¹/₄ cup dry white wine

1 teaspoon grated lemon zest

2 tablespoons fresh lemon juice

1 tablespoon minced fresh oregano, or ¹/₂ teaspoon dried

1 tablespoon capers, drained

2 teaspoons olive oil

2 anchovy fillets, rinsed and chopped, or 1 teaspoon anchovy paste

Freshly ground pepper, to taste

1. Spray the broiler rack with nonstick spray; preheat the broiler. Broil the fish 5 minutes; turn and broil 2 minutes longer.

2. Meanwhile, pulse the bread crumbs, wine, lemon zest, lemon juice, oregano, capers, oil, anchovies, and pepper in a food processor until thoroughly combined. Spread the crumb mixture over the fish; broil until the fish is just opaque in the center and the crust is a deep gold, 3–4 minutes. Serve at once.

Per serving: 206 Calories, 7 g Total Fat, 2 g Saturated Fat, 43 mg Cholesterol, 312 mg Sodium, 8 g Total Carbohydrate, 0 g Dietary Fiber, 23 g Protein, 37 mg Calcium.

POINTS per serving: 5.

Di Giorno   Capers, called *capperi* in Italian, are flower buds from a shrub native to the Mediterranean and parts of Asia. They can range in size from very small (called nonpareil; these delicately flavored capers are from the South of France) to about the size of the tip of a pinky (these more robust capers are usually from Italy); if yours are the larger variety, you may wish to chop them. Their flavor marries well with olives, anchovies, lemons, and tomatoes. Capers are often packed in a vinegar brine, but sometimes you'll find them packed in salt, in which case they should be rinsed before you use them. Capers bottled in vinegar brine will keep indefinitely in the refrigerator. Those stored in salt perish more quickly.

Sea Bass in Acqua Pazza

Fish poached in a crushed red pepper–spiked broth is popular throughout the Mediterranean basin. In Spain, the broth is called *agua loco*, in Italy, *acqua pazza;* both mean "crazy water." The Italian version hails from Naples. Serve this in soup plates or shallow bowls, with lots of crusty bread to soak up the acqua pazza.

Makes 4 servings

1 (14 1/2-ounce) can diced tomatoes

1/4 teaspoon crushed red pepper, or to taste

1/4 teaspoon salt

3 large garlic cloves, minced

1 cup dry white wine

3/4 cup water

2 teaspoons olive oil

4 (6-ounce) sea bass fillets

Combine the tomatoes, crushed red pepper, salt, garlic, wine, and water in a nonstick skillet. Bring to a boil and boil 5 minutes. Stir in the oil. Reduce the heat and simmer, uncovered, 10 minutes. Add the fish and cook, covered, until opaque in the center, about 8 minutes.

Per serving: 249 Calories, 6 g Total Fat, 1 g Saturated Fat, 70 mg Cholesterol, 562 mg Sodium, 5 g Total Carbohydrate, 1 g Dietary Fiber, 33 g Protein, 33 mg Calcium.

POINTS per serving: 5.

Di Giorno   This cooking method works well with a firm white flesh fish, such as Chilean sea bass, but halibut, sole, or red snapper are also good choices.

Salmon in Green Sauce

This is a perfect make-ahead meal. Refrigerate the sauce and the poached fillets separately for up to 24 hours, then serve cold on a bed of greens, as they would on the Amalfi coast. Bring the sauce back to room temperature before serving.

Makes 4 servings

1 1/2 cups + 1 tablespoon water

1 bay leaf

12 whole black peppercorns

4 (6-ounce) salmon fillets

2/3 cup flat-leaf parsley leaves

1/4 cup basil leaves

1 garlic clove, peeled

1/2 tablespoon plain dried bread crumbs

2 tablespoons fresh lemon juice

1 tablespoon white wine vinegar

1. Combine 1 1/2 cups of the water, the bay leaf, and peppercorns in a large straight-sided skillet. Bring to a boil, then add the salmon in a single layer. Reduce the heat and simmer, covered, until opaque in the center, 10–12 minutes.

2. Meanwhile, puree the parsley, basil, garlic, bread crumbs, lemon juice, vinegar, and the remaining tablespoon water in a food processor. Remove the skin from the fillets and serve, topped with the sauce.

Per serving: 255 Calories, 11 g Total Fat, 2 g Saturated Fat, 94 mg Cholesterol, 89 mg Sodium, 3 g Total Carbohydrate, 1 g Dietary Fiber, 34 g Protein, 46 mg Calcium.

POINTS *per serving: 6.*

D i G i o r n o   When making herb-based sauces, using a food processor is your best bet for chopping the herbs as finely as possible. To boost the flavor of the poaching liquid, add onion, celery leaves, or carrots if you like.

Prawns Fra Diavolo

Fra diavolo, which translates as "brother devil," is the term given to spicy dishes made with tomato sauce and hot chile peppers. Serve this dish as an entrée, over pasta (it's enough for 1 pound of pasta), or as a first course for six.

Makes 4 servings

1/2 tablespoon olive oil

1 large onion, chopped

3 large garlic cloves, chopped

1/4 cup red-wine vinegar

1/3 cup chopped flat-leaf parsley

1 (28-ounce) can diced tomatoes

1/4 teaspoon crushed red pepper, or to taste

1 1/2 pounds freshwater prawns

1. Heat a nonstick skillet. Swirl in the oil, then add the onion. Sauté until golden. Add the garlic and sauté until fragrant. Add the vinegar and parsley and stir until bubbling, about 30 seconds longer. Add the tomatoes and crushed red pepper; bring just to a boil. Reduce the heat and simmer, uncovered, until thickened, about 15 minutes.

2. With scissors, slit each prawn through the shell along the outer curve. Rinse under cold water to remove the veins. When the sauce is thick, add the prawns and simmer until bright red and opaque in the center, 6–8 minutes, turning halfway through.

Per serving: 275 Calories, 5 g Total Fat, 0 g Saturated Fat, 0 mg Cholesterol, 581 mg Sodium, 20 g Total Carbohydrate, 3 g Dietary Fiber, 36 g Protein, 115 mg Calcium.

POINTS per serving: 5.

Sicilian Braised Baby Octopus

In ancient Sicily, the octopus would have been cooked in an earthenware jug with a chimney called a *quartara*, which was placed directly in the embers of a fire. Serve this on toasted slices of bread or polenta.

Makes 4 servings

1 (14 1/2-ounce) can diced tomatoes

3 garlic cloves, minced

2 tablespoons chopped flat-leaf parsley

1/2 teaspoon salt

1/2 teaspoon crushed red pepper

1 1/2 pounds cleaned baby octopus

Bring the tomatoes, garlic, parsley, salt, and crushed red pepper to a boil, then stir in the octopus. Reduce the heat to the lowest possible setting and cook, covered, until the octopus is fork-tender, 40–50 minutes. Uncover, raise the heat to medium, and cook until the sauce thickens, 20–30 minutes longer.

Per serving: 165 Calories, 2 g Total Fat, 0 g Saturated Fat, 82 mg Cholesterol, 981 mg Sodium, 8 g Total Carbohydrate, 1 g Dietary Fiber, 27 g Protein, 104 mg Calcium.

POINTS per serving: 3.

Grilled Stuffed Calamari

Variations on this dish are common throughout coastal Italy. Wrapping the stuffing in a leaf is a technique borrowed from Asian cooking. It simplifies stuffing the calamari and makes for a prettier dish. Use as many large escarole leaves as you can. If you run short, use two smaller leaves, overlapping them slightly.

Makes 6 servings

²/₃ cup quick-cooking barley

¹/₂ cup chopped cremini mushrooms

2 ²/₃ cups chicken broth

12 large escarole leaves, stemmed

12 large cleaned squid bodies (about ³/₄ pound)

1 lemon, cut into wedges

1. Bring the barley, mushrooms, and broth in a medium saucepan to a boil. Reduce the heat and simmer, covered, until all the broth is absorbed, 10–12 minutes.

2. Meanwhile, put the escarole in a colander. Pour boiling water over it to wilt the leaves, then drain well. Lay the escarole leaves flat. Divide the barley mixture among the leaves. Roll each leaf up and stuff it into a squid body. Secure closed with toothpicks. Spray with nonstick spray.

3. Preheat a grill or broiler. Cook the squid until opaque and lightly browned, about 1 minute on each side. Serve with the lemon wedges. Remove toothpicks before eating.

Per serving: 145 Calories, 3 g Total Fat, 1 g Saturated Fat, 134 mg Cholesterol, 473 mg Sodium, 17 g Total Carbohydrate, 4 g Dietary Fiber, 12 g Protein, 30 mg Calcium.

POINTS *per serving: 2.*

Di Giorno   Calamari, or squid, is highly perishable and usually previously frozen. You'll find it in many supermarkets. Look for precleaned squid that smells sweet, and plan to use it within 24 hours of purchase.

Grilled Stuffed Calamari

Steamed Clams

Littleneck clams are the smallest and sweetest variety, and the most like those available in Italy.

Makes 4 servings

1 1/2 ounces pancetta, diced
 (1/4 cup), or 3 slices bacon,
 chopped

2 large garlic cloves, minced

1 1/4 cups Pinot Grigio or other
 dry white wine

2 pounds littleneck clams,
 scrubbed

Heat a nonstick saucepan. Add the pancetta and sauté until it just begins to brown, then add the garlic and sauté until golden. Add the wine and bring to a boil. Add the clams and cook, covered, shaking the pan occasionally, until they open, 5–8 minutes; discard any clams that don't open.

Per serving: 279 Calories, 8 g Total Fat, 3 g Saturated Fat, 84 mg Cholesterol, 209 mg Sodium, 7 g Total Carbohydrate, 0 g Dietary Fiber, 30 g Protein, 114 mg Calcium.

POINTS per serving: 6.

D i G i o r n o   Raw clams can be stored in the refrigerator for up to 24 hours. If the clams you have purchased are packaged in plastic, punch holes in the plastic so that they can breathe. To scrub clams, place them in a colander and rinse under cold running water, discarding any with broken shells.

Steamed Mussels

Debearding mussels can be a tedious process, but you can buy already debearded mussels (they're usually sold in mesh bags). To clean the mussels, place them in a colander and scrub clean under cold running water, discarding any that do not close tightly. And don't soak mussels in a bowl of tap water to dislodge sand; by doing so, you run the risk of killing the mussels.

Makes 4 servings

1 teaspoon olive oil

1 small onion, chopped

3 large garlic cloves, minced

1 (14^1/$_2$-ounce) can diced tomatoes

^{3}/$_4$ cup dry white wine

2 tablespoons chopped basil

2 pounds debearded mussels, scrubbed

Heat a nonstick saucepan. Swirl in the oil, then add the onion. Sauté until golden. Add the garlic and sauté until fragrant. Stir in the tomatoes, wine, and basil and bring to a boil. Add the mussels and cook, covered, shaking the pan occasionally, until they open, about 5 minutes; discard any mussels that don't open.

Per serving: 270 Calories, 6 g Total Fat, 1 g Saturated Fat, 64 mg Cholesterol, 950 mg Sodium, 15 g Total Carbohydrate, 2 g Dietary Fiber, 29 g Protein, 81 mg Calcium.

POINTS per serving: 6.

eight

poultry

Roasted Basil Chicken

Use a metal roasting pan that can go from oven to stovetop, rather than a glass baking dish. For a preparation this simple, splurge on a good quality, free-range chicken—which would be called *pollo ruspante* in Italy.

Makes 6 servings

3–4 garlic cloves, peeled

1/3 cup packed basil leaves

1/2 teaspoon grated lemon zest

1 tablespoon fresh lemon juice

2 teaspoons olive oil

1 (3 1/2 to 4-pound) chicken, rinsed, patted dry, and trimmed of all visible fat

1 cup dry white wine

1 garlic clove, minced

1 teaspoon chopped basil

1/4 teaspoon salt

1/8 teaspoon freshly ground pepper

1. Preheat the oven to 400°F. Set a roasting rack inside a roasting pan.

2. Combine the peeled garlic, basil leaves, lemon zest, and lemon juice in a food processor. With the machine running, drizzle the oil through the feed tube to form a paste. Gently lift the skin from the breast of the chicken and push the paste under the skin, spreading to cover the meat. Set the chicken, breast-side up, on the rack, tucking the wings under. Roast until an instant-read thermometer, inserted in the thigh not touching bone, registers 180°F, about 1–1 1/2 hours. Transfer the chicken to a plate, wrap it in foil, and let stand while you make the sauce.

3. Pour the fat from the roasting pan. Combine the wine, minced garlic, and chopped basil in the pan. Bring to a boil, stirring occasionally to scrape the browned bits from the bottom of the pan, and cook until the sauce is reduced by about half, about 5 minutes. Stir in the salt and pepper.

4. Carve the chicken, removing the skin before eating. Serve with the sauce on the side.

Per serving: 159 Calories, 4 g Total Fat, 1 g Saturated Fat, 66 mg Cholesterol, 175 mg Sodium, 2 g Total Carbohydrate, 0 g Dietary Fiber, 21 g Protein, 25 mg Calcium.

POINTS per serving: 4.

Roasted Basil Chicken with Ruby Risotto (page 117)

Fennel-Roasted Capon

Succulent capons are particularly well suited to roasting. Pancetta is an Italian bacon that is cured rather than smoked. It is sold rolled into a sausage shape, often with peppercorns. It should last for up to three weeks in the refrigerator and can be frozen.

Makes 8 servings

1 1/2 ounces pancetta, finely chopped

2 large garlic cloves, peeled

1 tablespoon rosemary leaves

1 teaspoon fennel seed

1/2 teaspoon freshly ground pepper

2 teaspoons olive oil

1 (5–6 pound) capon, rinsed, patted dry, and trimmed of all visible fat

1. Preheat the oven to 425°F. Set a roasting rack inside a roasting pan.

2. Combine the pancetta, garlic, rosemary, fennel seed, and pepper in a food processor. With the machine running, drizzle the oil through the feed tube to form a paste. Gently lift the skin from the breast of the capon and push the paste under the skin, spreading to cover the meat. Set the capon, breast-side up, on the rack, tucking the wings under. Roast 15 minutes, then reduce the oven temperature to 350°F. Continue to roast until an instant-read thermometer, inserted in the thigh not touching bone, registers 180°F, about 1 1/2 hours longer. Let stand 10 minutes before carving. Remove the skin before eating.

Per serving: 171 Calories, 7 g Total Fat, 2 g Saturated Fat, 77 mg Cholesterol, 124 mg Sodium, 1 g Total Carbohydrate, 0 g Dietary Fiber, 24 g Protein, 27 mg Calcium.

POINTS *per serving: 4.*

Braised Lemon Chicken

Don't crush the garlic clove in a press; just press it with the flat side of a large knife so it's easier to retrieve when the chicken is done simmering.

Makes 4 servings

5 lemons

2 pounds bone-in chicken parts, skinned and trimmed of any visible fat

1 pound all-purpose potatoes, peeled and chopped

1 garlic clove, bruised and peeled

$1/2$ teaspoon salt

3 zucchini, cubed

1 teaspoon instant chicken bouillon granules

2 teaspoons minced tarragon

1. Cut the zest from 2 of the lemons into strands, then squeeze the juice from all 5 lemons.

2. Heat a nonstick saucepan and combine the chicken, potatoes, garlic, and 4–5 tablespoons of the lemon juice. Cook, turning the chicken occasionally, until it is browned. Season with the salt. Stir in the zucchini and cook about 5 minutes, then add the remaining lemon juice and bouillon. Reduce the heat and simmer until the chicken is cooked through, about 25 minutes. Discard the garlic. Serve, topped with any pan juices and sprinkled with the tarragon.

Per serving: 284 Calories, 5 g Total Fat, 1 g Saturated Fat, 99 mg Cholesterol, 633 mg Sodium, 27 g Total Carbohydrate, 2 g Dietary Fiber, 34 g Protein, 54 mg Calcium.

POINTS per serving: 6.

Di Giorno   Tarragon, called *dragoncello* in Italy, has a strong anise-like flavor. Use it sparingly, otherwise it will overpower the other flavors in this dish.

Roasted Chicken with Potatoes and Onions

This one-pot meal takes just minutes to prepare and about an hour to bake. Fix it for Sunday dinner and brown-bag any leftovers during the week.

Makes 8 servings

1 cup low-sodium chicken broth

1/2 cup fresh lemon juice

2 tablespoons fresh thyme, or 2 teaspoons dried leaves, crumbled

3 tablespoons olive oil

1/4 teaspoon salt

Freshly ground pepper, to taste

2 1/2 pounds all-purpose potatoes, peeled and cubed

4 onions, coarsely chopped

8 (3-ounce) skinless boneless chicken breast halves

1. Preheat the oven to 350°F. Spray a 9 × 13-inch baking dish with nonstick spray.

2. Combine the broth, lemon juice, thyme, oil, salt, and pepper in a large bowl. Add the potatoes and onions; toss to coat. With a slotted spoon, transfer the vegetables to the baking dish. Add the chicken to the broth mixture; toss to coat. Transfer the chicken to the baking dish, arranging the chicken and vegetables in a single layer; pour the broth mixture over all. Cover with foil.

3. Roast 30 minutes, turning the chicken occasionally, until the juices run pink when the chicken is pierced with a fork. Remove the foil and roast 30 minutes more, until the vegetables are golden and the juices run clear when the chicken is pierced with a fork.

Per serving: 270 Calories, 6 g Total Fat, 1 g Saturated Fat, 49 mg Cholesterol, 147 mg Sodium, 31 g Total Carbohydrate, 3 g Dietary Fiber, 24 g Protein, 38 mg Calcium.

***POINTS** per serving: 5.*

D i   G i o r n o   If you use a glass baking dish, you may want to reduce the oven temperature to 325°F, and you might need to increase the cooking time somewhat. Glass is a very poor conductor of heat, so it heats up very slowly, but once hot, it retains the heat much more than metal does.

Chicken Marsala

Add a light pasta or risotto and Sautéed Peas with Prosciutto (page 239) and you're all set for company.

Makes 4 servings

1 tablespoon olive oil

3 tablespoons all-purpose flour

1/4 teaspoon salt

Freshly ground pepper, to taste

4 (3-ounce) thin-sliced skinless chicken breast halves (1/4-inch thick)

2 cups thinly sliced mushrooms

1 cup dry Marsala wine

2 tablespoons minced flat-leaf parsley

1 tablespoon minced fresh basil, or 1/2 teaspoon dried

1 garlic clove, bruised and peeled

1. Heat the oil in a large nonstick skillet. Combine the flour, salt, and pepper in a zip-close plastic bag. Add the chicken and shake to coat.

2. Transfer the chicken to the skillet, shaking off any excess flour. Sauté until cooked through, about 3 minutes on each side. Transfer to a warm platter.

3. In the skillet, combine the mushrooms, wine, parsley, basil, and garlic; cook, stirring frequently and scraping up any browned bits from the bottom of the pan, until the liquid is reduced to 1/3 cup, about 5 minutes. Discard the garlic. Reduce the heat, return the chicken and any juices to the skillet, and heat to serving temperature. Serve the chicken, topped with the sauce.

Per serving: 261 Calories, 6 g Total Fat, 1 g Saturated Fat, 49 mg Cholesterol, 226 mg Sodium, 14 g Total Carbohydrate, 1 g Dietary Fiber, 21 g Protein, 25 mg Calcium.

POINTS per serving: 6.

D i   G i o r n o   Marsala is a fortified wine that originated in the Sicilian city of the same name. "Fortified" means that ingredients are added to boost the alcohol content (Marsala's alcohol content ranges between 12 and 20 percent alcohol; table wines, between 7 and 14 percent). You'll find it labeled dry (*secco*), semi-dry (*semisecco*) or sweet (*dolce*). The sweet version is used in desserts like zabaglione; dry Marsala is an excellent apéritif, and it's used in meat dishes.

Chicken Cutlets Bolognese

Chicken, ham, and cheese are a delectable combination—think of the French classic chicken Cordon Bleu. In Bologna, cooks prepare this dish with veal rather than chicken, and they fry it rather than bake it in a hot oven.

Makes 4 servings

¹/₄ cup buttermilk

¹/₈ teaspoon freshly ground pepper

¹/₂ cup dried Italian-style bread crumbs

4 (¹/₄-pound) skinless boneless chicken breast halves

2 slices prosciutto (about 1 ounce), each halved crosswise

4 tablespoons shredded part-skim mozzarella cheese

1. Put a nonstick baking sheet in the oven and preheat it to 475°F.

2. Mix the buttermilk and pepper in a shallow bowl. Put the bread crumbs on wax paper. Dip the chicken breasts into the buttermilk, then roll to coat in the bread crumbs.

3. Spray the baking sheet with nonstick spray and set the chicken on it. Bake 4 minutes, spray the top of the breasts, and turn them over. Top each with a piece of prosciutto and 1 tablespoon of cheese. Bake until the chicken is cooked through and the cheese is melted and lightly browned, about 3 minutes longer.

Per serving: 223 Calories, 5 g Total Fat, 2 g Saturated Fat, 74 mg Cholesterol, 433 mg Sodium, 11 g Total Carbohydrate, 1 g Dietary Fiber, 32 g Protein, 103 mg Calcium.

***POINTS** per serving: 5.*

D i G i o r n o   Preheating the baking sheet and spraying it just before setting the food on is a great fake for deep-frying. The heat helps to give the food a crisp, crunchy crust, and the spray imparts the flavor without greasiness.

Chicken Breasts in Tuna Sauce

We substitute chicken breasts for the traditional veal roast in this rendition of Vitello Tonnato, a French-inspired dish long popular in the northern regions of Lombardy and Piedmont. Like the original, this dish is good both hot and chilled.

Makes 4 servings

1 (6 1/2-ounce) can albacore tuna in water, drained

6 sage leaves

1/4 cup low-fat mayonnaise

2 tablespoons fresh lemon juice

1 tablespoon large capers, drained

1 teaspoon anchovy paste

6 drops green hot pepper sauce

4 (3-ounce) skinless boneless chicken breast halves

1. Preheat the oven to 375°F.

2. Puree the tuna, sage, mayonnaise, lemon juice, capers, anchovy paste, and hot pepper sauce in a food processor. Put the chicken breasts in a baking dish in a single layer and spread the puree over each. Bake until the chicken is cooked through and the tuna sauce is bubbling, about 25 minutes.

Per serving: 275 Calories, 6 g Total Fat, 2 g Saturated Fat, 124 mg Cholesterol, 427 mg Sodium, 2 g Total Carbohydrate, 0 g Dietary Fiber, 50 g Protein, 33 mg Calcium.

POINTS per serving: 6.

Chicken Breasts Stuffed with Hazelnuts

Hazelnut stuffings are common in Piedmont. If you like, chill the chicken after you've cooked it, then slice it and serve atop a bed of arugula or spinach as a main dish salad; the sauce can double as a salad dressing.

Makes 4 servings

2 ounces hazelnuts (about 1/2 cup)

1/4 cup golden raisins

2 tablespoons flat-leaf parsley leaves

2 tablespoons Italian-style dried bread crumbs

1/4 cup + 3 tablespoons orange juice

4 (1/4-pound) thin-sliced skinless boneless chicken breast halves (1/4-inch thick)

3 tablespoons honey

2 tablespoons Dijon mustard

1. Preheat the oven to 375°F. Put the hazelnuts on a baking sheet and bake 4 minutes. Transfer the nuts to a clean dish towel, cover, and cool about 2 minutes, then rub off the skins with the towel. Transfer the nuts to a food processor. Add the raisins, parsley, bread crumbs, and 3 tablespoons of the orange juice and pulse 3–5 times to chop finely.

2. Spread about 2 tablespoons of the nut mixture on each of the chicken breasts and roll them up, starting at the short ends and securing closed with toothpicks. Put in a baking dish and spray with nonstick spray. Bake until cooked through, about 20 minutes.

3. To make the sauce, mix together the honey, the mustard, and the remaining 1/4 cup of orange juice. Serve the chicken, with the sauce on the side.

Per serving: 330 Calories, 11 g Total Fat, 1 g Saturated Fat, 66 mg Cholesterol, 320 mg Sodium, 30 g Total Carbohydrate, 2 g Dietary Fiber, 30 g Protein, 67 mg Calcium.

POINTS per serving: 7.

D i G i o r n o   You can purchase chicken breast halves that are "thin-sliced" so they're only 1/4-inch thick, or you can pound regular breast halves. To pound them, lay the breasts between 2 sheets of wax paper or put in a zip-close plastic bag (don't seal the bag completely or it will pop) and pound with a meat tenderizer, rubber mallet, or heavy skillet.

Chicken Breasts Stuffed with Hazelnuts with Braised Fennel
(pages 252)

Olive-Stuffed Chicken Breasts

Stuffed rolls of meat or fish, called *involtini*, are very popular throughout Italy. Our rendition is based on a recipe from Marche for a whole chicken stuffed with olives. Use plump, firm-fleshed olives packed in a light saltwater or vinegar brine, not in oil.

Makes 4 servings

- ¹/₄ cup nonfat ricotta cheese
- 4 green olives, pitted
- 2 teaspoons thyme leaves
- ¹/₄ cup plain dried bread crumbs
- 4 (3-ounce) thin-sliced skinless boneless chicken breast halves (¹/₄-inch thick)
- ¹/₂ cup chicken broth
- 1 tablespoon balsamic vinegar
- 1 tablespoon granulated light brown sugar

1. Preheat the oven to 350°F.

2. Puree the ricotta, olives, thyme, and 2 tablespoons of the bread crumbs in a food processor. Spread the puree over the chicken breasts and roll them up, starting at the long sides and securing closed with toothpicks. Roll the breasts in the remaining 2 tablespoons of bread crumbs to coat. Put in a baking dish, spray with olive oil, and bake until cooked through, about 25 minutes.

3. Meanwhile, bring the broth, vinegar, and brown sugar to a boil and boil 1 minute. Cut each chicken breast into four slices. Arrange the slices on plates and serve, drizzled with the sauce.

Per serving: 158 Calories, 2 g Total Fat, 1 g Saturated Fat, 50 mg Cholesterol, 342 mg Sodium, 10 g Total Carbohydrate, 1 g Dietary Fiber, 23 g Protein, 53 mg Calcium.

POINTS per serving: 3.

D i G i o r n o   Granulated brown sugar is processed in such a way that it's pourable and doesn't clump the way brown sugar typically does. It's ideal for sauces and dressings because it dissolves almost instantly.

Stewed Chicken with Lima Beans

In Lombardy, this dish is traditionally made with fava beans, which are highly seasonal and can be hard to find throughout much of the United States. Use only fresh ones, available in late spring and early summer. If you find them, start with 1¹/2 pounds of beans in their pods. Remove the beans from the pods, blanch in boiling water, and peel.

Makes 4 servings

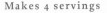

¹/4 cup all-purpose flour

1 teaspoon Italian seasoning

¹/2 teaspoon salt

¹/4 teaspoon freshly ground pepper

4 (¹/4-pound) skinless boneless chicken breast halves

1 garlic clove, minced

1 (10-ounce) box frozen lima beans, thawed

1 tablespoon chopped basil

1 cup dry white wine

1. Mix the flour, Italian seasoning, salt, and pepper on wax paper. Dredge the chicken in the mixture and spray with nonstick spray.

2. Heat a nonstick skillet. Add the chicken breasts and cook until browned, about 2 minutes. Turn over and add the garlic, lima beans, basil, and wine. Reduce the heat and cook, covered, until the chicken is cooked through, about 10 minutes.

Per serving: 270 Calories, 2 g Total Fat, 0 g Saturated Fat, 66 mg Cholesterol, 990 mg Sodium, 21 g Total Carbohydrate, 4 g Dietary Fiber, 32 g Protein, 40 mg Calcium.

POINTS per serving: 5.

Di Giorno   We like the convenience of wax paper for dredging meat and poultry. When you're done, simply fold up the wax paper with any flour inside and toss—one less dish to wash.

Turkey alla Romana

In Rome, the turkey is often poached in a tomato and bell pepper sauce. Although the meat is often sliced before poaching, we've left it whole to keep it moist.

Makes 6 servings

1 teaspoon olive oil

1 (1 1/2-pound) lean boneless turkey breast roast

2 (10-ounce) jars mixed roasted peppers, rinsed and drained

1 (28-ounce) can diced tomatoes

2 garlic cloves, minced

1/2 teaspoon salt

2 teaspoons arrowroot, dissolved in 2 tablespoons water

1. Heat a straight-sided nonstick skillet. Swirl in the oil, then add the turkey breast. Brown about 2 minutes, then turn over and brown on the other side, about 1 minute. Transfer to a plate. Add the roasted peppers, tomatoes, and garlic to the skillet. Bring to a boil, return the turkey to the pan, and spoon the sauce over it. Reduce the heat and simmer, covered, until the turkey is cooked through, about 1 hour. Let stand 10 minutes before slicing.

2. Add the salt and the dissolved arrowroot to the pan juices. Stir to mix and cook until the sauce is thick and clear, about 2 minutes. Serve the turkey, topped with the sauce. Remove the skin before eating.

Per serving: 198 Calories, 1 g Total Fat, 0 g Saturated Fat, 70 mg Cholesterol, 678 mg Sodium, 10 g Total Carbohydrate, 1 g Dietary Fiber, 29 g Protein, 35 mg Calcium.

POINTS per serving: 4.

D i G i o r n o   Use a straight-sided skillet, sometimes called a sauté pan, for poaching, which will better accommodate the large turkey breast.

Milk-Braised Turkey with Arugula Pesto

Milk-braising is very popular in Lombardy and Piedmont. It's a technique that yields a wonderfully moist and dramatically white turkey breast, here set off by a vibrant arugula pesto. Slice any leftovers for sandwiches, and use the pesto as a spread.

Makes 6 servings

1 (2-pound) lean boneless turkey
    breast roast

10 sage leaves

1/4 teaspoon salt

1/8 teaspoon freshly ground
    pepper

1/2 cup fat-free milk

3/4 cup chicken broth

1 bunch arugula, cleaned and
    stemmed

2 garlic cloves, peeled

1/2 tablespoon pine nuts

1 tablespoon olive oil

2 tablespoons flat-leaf parsley
    leaves

2 tablespoons low-fat mayonnaise

1. Gently lift the skin from the turkey breast and stuff the sage leaves under the skin. Season the breast with the salt and pepper.

2. Bring the milk and $1/2$ cup of the broth to a boil in a straight-sided nonstick skillet. Add the turkey breast, reduce the heat, and simmer, covered, until cooked through, about 1 hour. Let stand 10 minutes before slicing.

3. To make the pesto, puree the arugula, garlic, pine nuts, oil, parsley, mayonnaise, and the remaining $1/4$ cup of broth in a food processor. Serve the turkey with the pesto on the side. Remove the skin before eating.

Per serving: 236 Calories, 5 g Total Fat, 1 g Saturated Fat, 96 mg Cholesterol, 336 mg Sodium, 5 g Total Carbohydrate, 2 g Dietary Fiber, 40 g Protein, 164 mg Calcium.

POINTS per serving: 5.

Cornish Hens Vesuvio

The origins of Italian-American Vesuvio-style preparations—characterized by large eruptions of garlic and rosemary—are shrouded in mystery, but they have become signature dishes in Chicago restaurants. Feel free to increase the amounts of garlic and rosemary to suit your taste, up to double the measures we call for.

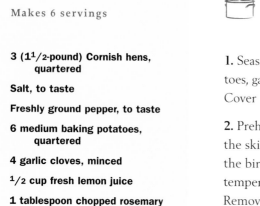

Makes 6 servings

3 (1^1/$_2$-pound) Cornish hens, quartered

Salt, to taste

Freshly ground pepper, to taste

6 medium baking potatoes, quartered

4 garlic cloves, minced

^{1}/$_2$ cup fresh lemon juice

1 tablespoon chopped rosemary

1. Season the hens with the salt and pepper. Combine the hens, potatoes, garlic, lemon juice, and rosemary in a nonreactive baking pan. Cover and marinate in the refrigerator for at least 30 minutes.

2. Preheat the oven to 425°F. Uncover the baking pan and roast until the skin of the hens is well browned and the juices run clear when the birds are pierced with a fork, about 30 minutes. Increase the oven temperature to broil. Broil until the potatoes brown, about 2 minutes. Remove the skin before eating.

Per serving: 274 Calories, 4 g Total Fat, 1 g Saturated Fat, 103 mg Cholesterol, 88 mg Sodium, 33 g Total Carbohydrate, 3 g Dietary Fiber, 26 g Protein, 35 mg Calcium.

POINTS per serving: 5.

Di Giorno   Be sure to choose a baking pan that's both nonreactive—that is, one that won't react to the acid in the lemon juice—and able to withstand the broiler's direct heat. A shallow stainless steel roasting pan is a good choice, as is porcelain-coated cast iron.

Cornish Hens alla Cacciatora

Cornish hens are almost all moderately low-fat breast meat; the little taste of dark meat in the legs adds an insignificant amount of fat. Although the hens are now farm-raised, they are still considered game birds. They are delicious served up in a hearty tomato and wine "hunter's-style" stew, which is the translation of *cacciatora*.

Makes 4 servings

1 teaspoon olive oil

2 (1¹/₂-pound) Cornish hens, quartered

1 onion, chopped

1 green bell pepper, seeded and chopped

2 garlic cloves, minced

1 (15-ounce) can tomato sauce

4 plum tomatoes, seeded and chopped

2 bay leaves

1 teaspoon dried oregano

¹/₂ teaspoon salt

¹/₄ teaspoon freshly ground pepper

¹/₂ teaspoon celery seed

¹/₄ cup dry red wine

Heat a large nonstick skillet. Swirl in the oil, then brown the hens, skin-side down, about 3 minutes. Transfer to a plate. Add the onion and bell pepper and sauté until the onion turns golden. Add the garlic and sauté until fragrant. Stir in the tomato sauce, tomatoes, bay leaves, oregano, salt, pepper, and celery seed. Return the hens to the pan, reduce the heat, and simmer, covered, 10 minutes. Uncover and simmer 10 minutes longer. Stir in the wine and boil until the sauce thickens and the hens are cooked through, about 3 minutes. Remove the bay leaves and the skin before serving.

Per serving: 240 Calories, 6 g Total Fat, 1 g Saturated Fat, 120 mg Cholesterol, 1,014 mg Sodium, 16 g Total Carbohydrate, 4 g Dietary Fiber, 29 g Protein, 59 mg Calcium.

POINTS per serving: 5.

Cornish Hens with Olives

The small purple-black gaeta olives, from Campania, are tasty in this dish; use them if you can find them. Serve this savory entrée on a bed of Polenta (page 131) with Tricolor Salad (page 148) on the side.

Makes 4 servings

2 (1½-pound) Cornish hens
½ teaspoon salt
Freshly ground pepper, to taste
4 teaspoons olive oil
2 garlic cloves, peeled
½ cup dry white wine
10 small green olives, pitted
10 small black olives, pitted
2 tablespoons minced parsley

1. Season the hen cavities with half of the salt and some pepper.

2. Heat the oil in a nonstick skillet over medium-low heat, then add the garlic. Cook, stirring constantly, until golden, about 5 minutes; reduce the heat if it cooks too quickly. Add the hens and brown on all sides. Discard the garlic. Sprinkle the hens with the remaining salt and more pepper to taste, then stir in the wine and olives. Reduce the heat and cook, covered, turning the hens occasionally and adding water if necessary, until cooked through, about 45 minutes.

3. Cut the hens in half and remove the skin. Serve with the olives and any pan juices, sprinkled with the parsley.

Per serving: 241 Calories, 12 g Total Fat, 3 g Saturated Fat, 76 mg Cholesterol, 581 mg Sodium, 1 g Total Carbohydrate, 1 g Dietary Fiber, 25 g Protein, 33 mg Calcium.

POINTS *per serving: 6.*

Di Giorno   Cooking the garlic in the oil imparts a subtle flavor to the oil and, in turn, the hens. If you prefer, you could make this with bone-in chicken breasts (discard the skin before eating).

meats

Beef-Stuffed Peppers

Stuffed peppers are freezer and lunch box friendly. Delicious hot or cold and colorful as well, they're also perfect for a buffet supper or picnic.

Makes 4 servings

³/4 pound lean ground beef (10% or less fat)

1 tomato, finely chopped

2 onions, finely chopped

1 large Italian frying pepper (see Di Giorno, page 137), seeded and finely chopped

3 egg whites

3 tablespoons plain dried bread crumbs

1 tablespoon minced fresh oregano, or 1 teaspoon dried

¹/4 teaspoon salt

Freshly ground pepper, to taste

4 yellow, red, or green bell peppers, halved lengthwise and seeded

1 cup tomato sauce (no salt added)

1. Preheat the oven to 400°F. Spray a 9 × 13-inch baking dish with nonstick spray.

2. Combine the ground beef, tomato, onions, frying pepper, egg whites, bread crumbs, oregano, salt, and pepper; set aside.

3. Put the bell peppers in a microwavable dish. Cover with plastic wrap, then prick a few holes in the plastic. Microwave on medium until tender, 6 minutes. Uncover and let cool. Fill the peppers with the beef mixture, pressing in the mixture lightly. Transfer to the baking dish and bake until the filling is slightly browned, 25–30 minutes. Spoon the tomato sauce over the peppers and bake until the sauce is bubbling and slightly browned, 15–20 minutes longer. Let stand 5 minutes before serving.

Per serving: 240 Calories, 8 g Total Fat, 3 g Saturated Fat, 44 mg Cholesterol, 294 mg Sodium, 23 g Total Carbohydrate, 4 g Dietary Fiber, 21 g Protein, 47 mg Calcium.

POINTS per serving: 5.

Bollito Misto

Despite the 15 ingredients, this is a simplified version of the Piedmontese classic: Some recipes for Bollito Misto call for seven cuts of beef, seven other kinds of meat (sausage, capon, and so forth), seven kinds of vegetables, and three sauces!

Makes 8 servings

1/2 cup chopped flat-leaf parsley

1 tablespoon chopped mint

1 tablespoon capers, drained

1 tablespoon white horseradish

2 teaspoons olive oil

1 teaspoon white-wine vinegar

1 anchovy fillet, rinsed, or 1/2 teaspoon anchovy paste

4 onions, chopped

3 celery stalks, chopped

2 carrots, diced

1 small head green cabbage, cored and cut into 8 wedges

2 pounds lean beef (brisket, rump, bottom round, or lean chuck)

1 (14 1/2-ounce) can diced plum tomatoes (no salt added), with juice

1/4 teaspoon salt

Freshly ground pepper, to taste

1. To prepare the sauce, puree the parsley, mint, capers, horseradish, oil, vinegar, and anchovy in a mini food processor or blender. Let stand at room temperature to blend the flavors.

2. Bring the onions, celery, carrots, cabbage, and cold water to cover to a boil. Add the beef, cover the pot, and bring back to a boil. Reduce the heat and simmer, skimming off any foam, about 15 minutes. Stir in the tomatoes, salt, and pepper; simmer until the meat and vegetables are very tender, about 2 hours longer. Transfer the meat and vegetables to a platter, reserving the broth (and some vegetables, if desired) for later. Serve the beef and vegetables, with the sauce on the side.

Per serving: 246 Calories, 10 g Total Fat, 3 g Saturated Fat, 71 mg Cholesterol, 260 mg Sodium, 13 g Total Carbohydrate, 4 g Dietary Fiber, 26 g Protein, 83 mg Calcium.

POINTS *per serving: 5.*

D i G i o r n o   If you've eaten all the meat and still have broth and vegetables remaining, reheat them with pasta, diced potatoes, or rice for a delicious soup.

Braciola in Tomato Sauce

The authentic Calabrian *braciola alla brugia* is a cut of meat that's rolled around a filling, cooked in lard, and served with a tomato sauce. Our considerably lightened version of this old-fashioned dish is delicious served on a bed of rigatoni or penne with a sprinkling of cheese. For its intense flavor, be sure to use real Parmigiano-Reggiano cheese in this dish.

Makes 4 servings

1 (1-pound) boneless lean beef round steak (about $1/2$-inch thick)

1 teaspoon olive oil

1 small onion, minced

$1/4$ cup minced celery

2 garlic cloves, minced

$1/4$ cup + 2 tablespoons plain dried bread crumbs

3 tablespoons minced flat-leaf parsley

3 tablespoons grated Parmesan cheese

$1/2$ teaspoon dried oregano

$1/4$ teaspoon salt

Freshly ground pepper, to taste

1 cup tomato sauce (no salt added)

1 cup stewed tomatoes, pureed

$1/2$ cup low-sodium beef broth

1. Preheat the oven to 350°F. Spray an 8-inch square baking dish with nonstick spray.

2. Put the steak between 2 sheets of wax paper and pound to $1/8$-inch thick.

3. Heat the oil in a nonstick skillet, then add the onion, celery, and garlic. Sauté until softened, then transfer to a bowl. Stir in the bread crumbs, 2 tablespoons of the parsley, 2 tablespoons of the cheese, the oregano, salt, and pepper. Spread the mixture over the steak, leaving about $1/2$-inch border. Roll up the steak, jelly-roll fashion, and tie at 1 inch intervals with kitchen twine. Transfer to the baking dish. Roast 15 minutes.

4. Meanwhile, combine the tomato sauce, stewed tomatoes, and broth. Pour over the steak roll after 15 minutes. Continue to roast, basting with the sauce every 15 minutes, until the beef is cooked through and very tender, $1 1/2$–2 hours. Transfer to a platter, spooning the sauce over. Serve, sprinkled with the remaining parsley and cheese.

Per serving: 260 Calories, 8 g Total Fat, 3 g Saturated Fat, 65 mg Cholesterol, 493 mg Sodium, 18 g Total Carbohydrate, 3 g Dietary Fiber, 28 g Protein, 102 mg Calcium.

POINTS *per serving: 5.*

Salute! Some Notable Fruits of Italian Vines

RED WINES

Type	Characteristics	Pair It With
Barolo	A big, rich wine that can stand lots of aging, Barolo has intensely intensely concentrated fruit and a bouquet redolent of truffles, pepper, and tobacco.	Strongly flavored foods, such as roasted meats or game, aged cheeses, hearty stews.
Barbaresco	Like its neighbor Barolo, Barbaresco is made from the nebbiolo grape, so it's full-bodied and complex. With its slightly lower alcohol content, it needs less aging than Barolo.	Roasted meats or game, richly sauced pastas, hearty casseroles, aged cheeses.
Chianti	Made from a blend of red and white grapes, Chianti varies greatly from producer to producer. Young Chiantis tend to be light, fruity, and refreshing; older versions can be full-bodied and complex.	Young Chiantis: pizza, grilled foods, game birds, turkey, prosciutto, and pastas with meat sauces. Older Chiantis: roasted red meats and steak.

WHITE WINES

Type	Characteristics	Pair It With
Orvieto	This golden, lively wine tastes of fresh apples and pears when well made, but poor quality Orvietos can be dull. Best bet: Orvieto Classicos, which are often nutty and complex.	Simple, light foods: fish and poultry, pastas, sandwiches—it's a good everyday and picnic wine.
Gavi	A medium-bodied, pleasantly dry, fruity wine made from the Cortese grape.	Fish, poultry, simple veal dishes, lightly flavored pastas and risottos.
Greco di Tufo	A fine, dry white with a distinctive almondlike character, it can be quite full-bodied and interesting.	Fish, shellfish, poultry, risottos, mild cheeses.

SPECIALTY WINES

Type	Characteristics	Pair It With
Asti Spumante	A light sparkling white dessert wine made from the *moscato* grape. American spumantes tend to be cloyingly sweet; don't let them dissuade you from the Italian versions, which can be well-balanced and sophisticated.	Biscotti, fresh fruit, and other not-too-sweet desserts.
Vin Santo ("holy wine")	A Tuscan specialty, made from slightly dried grapes, which are fermented in small barrels in attics. The changes in temperature (freezing in winter, sweltering in summer) create an unusual, amber-colored dessert wine that may be dry, semi-dry, or sweet.	Biscotti (a classic combination), peaches or strawberries, pastries.
Grappa	A brandy made from the solids that remain after the wine grapes have fermented. These are soaked and fermented again, and the resulting wine distilled into a spirit that varies greatly from town to town. Depending on how long it has aged and what has been added, it can have flavors of herbs, anise, lavender, or raisins (to name a few).	Grappa is said to enhance digestion; serve it plain as an apéritif.

Osso Buco

This dish is a specialty of northern Italy's Lombardy region. It's traditionally served with Risotto alla Milanese (page 112) and *gremolata*, a mixture of garlic, parsley, and lemon. If you have the option, grate the zest into skinny strips rather than tiny bits; it makes a prettier garnish.

Makes 4 servings

4 (1/2-pound) veal shanks, trimmed of all visible fat and cut about 1-inch thick

1/4 cup + 2 tablespoons all-purpose flour

4 teaspoons olive oil

1 1/2 cups sliced mushrooms

2 shallots, finely chopped

1 carrot, thinly sliced

2 celery stalks, finely chopped

1/2 cup dry white wine

1 garlic clove, minced

1 cup low-sodium beef broth

1/4 cup minced flat-leaf parsley

2 tablespoons grated lemon zest

2 tablespoons fresh lemon juice

1 tablespoon minced fresh rosemary, or 1/2 teaspoon dried leaves, crumbled

1 tablespoon minced fresh sage, or 1/2 teaspoon dried leaves, crumbled

1 anchovy fillet, rinsed and chopped, or 1/2 teaspoon anchovy paste

Freshly ground pepper, to taste

1 garlic clove, minced

1. Dredge the veal in the flour; set aside.

2. Heat the oil in a nonstick saucepan, then add the veal and brown on all sides. Transfer to a plate. Sauté the mushrooms, shallots, carrot, celery, wine, and garlic in the saucepan, scraping up any browned bits from the bottom of the pan, until the liquid is reduced to about 1/4 cup. Add the broth, half of the parsley, half of the lemon zest, the lemon juice, rosemary, sage, anchovy, and pepper. Return the veal to the saucepan. Reduce the heat and simmer, covered, until the veal is very tender, 1–1 1/2 hours; add water, 1/4 cup at a time, if the sauce looks too thick.

3. Meanwhile, make the gremolata: Mix the remaining parsley and lemon zest with the garlic. Serve the veal, topped with the sauce and sprinkled with the gremolata.

Per serving: 273 Calories, 8 g Total Fat, 2 g Saturated Fat, 89 mg Total Cholesterol, 207 mg Sodium, 17 g Total Carbohydrate, 2 g Dietary Fiber, 28 g Protein, 40 mg Calcium.

POINTS per serving: 6.

D i G i o r n o   Ask your butcher for meat from the center part of the shank, where the bone is smaller. You'll get more meat for your money.

Osso Buco

Veal Piccata

Just a little lemon goes a long way toward enhancing the flavor of this northern Italian dish. Accompanied by Arugula and Potato Salad (page 150), it becomes an exquisite luncheon or light dinner.

Makes 4 servings

4 teaspoons olive oil

3 egg whites

1/4 cup + 2 tablespoons plain dried bread crumbs

1/4 teaspoon salt

Freshly ground pepper, to taste

4 (3-ounce) thin-sliced veal cutlets (1/4-inch thick)

2 tablespoons minced flat-leaf parsley

1 lemon, quartered

1. Heat the oil in a large nonstick skillet. Beat the egg whites until foamy in a shallow bowl. Combine the bread crumbs, salt, and pepper on wax paper. Quickly dip the cutlets, one at a time, into the egg whites, then the bread crumbs, coating them evenly.

2. Transfer the cutlets to the skillet and sauté until golden brown and cooked through, about 3 minutes on each side. Serve at once, sprinkled with the parsley, with the lemon wedges on the side.

Per serving: 196 Calories, 7 g Total Fat, 2 g Saturated Fat, 66 mg Cholesterol, 376 mg Sodium, 11 g Total Carbohydrate, 1 g Dietary Fiber, 22 g Protein, 49 mg Calcium.

POINTS per serving: 4.

Veal Scallopine with Lemon and Capers

This elegant dish is deceptively simple—and lightning fast. Don't coat the scallopine until just before you put them into the pan, otherwise they won't form their delicious crust.

Makes 4 servings

2 teaspoons olive oil

4 (3-ounce) thin-sliced veal cutlets (1/4-inch thick)

2 tablespoons all-purpose flour

Pinch salt

Freshly ground pepper, to taste

3 tablespoons fresh lemon juice

2 tablespoons water

1 teaspoon unsalted butter

1 teaspoon capers, drained and chopped

1/4 cup minced parsley

1. Heat a nonstick skillet. Swirl in 1 teaspoon of oil. Dredge 2 cutlets in the flour, coating on both sides; shake off the excess flour. Transfer the veal to the skillet and cook until lightly browned, about 1 minute on each side. Transfer to a plate and keep warm. Repeat with the remaining oil, cutlets, and flour. Sprinkle the cutlets with the salt and pepper.

2. Add the lemon juice, water, and any juices that have accumulated around the cutlets to the skillet; bring to a boil. Remove from the heat and swirl in the butter until it melts, then stir in the capers. Add the cutlets and stir to coat with the sauce. Serve with the pan juices, sprinkled with the parsley.

Per serving: 123 Calories, 4 g Total Fat, 1 g Saturated Fat, 58 mg Cholesterol, 80 mg Sodium, 4 g Total Carbohydrate, 0 g Dietary Fiber, 16 g Protein, 10 mg Calcium.

POINTS per serving: 3.

Stuffed Rolled Veal Roast

When you're browning or searing meat, choose your pan carefully. A darker metal, like cast-iron or anodized aluminum, can withstand high temperatures and will retain heat, both properties necessary to developing a nice crust on the meat. Lighter metals, such as stainless steel, will reflect the heat, so the meat won't brown as well, and lightweight metals like regular aluminum can warp at very high temperatures.

Makes 8 servings

1 slice bread, crusts removed

$1/2$ cup fat-free milk

1 bunch chicory, cleaned and chopped

1 (10-ounce) bag triple-washed spinach, cleaned and chopped

1 garlic clove, bruised and peeled

1 cup thawed frozen green peas

2 tablespoons grated Parmesan cheese

1 tablespoon minced parsley

2 teaspoon minced marjoram

$1/4$ teaspoon salt

Freshly ground pepper, to taste

1 (2-pound) boneless lean veal shoulder

2 carrots, halved if thick

4 teaspoons olive oil

$1/2$ cup dry red wine

1 ($14 1/2$-ounce) can tomato puree (no salt added)

1. Soak the bread in the milk.

2. Spray a saucepan with nonstick spray and set over medium heat. Sauté the chicory, spinach, and garlic until the greens wilt. Discard the garlic and let the greens cool. Stir in the bread and milk, peas, cheese, parsley, marjoram, salt, and pepper.

3. Put the veal between wax paper and pound to an even thickness. Remove the top sheet of wax paper and spread the greens mixture over the veal, leaving a border. Top with the carrots, then roll up the veal and tie every 2 inches with kitchen twine.

4. Heat the oil in a pan, then add the veal. Brown on all sides, then add the wine and cook until most of it evaporates. Stir in the tomato puree. Reduce the heat and simmer, covered, until cooked through, about 1 hour. Let cool to room temperature, then cut into 8 slices. Serve with the sauce on the side.

Per serving: 237 Calories, 7 g Total Fat, 2 g Saturated Fat, 92 mg Cholesterol, 490 mg Sodium, 14 g Total Carbohydrate, 4 g Dietary Fiber, 27 g Protein, 121 mg Calcium.

POINTS per serving: 5.

Stuffed Rolled Veal Roast

Braised Veal Roast

Because ovens in homes have only recently become common throughout Italy, braising meats is a long-standing tradition. The cooking liquid differs by region: In the north, cooks braise in milk or stock, while in central Italy, some combination of stock and wine are typical, and cream might be added at the end of cooking to thicken and enrich. We use pureed vegetables to thicken a stock-and-wine base.

Makes 10 servings

1 (2 1/2–3-pound) veal shoulder roast

1 large onion, finely chopped

2 celery stalks, finely chopped

2 carrots, finely chopped

1 scant ounce pancetta, chopped (about 2 tablespoons)

2 large garlic cloves, minced

1 1/2 cups beef or chicken broth

1 cup dry white wine

2 large thyme sprigs

2 bay leaves

Salt, to taste

Freshly ground pepper, to taste

1. Heat a nonstick saucepan, then add the veal and brown on all sides. Transfer to a plate. Add the onion, celery, carrots, pancetta, and garlic to saucepan and sauté until the onion is softened. Return the veal to the pan, then add the broth, wine, thyme, bay leaves, salt, and pepper; bring to a boil. Reduce the heat and simmer, covered, until the veal is cooked through and very tender, about 1 1/2 hours.

2. Transfer the roast to a cutting board; cover it with foil to keep warm. Discard the thyme and bay leaves. Transfer about 2 cups of vegetables and stock to a food processor and puree, then stir back into the pan. Thinly slice the veal and serve, drizzled with the sauce.

Per serving: 200 Calories, 6 g Total Fat, 2 g Saturated Fat, 119 mg Cholesterol, 309 mg Sodium, 3 g Total Carbohydrate, 1 g Dietary Fiber, 28 g Protein, 44 mg Calcium.

POINTS per serving: 4.

D i G i o r n o   Rather than fish out the herbs after cooking the roast, tie the stem ends of the thyme and bay leaves together with kitchen twine to make a bouquet garni. Or, crumble the herbs and suspend them in the pot in a tea ball.

Stuffed Boneless Veal Chops

Rib chops are 1¹/₄ to 1¹/₂ inches thick, so they're perfect for stuffing.

Makes 4 servings

4 (3-ounce) boneless veal rib chops

1 onion, cut into 4 slices

¹/₄ cup low-sodium beef broth

¹/₄ pound part-skim mozzarella cheese, cut into 4 thin slices

1 teaspoon minced oregano

4 teaspoons olive oil

1 tablespoon all-purpose flour

¹/₄ cup dry Marsala wine

¹/₄ teaspoon salt

Freshly ground pepper, to taste

1. Butterfly the veal chops by cutting them almost in half horizontally; leave them attached by ¹/₂ inch. Put them between wax paper and pound them to ¹/₄–¹/₂-inch thickness.

2. Simmer the onion slices in 1 tablespoon of the beef broth until softened, about 10 minutes. Put an onion slice and a slice of cheese on one half of each of the chops. Sprinkle with the oregano, then fold the chops to enclose. Press the edges together and seal with toothpicks.

3. Heat the oil in a nonstick skillet. Dredge the chops in the flour, coating on both sides; shake off the excess flour. Transfer the veal to the skillet and cook, shaking the skillet occasionally so the chops don't stick, until browned, 2–3 minutes on each side. Reduce the heat and add the wine, the remaining broth, the salt, and pepper. Simmer, turning the veal occasionally, until cooked through, about 15 minutes. Serve with the pan juices.

Per serving: 222 Calories, 10 g Total Fat, 4 g Saturated Fat, 80 mg Cholesterol, 362 mg Sodium, 5 g Total Carbohydrate, 0 g Dietary Fiber, 23 g Protein, 162 mg Calcium.

***POINTS** per serving: 5.*

Veal Chops alla Calabrese

In Calabria, located at the "toe" of Italy, bell peppers are a common sauce ingredient. For this low-fat rendition of a traditional Calabrian dish, we dip the meat in buttermilk rather than egg and bake it in a hot oven instead of fry it.

Makes 4 servings

4 (1/4-pound) veal rib chops, trimmed of all visible fat

1/4 cup buttermilk

1/2 cup Italian-style dried bread crumbs

1 (7-ounce) jar roasted red peppers, rinsed and drained

1 tablespoon sun-dried tomato paste

2 garlic cloves, chopped

1. Put a nonstick baking sheet into the oven and preheat it to 475°F.

2. Dip the veal chops into the buttermilk, then roll them in the bread crumbs. Spray the baking sheet with nonstick spray. Put the chops on the sheet and spray them. Bake 4 minutes.

3. Meanwhile, puree the roasted peppers, sun-dried tomato paste, and garlic in a food processor. Turn the veal chops over, spread the puree over each, and bake on the second side until the veal is cooked through and the sauce bubbling, about 6 minutes.

Per serving: 221 Calories, 5 g Total Fat, 1 g Saturated Fat, 91 mg Cholesterol, 471 mg Sodium, 14 g Total Carbohydrate, 1 g Dietary Fiber, 26 g Protein, 60 mg Calcium.

POINTS *per serving: 5.*

Di Giorno   We like tubes of concentrated tomato paste for several reasons. Because it is concentrated, you can get away with using half the amount of traditional paste. Unlike cans of paste, the tubes are resealable, so they'll keep in the refrigerator for several months. Look for tubes of sun-dried tomato paste imported from Italy in the Italian section of your supermarket.

Lamb Shanks alla Trastevere

Although Italy does not have a large Jewish population, its influence can be seen in dishes such as this. Sephardic Jews migrated from the Middle East to Spain, coming to Italy after the Inquisition; through their migrations, they helped to introduce typically Middle Eastern ingredients like lamb and eggplant throughout the Mediterranean basin (as well as many foods brought back from the New World by explorers). This dish gets its name from the Roman neighborhood where the Jews settled in medieval times, *Trastevere* (a corruption of *"tra Tevere"*—across the Tiber—from the center of ancient Rome).

Makes 4 servings

4 (6–8 ounce) lamb shanks, trimmed of all visible fat

2 carrots, chopped

2 onions, chopped

5 garlic cloves, minced

1 (28-ounce) can crushed tomatoes

2 tablespoons chopped basil

1 tablespoon chopped oregano, or 1 teaspoon dried

1 (4 × 1-inch) strip orange zest

$^1/_8$ teaspoon crushed red pepper

$^1/_2$ teaspoon salt

$^1/_2$ teaspoon grated orange zest

$^1/_4$ cup chopped flat-leaf parsley

1. Heat a nonstick saucepan. Add the lamb and brown about 4 minutes on each side. Transfer to a plate. Add the carrots, onions, and about half of the garlic to the saucepan. Sauté until the onions turn golden, then stir in the tomatoes, basil, oregano, orange zest, crushed red pepper, and salt. Return the shanks to the pan and spoon the sauce over them. Reduce the heat and simmer, covered, 1 hour. Turn the shanks over, cover again, and cook until fork-tender, about 30 minutes longer.

2. Transfer the shanks to dinner plates. Stir the orange zest, parsley, and the remaining garlic into the sauce, then spoon the sauce over the shanks.

Per serving: 381 Calories, 8 g Total Fat, 4 g Saturated Fat, 156 mg Cholesterol, 749 mg Sodium, 25 g Total Carbohydrate, 6 g Dietary Fiber, 53 g Protein, 127 mg Calcium.

POINTS *per serving: 7.*

D i G i o r n o   Our mixture of orange zest, parsley, and garlic is very similar to the lemon zest, parsley, and garlic mixture known as a *gremolata* that is commonly sprinkled over osso buco. Although orange zest is very untraditional, we think its flavor marries better with lamb than that of lemon zest.

Lamb alla Cacciatora

Cacciatora-style dishes are often served on grilled polenta rounds, over mounds of soft polenta, or on a broad pasta such as penne or rigatoni. The wine plays an integral part in this stew—use a good quality, full-bodied, dry red wine, such as Chianti.

Makes 8 servings

1 teaspoon olive oil

1³/₄ pounds lamb stew meat, cut in 1-inch chunks

1 cup dry red wine

¹/₂ cup tomato sauce

1 large onion, peeled and sliced

1 red bell pepper, seeded and sliced

1 green bell pepper, seeded and sliced

1 (8-ounce) package white mushrooms, cleaned and quartered

¹/₄ cup chopped rosemary

1 teaspoon salt

¹/₂ teaspoon freshly ground pepper

4 garlic cloves, minced

¹/₂ tablespoon arrowroot, dissolved in 1 tablespoon water

Heat a nonstick saucepan. Swirl in the oil, then add the lamb. Sauté until the lamb is browned and begins to release its juices. Stir in the wine and tomato sauce, scraping to dislodge the browned bits from the bottom of the pan. Add the onion, both bell peppers, the mushrooms, rosemary, salt, pepper, and garlic. Reduce the heat and simmer, covered, until the lamb is fork-tender, about 45 minutes. Stir in the dissolved arrowroot and cook, stirring constantly, until the sauce becomes thick and glossy, about 2 minutes.

Per serving: 184 Calories, 6 g Total Fat, 3 g Saturated Fat, 65 mg Cholesterol, 359 mg Sodium, 6 g Total Carbohydrate, 1 g Dietary Fiber, 21 g Protein, 32 mg Calcium.

POINTS per serving: 4.

D i   G i o r n o   For lamb stew meat, buy a small leg of lamb or a very large shank and cut the meat yourself, rather than buying precut stew meat. You'll end up with meat that's leaner and more tender.

Lamb alla Cacciatora with Polenta (page 131)

Stuffed Roast Pork Loin

Pork is one of Italy's favorite meats, and one of the most famous preparations is the boneless roast from Tuscany called *arista*, which is often prepared with dried fruit. Creating a cavity in the center of the loin to stuff is much quicker and easier than rolling a roast around stuffing. Commercial poultry seasoning is very similar to the sage mixture that Tuscan cooks use to season the roast.

Makes 8 servings

8 dried Calimyrna figs, stemmed and finely chopped

¹/₄ cup Italian-style dried bread crumbs

2 tablespoons chopped flat-leaf parsley

¹/₂ tablespoon chopped pine nuts

3 tablespoons dry Marsala wine

1 (1¹/₂–1³/₄-pound) pork loin roast, trimmed of all visible fat

1 teaspoon salt

¹/₂ teaspoon freshly ground pepper

1 teaspoon poultry seasoning

1. Preheat the oven to 375°F. Mix the figs, bread crumbs, parsley, pine nuts, and wine to make a paste.

2. Stand the roast on one end. Push the long handle of a wooden spoon through the center of the roast to create a hole, then insert a long knife into the hole and twist to enlarge it. Pack the fig mixture into the cavity from both ends.

3. Sprinkle the salt, pepper, and poultry seasoning over the roast; transfer to a roasting pan. Roast until the pork reaches an internal temperature of 150°F, about 1 hour; be sure the thermometer is in the meat, not the stuffing. Cover and let stand until the internal temperature rises to 160°F, about 5 minutes. Cut into eight slices.

Per serving: 202 Calories, 5 g Total Fat, 2 g Saturated Fat, 63 mg Cholesterol, 398 mg Sodium, 16 g Total Carbohydrate, 3 g Dietary Fiber, 22 g Protein, 49 mg Calcium.

POINTS per serving: 4.

Friulian Broiled Pork Chops

This dish features a tomato-basil sauce in the style of Friuli, where they would add plenty of cherry peppers for plenty of fire. If you like spicy foods, add up to $1/2$ teaspoon of crushed red pepper with the tomatoes. Take care not to overcook the sauce and break down the tomatoes: You want only to heat them through and soften them a bit.

Makes 4 servings

4 (5-ounce) center-cut pork loin chops (with bone), trimmed of all visible fat

Salt, to taste

Freshly ground pepper, to taste

$1/4$ cup vegetable broth or chicken broth

1 (12-ounce) package cherry tomatoes, trimmed and cut into eighths

$1/4$ cup chopped basil

1. Preheat the broiler.

2. Season the pork chops with salt and pepper. Set them on a broiler rack and broil until well browned and cooked through, 3–4 minutes on each side.

3. Meanwhile, bring the broth to a boil in a small skillet. Add the tomatoes and basil and cook, stirring occasionally, until the tomatoes soften slightly, about 1 minute. Serve the chops, topped with the sauce.

Per serving: 218 Calories, 8 g Total Fat, 3 g Saturated Fat, 89 mg Cholesterol, 164 mg Sodium, 4 g Total Carbohydrate, 1 g Dietary Fiber, 32 g Protein, 38 mg Calcium.

POINTS *per serving: 5.*

Pork and Apple Stew

Friuli is in the far northeastern corner of Italy. The taste of this dish reflects the Austrian-Hungarian influence on the cooking of the region. Juniper berries lend a distinctively tart accent to this homey stew. Look for dried juniper berries in your supermarket spice section; they're also sold pickled at some deli counters.

Makes 8 servings

1 teaspoon olive oil

1 large fennel bulb, trimmed and thinly sliced

1 onion, chopped

2 Granny Smith apples, peeled, cored, and chopped

1 1/2 pounds pork loin, trimmed of all visible fat and cut into 1-inch cubes

1/2 cup dry white wine

1/2 teaspoon salt

1/4 teaspoon freshly ground pepper

1/2 tablespoon chopped juniper berries

1 tablespoon arrowroot, dissolved in 2 tablespoons water

2 tablespoons chopped flat-leaf parsley

Heat a nonstick saucepan. Swirl in the oil, then add the fennel and onion. Sauté until the onion begins to turn golden, about 2 minutes. Add the apples and pork. Cook, stirring constantly, until the pork is no longer pink, about 1 minute. Stir in the wine, salt, pepper, and juniper berries. Reduce the heat and simmer, covered, until the meat is fork-tender, about 40 minutes. Stir in the dissolved arrowroot and parsley and cook, stirring constantly, until the sauce thickens and turns clear, about 2 minutes.

Per serving: 175 Calories, 6 g Total Fat, 2 g Saturated Fat, 50 mg Cholesterol, 206 mg Sodium, 9 g Total Carbohydrate, 2 g Dietary Fiber, 19 g Protein, 36 mg Calcium.

POINTS *per serving: 4.*

Sausage, Escarole, and Lentils

In Marche, where this recipe hails from, the sausage would be removed from its casing and crumbled, and the lentils cooked separately. Serve this in bowls with Apple Salad and Feta (page 160) and chilled crisp white wine. Pass grated Parmesan cheese on the side.

Makes 6 servings

1 teaspoon olive oil

1 small white onion, chopped

6 links Italian-style turkey sausages (about 3/4 pound), cut into chunks

2 garlic cloves, chopped

1 1/4 cups dried lentils, picked over, rinsed, and drained

3 cups beef broth, or 3 cups water and 3 beef bouillon cubes

1 head escarole, cleaned and chopped (about 2 1/2 packed cups)

2 plum tomatoes, chopped

1/2 teaspoon salt (see Di Giorno)

1/4 teaspoon freshly ground pepper

1. Heat the oil in a straight-sided nonstick skillet, then add the onion. Sauté until translucent. Add the sausage and sauté until the sausage is lightly browned and the onion golden. Stir in the garlic and continue to cook until fragrant. Scatter the lentils evenly over the contents of the pan, then pour in the broth; bring just to a boil. Reduce the heat and simmer, until most of the liquid evaporates, about 20 minutes.

2. Stir in the escarole and tomatoes. Cook, covered, until the escarole is totally wilted, the lentils are tender, and the tomatoes begin to break down, about 5 minutes. Stir in the salt and pepper.

Per serving: 272 Calories, 7 g Total Fat, 2 g Saturated Fat, 43 mg Cholesterol, 1,188 mg Sodium, 29 g Total Carbohydrate, 15 g Dietary Fiber, 25 g Protein, 77 mg Calcium.

POINTS per serving: 3.

D i G i o r n o   Omit the salt if you use bouillon cubes and water rather than broth.

vegetables

Basil-Roasted Vegetables

Try these savory veggies at your next picnic: They travel well and taste wonderful at room temperature, or you can reheat them, tightly wrapped in foil, on an outdoor grill. If you're not at a picnic and want to reheat them, cover them with foil and bake in a 325°F oven for about 10 minutes.

Makes 4 servings

1 cup basil leaves

1/4 cup parsley leaves

2 teaspoons grated Parmesan cheese

2 teaspoons balsamic vinegar

2 garlic cloves

1/8 teaspoon salt

Freshly ground pepper, to taste

1/4 cup low-sodium vegetable or chicken broth

1 broccoli crown, cut into florets

1 cup quartered mushrooms

1/4 pound green beans, cut into 2-inch lengths

1 small onion, thinly sliced and separated into rings

1/4 cup chopped pimientos

1. Preheat the oven to 425°F. Spray an 8-inch square baking dish with nonstick spray.

2. Chop the basil, parsley, cheese, vinegar, garlic, salt, and pepper in a food processor. Add the broth and process until combined.

3. Put the broccoli, mushrooms, green beans, and onion in the baking dish. Pour in the basil sauce and toss to coat. Cover with foil and bake, stirring frequently, until the vegetables are tender, 15–20 minutes. Stir in the pimientos.

Per serving: 60 Calories, 1 g Total Fat, 0 g Saturated Fat, 1 mg Cholesterol, 126 mg Sodium, 11 g Total Carbohydrate, 3 g Dietary Fiber, 4 g Protein, 155 mg Calcium.

POINTS per serving: 1.

D i   G i o r n o   Although broccoli stems are edible, many people discard them rather than peel their tough skins. If you do too, you might want to look for broccoli crowns in your supermarket. Crowns often cost a bit more per pound, but there's less waste, so you may actually save money.

Roasted Potatoes with Oregano

Crisp on the outside and tender on the inside, roasted potatoes are always wonderful. With oregano, they're especially fragrant and delicious—and they couldn't be easier to prepare.

Makes 4 servings

2 tablespoons minced fresh
    oregano, or 1 teaspoon dried

2 teaspoons olive oil

1/4 teaspoon salt

Freshly ground pepper, to taste

4 medium all-purpose potatoes,
    peeled and cut into chunks

Preheat the oven to 400°F. Combine the oregano, oil, salt, and pepper in an 8-inch square baking dish. Add the potatoes; toss to coat. Roast, turning the potatoes once, until they are golden and crisp on the outside and tender on the inside, about 45 minutes.

Per serving: 133 Calories, 2 g Total Fat, 0 g Saturated Fat, 0 mg Cholesterol, 144 mg Sodium, 26 g Total Carbohydrate, 2 g Dietary Fiber, 3 g Protein, 17 mg Calcium.

POINTS per serving: 2.

Di Giorno   Don't stir the potatoes too often—a lot of stirring keeps them from developing that appealing crust.

Rosemary-Roasted Vegetables

Italian cooks are experts at waking up the flavors of ordinary dishes with herbs. With a generous sprinkling of rosemary and sage, that's just what happens to these three vegetables.

Makes 4 servings

2 tablespoons low-sodium vegetable or chicken broth

4 teaspoons olive oil

1 tablespoon minced fresh rosemary leaves, or $^1/_2$ teaspoon dried

1 tablespoon minced fresh sage leaves, or $^1/_2$ teaspoon dried

$^1/_4$ teaspoon salt

Freshly ground pepper, to taste

4 medium all-purpose potatoes, scrubbed and sliced $^1/_4$-inch thick

2 onions, sliced

1 carrot, diced

Preheat the oven to 425°F. Combine the broth, oil, rosemary, sage, salt, and pepper in a 9 × 13-inch baking dish. Add the potatoes, onions, and carrot; toss to coat. Cover with foil and roast 30 minutes, then remove the foil and roast until crisp and golden, about 30 minutes longer.

Per serving: 182 Calories, 5 g Total Fat, 1 g Saturated Fat, 0 mg Cholesterol, 157 mg Sodium, 32 g Total Carbohydrate, 4 g Dietary Fiber, 4 g Protein, 30 mg Calcium.

POINTS per serving: 3.

Roasted Radicchio and Endive with Mozzarella

Italians roast, bake, and grill vegetables that most Americans haven't let out of their salad bowls. If you've never tried either of these vegetables cooked, this recipe is a perfect introduction.

Makes 4 servings

1 head radicchio, cleaned and cut into 4 wedges

2 heads Belgian endive, cleaned and halved lengthwise

2 teaspoons olive oil

3/4 cup shredded skim-milk mozzarella cheese

Preheat the oven to 400°F. Spray a 9 × 13-inch baking dish with nonstick spray. Place the radicchio and endive, cut-sides up, in the dish. Drizzle evenly with the oil. Roast until tender, 10–15 minutes. Sprinkle with the mozzarella; roast until the cheese melts, about 5 minutes longer.

Per serving: 70 Calories, 3 g Total Fat, 0 g Saturated Fat, 2 mg Cholesterol, 165 mg Sodium, 5 g Total Carbohydrate, 2 g Dietary Fiber, 8 g Protein, 172 mg Calcium.

POINTS per serving: 1.

Roasted Sunchokes and Brussels Sprouts

Also called a Jerusalem artichoke, the sunchoke has nothing to do with Jerusalem, nor is it related to the artichoke. To confuse things even more, its brown, lumpy appearance makes it resemble fresh ginger. It is actually a tuber and a member of the sunflower family; its name is derived from the Italian *girasole*, which means sunflower. When roasted, it has a potato-like texture but a sweeter taste.

Makes 6 servings

1 pound sunchokes, scrubbed

2 tablespoons olive oil

3 large garlic cloves, thinly sliced

1 pound Brussels sprouts, trimmed

1. Preheat the oven to 400°F. Cut the sunchokes into pieces about the size of the Brussels sprouts.

2. Combine the oil and garlic in a saucepan. Cook over low heat until the garlic is fragrant, about 5 minutes. Add the sunchokes and Brussels sprouts and toss to coat. Transfer to a baking sheet and roast, tossing occasionally, until well browned and very tender, about 25 minutes.

Per serving: 132 Calories, 5 g Total Fat, 1 g Saturated Fat, 0 mg Cholesterol, 22 mg Sodium, 20 g Total Carbohydrate, 4 g Dietary Fiber, 4 g Protein, 45 mg Calcium.

POINTS per serving: 2.

D i   G i o r n o   To trim Brussels sprouts, peel off the tough outer leaves, cut a thin slice off the bottom, then cut an "X" into the bottom.

Roasted Sunchokes and Brussels Sprouts with *Friulian Broiled Pork Chops (page 221)*

Giardinetto al Forno

Since *giardinetto* refers to a plate of vegetables arranged to resemble a garden, keep the vegetables separate when you cook them and on the serving platter (*al forno* means roasted or baked in the oven). If you like, sprinkle a tablespoon or two of your favorite herb over the veggies before serving.

Makes 6 servings

1 (1-pound) eggplant, cut into chunks

2 medium zucchini, cut into chunks

1 1/4 cups baby carrots, halved crosswise

1 (8-ounce) package white boiling onions, peeled

Preheat the oven to 375°F. Spray a baking sheet with nonstick spray. Arrange the eggplant, zucchini, carrots, and onions in separate piles on the baking sheet. Spray with nonstick spray. Roast until well browned, about 45 minutes, tossing every 15 minutes.

Per serving: 59 Calories, 0 g Total Fat, 0 g Saturated Fat, 0 mg Cholesterol, 22 mg Sodium, 13 g Total Carbohydrate, 4 g Dietary Fiber, 2 g Protein, 28 mg Calcium.

POINTS *per serving: 0.*

Stuffed Zucchini

Like other gourds, zucchini were brought to Italy from the New World in the 1500s. You'll now find stuffed zucchini in nearly every region in Italy, but the combination of pine nuts, raisins, and anchovies are a tip-off that this dish is from the south.

Makes 4 servings

4 medium zucchini

2 teaspoons olive oil

2 onions, minced

3 garlic cloves, minced

1/4 cup + 2 tablespoons plain dried bread crumbs

1/4 cup golden raisins, chopped

1/4 cup minced parsley

1/4 cup grated Parmesan cheese

3 tablespoons pine nuts, chopped

1 tablespoon anchovy paste

Freshly ground pepper, to taste

1. Preheat the oven to 375°F. Line a baking sheet with foil.

2. Trim the stem ends from the zucchini, then cut a paper-thin slice off one side so they don't roll. Cut 1/2-inch off the opposite side, then with a sharp knife or a spoon, hollow out the zucchini, leaving a 1/2-inch shell. Finely chop the long pieces and the zucchini insides.

3. Heat the oil in a nonstick skillet, then add the chopped zucchini and onions. Sauté until golden, about 10 minutes, then add the garlic and sauté until fragrant. Remove from the heat and stir in the bread crumbs, raisins, parsley, cheese, pine nuts, anchovy paste, and pepper. Stuff the filling into the zucchini and put on the baking sheet. Cover with foil and bake 20 minutes, then remove the foil and bake until the zucchini shells are tender and the filling is browned, about 10 minutes longer.

Per serving: 235 Calories, 10 g Total Fat, 3 g Saturated Fat, 10 mg Cholesterol, 436 mg Sodium, 29 g Total Carbohydrate, 4 g Dietary Fiber, 12 g Protein, 226 mg Calcium.

POINTS *per serving: 5.*

Di Giorno   Be sure to choose smallish zucchini; they have smaller and fewer seeds and more flavorful pulp.

Zucchini Agrodolce

This classic dish (the term *agrodolce* means "sour-sweet" in Italian) should be served at room temperature, with crusty bread, ripe tomatoes, and a bit of cheese.

Makes 4 servings

4 teaspoons olive oil

4 small zucchini, thinly sliced on
   the diagonal

1/4 cup balsamic vinegar

2 teaspoons sugar

Freshly ground pepper, to taste

Pinch cinnamon

Heat the oil in a very large nonstick skillet, then add the zucchini. Sauté until golden brown, then stir in the vinegar, sugar, pepper, and cinnamon. Toss to coat, then cook until most of the liquid evaporates. Cool to room temperature and serve, or cover and refrigerate until chilled.

Per serving: 68 Calories, 5 g Total Fat, 1 g Saturated Fat, 0 mg Cholesterol, 5 mg Sodium, 6 g Total Carbohydrate, 1 g Dietary Fiber, 2 g Protein, 21 mg Calcium.

POINTS per serving: 2.

Di Giorno   Sweet-and-sour sauces were very popular throughout Italy during the Renaissance; they were probably brought from the Middle East during the Crusades. You'll still find them used in pockets of northern Italy near the Austrian border and throughout southern Italy.

Sweet-and-Sour Onions

Pearl onions, simmered in vinegar and a bit of sugar, make a delectable accompaniment to meat or fowl, a great component to an antipasto platter, a garnish, or even a snack. In Lombardy, these are called *cipolline in agrodolce*.

Makes 4 servings

4 cups thawed frozen pearl onions

2 cups low-sodium beef broth

4 teaspoons olive oil

2 tablespoons white-wine vinegar

1 tablespoon sugar

Freshly ground pepper, to taste

1. Combine the onions, broth, and oil in a nonstick skillet. Cover and cook, stirring occasionally, until the onions begin to soften, about 30 minutes. If the onions get too dry, add water, 1 tablespoon at a time.

2. Stir in the vinegar, sugar, and pepper; cook, stirring frequently, until the onions are very tender, about 30 minutes longer; add water, 1 tablespoon at a time, as needed.

Per serving: 137 Calories, 5 g Total Fat, 1 g Saturated Fat, 0 mg Cholesterol, 110 mg Sodium, 19 g Total Carbohydrate, 0 g Dietary Fiber, 4 g Protein, 68 mg Calcium.

POINTS per serving: 3.

D i G i o r n o   Don't even think of peeling so many fresh onions; use frozen ones.

Sautéed Broccoli with Garlic and Lemon

Garlic and lemon are the classic dressing for many an Italian vegetable dish or salad. This dressing is good with cauliflower, broccoli rabe, or greens like Swiss chard or spinach, and it's a never-fail pasta topper.

Makes 4 servings

1 pound broccoli crowns, cut into florets (about 4 cups)

1/2 cup low-sodium chicken broth

4 teaspoons olive oil

6 garlic cloves, minced

1/4 teaspoon salt

2 tablespoons fresh lemon juice

1. Put the broccoli in a steamer basket; set in a saucepan over 1 inch of boiling water. Cover tightly and steam until barely tender, about 3 minutes.

2. Combine the broth and oil in a nonstick skillet over medium-high heat, then add the broccoli, garlic, and salt. Cook, stirring frequently, until the broccoli is tender and the liquid evaporates. Transfer to a serving bowl; sprinkle with the lemon juice. Let stand until slightly warm or at room temperature before serving.

Per serving: 71 Calories, 5 g Total Fat, 1 g Saturated Fat, 0 mg Cholesterol, 169 mg Sodium, 6 g Total Carbohydrate, 2 g Dietary Fiber, 3 g Protein, 45 mg Calcium.

POINTS *per serving: 1.*

D i G i o r n o   When you buy broccoli, choose heads with dark green, very tiny buds. Avoid any with a yellow tinge (which is a sign they're past their prime).

Broccoflower and Onion Sauté

A North American hybrid of two of Italy's most popular vegetables, broccoli and cauliflower, broccoflower pairs well with the bold flavors of crushed red pepper and pecorino Romano. You could easily substitute 4 cups broccoli florets for the broccoflower. Serve with Osso Buco (page 208) and Risotto alla Milanese (page 110).

Makes 6 servings

1 onion, sliced

1 1/2 pounds broccoflower, cut into florets (about 6 cups)

1 large garlic clove, chopped

1/8 teaspoon crushed red pepper

1/2 cup dry white wine

2 tablespoons grated pecorino Romano cheese

Heat a nonstick skillet. Sauté the onion until limp and dry, 1–2 minutes. Add the broccoflower in as thin a layer as possible, then sprinkle with the garlic and crushed red pepper. Add the wine, reduce the heat and cook, covered, until the broccoflower is fork-tender and the wine evaporates, 10–12 minutes. Serve, sprinkled with the cheese.

Per serving: 67 Calories, 1 g Total Fat, 0 g Saturated Fat, 2 mg Cholesterol, 66 mg Sodium, 9 g Total Carbohydrate, 4 g Dietary Fiber, 4 g Protein, 71 mg Calcium.

POINTS *per serving: 1.*

Sautéed Mushrooms with Mint and Parsley

Mint is a popular seasoning in Rome; throughout Italy, mint, or even catmint (a wild mint related to catnip), is sometimes used with mushrooms.

Makes 4 servings

2 teaspoons olive oil

3 shallots, finely chopped

2 garlic cloves, minced

1/2 pound mushrooms, trimmed and very thinly sliced

2 portobello mushrooms, trimmed and very thinly sliced

1/4 teaspoon salt

1/4 teaspoon ground white pepper

2 tablespoons minced mint

2 tablespoons minced flat-leaf parsley

Heat the oil in a nonstick skillet, then add the shallots and garlic. Sauté until fragrant, then add the mushrooms, salt, and pepper. Sauté until the mushrooms have released some of their liquid, about 5 minutes. Add the mint and parsley. Increase the heat to high and sauté until the liquid evaporates. Serve warm or at room temperature.

Per serving: 56 Calories, 3 g Total Fat, 0 g Saturated Fat, 0 mg Cholesterol, 141 mg Sodium, 7 g Total Carbohydrate, 1 g Dietary Fiber, 2 g Protein, 16 mg Calcium.

POINTS per serving: 1.

D i G i o r n o   White, black, and green peppercorns are actually the same berry in different stages of ripeness. Green peppercorns are unripened; they turn black when ripe. When the outer shell is removed from a black peppercorn, you're left with white pepper. Ground white pepper is used most often in white sauces or pale soups when black pepper's dark flecks might be distracting. Its flavor is somewhat milder than black pepper's, so it can also be used when you want a little less kick.

Sautéed Peas with Prosciutto

In Florence, they use the tiniest fresh peas imaginable in this dish. If you don't have the time to shell fresh peas, use frozen, but be sure you buy the really small ones.

Makes 4 servings

4 teaspoons olive oil

2 shallots, minced

2 garlic cloves, minced

1 ounce prosciutto, minced

2 cups fresh or partially thawed frozen young green peas

1 tablespoon minced mint

1/4 teaspoon salt

Freshly ground pepper, to taste

3 tablespoons water

Heat the oil in a nonstick skillet, then add the shallots, garlic, and prosciutto. Sauté until the shallots wilt. Add the peas, mint, salt, pepper, and water. Cover and cook until the peas are tender but not mushy, 10 minutes if using fresh peas or 3–5 minutes if using frozen.

Per serving: 122 Calories, 6 g Total Fat, 1 g Saturated Fat, 6 mg Cholesterol, 271 mg Sodium, 12 g Total Carbohydrate, 3 g Dietary Fiber, 6 g Protein, 25 mg Calcium.

POINTS per serving: 2.

Sautéed Peppers

When you taste the soft, creamy texture and the concentrated flavor of these peppers, you'll swear there has to be more than just half a teaspoon of oil per serving. Serve them as an appetizer or a side dish, or cut them into thin slices to layer on your favorite sandwich or toss into a salad. If you find red frying peppers, use a combination of the red and green,

Makes 4 servings

4 Italian frying peppers (see Di Giorno, p. 137), quartered and seeded

1 cup hot water

4 garlic cloves, sliced

2 teaspoons olive oil

¹/₄ teaspoon salt

Freshly ground pepper, to taste

1 teaspoon balsamic vinegar

1. Combine the frying peppers, water, garlic, oil, salt, and pepper in a nonstick skillet. Cover and cook, stirring occasionally, until the peppers are tender and the liquid evaporates, about 20 minutes.

2. Add the balsamic vinegar; toss lightly. Serve hot, warm, or at room temperature.

Per serving: 58 Calories, 2 g Total Fat, 0 g Saturated Fat, 0 mg Cholesterol, 141 mg Sodium, 9 g Total Carbohydrate, 1 g Dietary Fiber, 2 g Protein, 21 mg Calcium.

POINTS per serving: 1.

Sautéed Endive

The strong flavors of this dish marry well with Whole Roasted Fish in Balsamic Sauce (page 170) or Sea Bass in Acqua Pazza (page 176), but since it takes so little time to whip this up, it's sure to become part of your regular repertoire.

Makes 4 servings

1/2 tablespoon olive oil

2 heads Belgian endive, cleaned and sliced crosswise

1/2 cup packed chopped arugula

1/2 teaspoon salt

2 tablespoons grated Parmesan cheese

Heat a nonstick skillet. Swirl in the oil, then add the endive. Sauté until it just begins to brown, then add the arugula and sauté until it is wilted and bright green. Stir in the salt and cheese.

Per serving: 34 Calories, 3 g Total Fat, 1 g Saturated Fat, 2 mg Cholesterol, 350 mg Sodium, 1 g Total Carbohydrate, 1 g Dietary Fiber, 2 g Protein, 52 mg Calcium.

POINTS *per serving: 1.*

Di Giorno   Be sure to use Belgian endive, the variety with long, off-white leaves packed tightly into a head, not frilly, green curly endive (sometimes called frisée). Store Belgian endive for no more than a day in the refrigerator wrapped in paper towels, as exposure to light will make it more bitter.

Broccoli Rabe with Potatoes

Broccoli rabe has a pleasantly bitter flavor that stands up well to crushed red pepper and a hefty amount of garlic. With crisp potato slices, it's even more special, and a great accompaniment to meat or fowl.

Makes 4 servings

1 bunch broccoli rabe, cleaned and coarsely chopped

4 teaspoons olive oil

2 medium all-purpose potatoes, scrubbed and very thinly sliced

4 garlic cloves, minced

1/2 teaspoon crushed red pepper

1/4 teaspoon salt

1. Put the broccoli rabe in a steamer basket; set in a saucepan over 1 inch of boiling water. Cover tightly and steam until tender, about 10 minutes.

2. Heat a nonstick skillet. Swirl in the oil. Cover the bottom of the pan with the potato slices, overlapping as necessary. Sprinkle with the garlic, crushed red pepper, and salt. Cook over medium heat until the potatoes are browned on the bottom but are still not quite tender, about 10 minutes.

3. Spread the broccoli rabe over the potatoes. Reduce the heat, cover, and cook, adding 1/4 cup water at a time as needed, until the potatoes are tender, 10–15 minutes.

Per serving: 185 Calories, 5 g Total Fat, 1 g Saturated Fat, 0 mg Cholesterol, 195 mg Sodium, 32 g Total Carbohydrate, 5 g Dietary Fiber, 6 g Protein, 90 mg Calcium.

POINTS *per serving: 3.*

Broccoli Rabe and Cannellini with Red Pepper

Also called *broccoletti di rapa*, *rapini*, or *cime di rapa*—or broccoli raab in English—this vegetable is ample evidence that Italians like assertively flavored vegetables. Broccoli rabe is a winter vegetable, so try this dish when the garden is lying fallow.

Makes 6 servings

¹/₂ tablespoon olive oil

2 large garlic cloves, minced

1 pound broccoli rabe, cleaned and chopped

1 (16-ounce) can cannellini beans, rinsed and drained

¹/₄ teaspoon crushed red pepper

¹/₃ cup water

2 teaspoons fresh lemon juice

Heat a large nonstick skillet. Swirl in the oil, then add the garlic. Sauté until fragrant. Add the broccoli rabe, cannellini beans, crushed red pepper, and water. Cook, covered, until the water evaporates and the broccoli rabe is fork-tender, about 15 minutes. Stir in the lemon juice.

Per serving: 80 Calories, 1 g Total Fat, 0 g Saturated Fat, 0 mg Cholesterol, 161 mg Sodium, 13 g Total Carbohydrate, 3 g Dietary Fiber, 5 g Protein, 42 mg Calcium.

POINTS per serving: 1.

D i G i o r n o   Lemon adds a pleasant counterpoint to many vegetables, but always add it at the end of the cooking—its acidity can turn some veggies mushy or an unappetizing shade of green.

Cannellini-Stuffed Peppers

In Tuscany, beans—especially the white kidney beans called cannellini—are the staff of life. Combined with sage and tomatoes, they provide a hearty filling for colorful bell peppers.

Makes 4 servings

4 red or yellow bell peppers,
   halved lengthwise and
   seeded

4 teaspoons olive oil

4 plum tomatoes, chopped

2 onions, minced

2 tablespoons minced fresh sage,
   or 1 teaspoon dried

1 garlic clove, minced

1/4 teaspoon salt

Freshly ground pepper, to taste

1 (16-ounce) can cannellini
   beans, rinsed and drained

1. Preheat the oven to 425°F. Rinse the peppers under cold water and put them in a 9 × 13-inch baking dish; cover with foil and bake 20 minutes, until barely tender. Uncover and bake 15 minutes longer. Drain off any liquid.

2. Meanwhile, heat the oil in a nonstick skillet, then add the tomatoes, onions, sage, garlic, salt, and pepper. Sauté until the sauce is thickened and the onions are softened, 15–20 minutes. Remove from the heat and stir in the beans. Divide the bean mixture evenly among the pepper halves. Let stand 5 minutes before serving.

Per serving: 248 Calories, 6 g Total Fat, 1 g Saturated Fat, 0 mg Cholesterol, 150 mg Sodium, 41 g Total Carbohydrate, 8 g Dietary Fiber, 12 g Protein, 59 mg Calcium.

POINTS *per serving: 4.*

Pasta-Stuffed Peppers

If you're pressed for time, substitute a 14$^{1}/_{2}$-ounce can of diced tomatoes for the plum tomatoes. But no matter how rushed you are, always trim any woody ends from the mushroom stems before you chop them (if you've a particularly woody batch, you might find it easier to snap off the stems and just use the caps).

Makes 4 servings

4 teaspoons olive oil

1 onion, minced

2 garlic cloves, minced

4 plum tomatoes, peeled, seeded, and chopped

1 cup chopped white mushrooms

1 tablespoon minced fresh basil, or 1 teaspoon dried

1 tablespoon minced fresh oregano, or 1 teaspoon dried

1 tablespoon capers, drained and chopped

2 anchovy fillets, rinsed and chopped, or 1 teaspoon anchovy paste

Freshly ground pepper, to taste

$^{1}/_{2}$ cup orzo, small star, or tubetti pasta

$^{3}/_{4}$ cup shredded skim-milk mozzarella cheese

4 green, red, or yellow bell peppers, halved lengthwise and seeded

1. Preheat the oven to 350°F. Spray a 9 × 13-inch baking dish with nonstick spray.

2. Heat the oil in a nonstick skillet, then add the onion and garlic. Sauté until softened. Stir in the tomatoes, mushrooms, basil, oregano, capers, anchovies, and pepper and cook until thickened. Remove from the heat.

3. Cook the pasta according to package directions until barely tender, about 5 minutes. Drain and add to the tomato mixture. Add half the cheese and toss to combine. Divide among the pepper halves, then put in the baking dish. Pour $^{1}/_{2}$ inch of water in the bottom of the dish. Bake until the peppers are tender, about 45 minutes. Sprinkle the remaining cheese over the filling; bake until the cheese melts, about 5 minutes longer. Let stand 5 minutes before serving.

Per serving: 206 Calories, 6 g Total Fat, 1 g Saturated Fat, 3 mg Cholesterol, 296 mg Sodium, 28 g Total Carbohydrate, 3 g Dietary Fiber, 12 g Protein, 188 mg Calcium.

POINTS per serving: 4.

D i G i o r n o   The pasta will continue to cook as the peppers bake, so be sure to undercook it slightly.

Broiled Tomatoes

Although it's impossible to imagine Italian cooking without tomatoes, they were introduced to Italy in the sixteenth century when Jesuit priests brought them from Mexico; they didn't gain widespread use until about two hundred years ago. The plant flourished in the fertile Campania region, especially in the San Marzano area near Naples.

Makes 4 servings

2 large ripe tomatoes

1/2 teaspoon salt

3 tablespoons plain dried bread crumbs

1 tablespoon capers, drained and minced

1 tablespoon minced parsley

1 garlic clove, minced

4 teaspoons extra-virgin olive oil

2 tablespoons torn basil

1. Preheat the broiler. Line an 8-inch square baking pan with foil.

2. Cut the tomatoes in half horizontally and remove the seeds. Sprinkle with the salt and invert on a plate to drain while you make the filling.

3. Combine the bread crumbs, capers, parsley, and garlic. Spoon the filling into the tomatoes and put in the baking pan. Drizzle with the oil and basil. Broil 5 inches from the heat until the tomatoes are tender and the filling is browned, about 5 minutes. Serve hot or at room temperature.

Per serving: 87 Calories, 5 g Total Fat, 1 g Saturated Fat, 0 mg Cholesterol, 383 mg Sodium, 10 g Total Carbohydrate, 2 g Dietary Fiber, 2 g Protein, 34 mg Calcium.

POINTS per serving: 2.

Di Giorno   If you're grilling, make this on the grill, too: Just set the tomatoes directly on the grill rack and let them cook 20–25 minutes.

Cavolfiore alla Calabrese

Cauliflower is common in southern Italy. This recipe is a variation of a typical preparation in Calabria, where it's parboiled, then combined with a sauce of anchovies, capers, and, sometimes, bread crumbs.

Makes 4 servings

2 cups cauliflower florets

1 teaspoon olive oil

2 slices white bread, made into fine crumbs

1/2 teaspoon dried thyme leaves

1 green bell pepper, seeded and thinly sliced

2 tablespoons low-sodium chicken broth

1/2 tablespoon capers, drained and chopped

1 garlic clove, minced

1 anchovy fillet, rinsed and finely chopped

Freshly ground pepper, to taste

1. Cook the cauliflower in boiling water until barely tender, about 5 minutes. Drain.

2. Heat the oil in a nonstick skillet, then add the bread crumbs and thyme. Cook, stirring frequently, until lightly browned. Add the cauliflower and bell pepper; cook, stirring frequently, until the vegetables are tender. Stir in the broth, capers, garlic, anchovy, and pepper; cook, stirring, until the anchovy dissolves.

Per serving: 79 Calories, 3 g Total Fat, 1 g Saturated Fat, 1 mg Cholesterol, 214 mg Sodium, 11 g Total Carbohydrate, 2 g Dietary Fiber, 3 g Protein, 42 mg Calcium.

POINTS per serving: 1.

Asparagus Gratinata

The influence of French cooking is prevalent in northern Italy; gratins are common in Piedmont, Lombardy, and Emilia-Romagna. For variety, use Brussels sprouts or fennel.

Makes 4 servings

1 bunch asparagus, trimmed

2 teaspoons olive oil

1 cup fat-free milk

1/4 cup grated Parmesan cheese

1 egg

1 egg white

Pinch salt

1. Preheat the oven to 400°F.

2. Cook the asparagus in a pot of simmering water until tender, about 5 minutes. Drain and place in an ovenproof serving dish, then drizzle with the oil.

3. Whisk together the milk, cheese, egg, egg white, and salt. Pour over the asparagus. Bake until the gratinata is browned and bubbling, about 20 minutes.

Per serving: 131 Calories, 6 g Total Fat, 3 g Saturated Fat, 62 mg Cholesterol, 216 mg Sodium, 9 g Total Carbohydrate, 1 g Dietary Fiber, 12 g Protein, 196 mg Calcium.

POINTS per serving: 3.

Potatoes and Green Beans with Pesto

Pesto is used all over Italy, but it's most associated with Genoa, on the Ligurian coast. There, this dish is served over pasta ribbons called *trenette*.

Makes 4 servings

2 cups packed basil leaves

4 teaspoons olive oil

2 garlic cloves, chopped

1/4 teaspoon salt

Freshly ground pepper, to taste

4 medium all-purpose potatoes, peeled and chunked

1 pound green beans, cut into 1-inch lengths (about 3 cups)

1. Combine the basil, oil, garlic, salt, and pepper in a food processor; pulse several times until smooth.

2. Bring the potatoes and cold water to cover to a boil. Reduce the heat and simmer, covered, until tender, about 20 minutes. Drain and transfer to a large serving bowl.

3. Meanwhile, put the green beans in a steamer basket; set in a saucepan over 1 inch of boiling water. Cover tightly and steam until barely tender, about 5 minutes. Transfer to the bowl with the potatoes. Add the pesto and toss to coat. Serve warm or at room temperature.

Per serving: 222 Calories, 5 g Total Fat, 1 g Saturated Fat, 0 mg Cholesterol, 155 mg Sodium, 42 g Total Carbohydrate, 4 g Dietary Fiber, 7 g Protein, 339 mg Calcium.

POINTS *per serving: 4.*

Ciambotta

There are countless variations on this southern Italian vegetable stew (in Apulia, they add seafood), and there are almost as many names for it (you may see it called *cianfotta* or *giambotta*). Pronounced *chahm-BOH-tah*, this Calabrian specialty uses four different colors of bell peppers. If your market doesn't have all of them, use whatever is available. The stew can be partially prepared a few hours ahead of time.

Makes 4 servings

1/2 cup low-sodium vegetable broth

1 tablespoon olive oil

1/4 teaspoon salt

Freshly ground pepper, to taste

1 (1-pound) eggplant, cut crosswise into 1/4-inch slices

4 medium all-purpose potatoes, scrubbed and cut into 1/8-inch slices

1 green bell pepper, seeded and cut into 1/4-inch rings

1 yellow bell pepper, seeded and cut into 1/4-inch rings

1 red bell pepper, seeded and cut into 1/4-inch rings

1 orange bell pepper, seeded and cut into 1/4-inch rings

1 small zucchini, cut crosswise into 1/4-inch slices

3 tomatoes, chopped

3 garlic cloves, minced

1. Spray the broiler rack with nonstick spray; preheat the broiler.

2. Whisk the broth, oil, salt, and pepper. Brush lightly onto the eggplant, potatoes, bell peppers, and zucchini on both sides. Transfer to the broiler rack. Broil 5 inches from the heat until tender and slightly charred, about 5 minutes; turn and broil 4 minutes longer. Remove from the heat.

3. Reduce the oven temperature to 375°F. Spray a casserole with nonstick spray. Layer the vegetables in this order: eggplant, potatoes, peppers, then zucchini, sprinkling the tomatoes and garlic between each layer of roasted vegetables. (The dish can be prepared up to 2 hours ahead to this point; cover and keep at room temperature. Uncover before baking.)

4. Bake until bubbling, 30–40 minutes. Serve hot, warm, or at room temperature.

Per serving: 270 Calories, 8 g Total Fat, 1 g Saturated Fat, 0 mg Cholesterol, 172 mg Sodium, 48 g Total Carbohydrate, 7 g Dietary Fiber, 7 g Protein, 81 mg Calcium.

POINTS per serving: 5.

Stewed Artichokes

If you like artichokes, you'll love them stewed in white wine, garlic, lemon, and oil until they're meltingly tender. Rich in flavor, they're great paired with almost any pasta, or try them with your favorite meat, fish, or poultry. You can also try using baby artichokes, as we did for the photograph. Substitute $1^1/2$ pounds for the four full-size artichokes. One benefit: There's no choke to remove.

Makes 4 servings

1/4 cup fresh lemon juice

4 artichokes

4 teaspoons extra-virgin olive oil

6 shallots, chopped

1 cup dry white wine

2 tablespoons minced flat-leaf parsley

2 garlic cloves, minced

1/4 teaspoon salt

Freshly ground pepper, to taste

1. Fill a large bowl a little more than halfway with cold water; stir in the lemon juice.

2. Slice off the stem and upper third of the artichokes so they have flat bottoms and tops. Trim the tough outer leaves and remove the chokes with a teaspoon. Cut in half lengthwise; drop into the water to prevent discoloration.

3. Heat the oil in a nonstick saucepan, then add the shallots. Sauté until wilted. Drain the artichokes, then add to the shallots and stir in the wine, parsley, garlic, salt, and pepper. Reduce the heat and simmer, covered, until the artichokes are tender, about 40 minutes. Add water, 1 tablespoon at a time, if the liquid evaporates too quickly. Serve warm or at room temperature.

Per serving: 166 Calories, 5 g Total Fat, 1 g Saturated Fat, 0 mg Cholesterol, 270 mg Sodium, 20 g Total Carbohydrate, 7 g Dietary Fiber, 5 g Protein, 80 mg Calcium.

POINTS per serving: 2.

D i G i o r n o   When water is mixed with a mildly acidic ingredient (here, we use lemon juice), the culinary term for it is *acidulated water;* the acid keeps cut or peeled fruits and vegetables from discoloring. Be sure that your bowl is big enough so that the artichokes are completely submerged.

Braised Fennel

To prep a fennel bulb, first trim off the green stalks. Cut a thin slice off the root end, then thinly slice lengthwise. The thinner the slices, the sweeter the fennel will become when cooked; if you happen to own a mandoline, bring it out for this recipe.

Makes 6 servings

1 tablespoon olive oil

2 anchovy fillets, rinsed and chopped

1 large fennel bulb, trimmed and thinly sliced

Freshly ground pepper, to taste

Heat a nonstick skillet. Swirl in the oil, then add the anchovies. Cook, stirring constantly, until fragrant, about 30 seconds. Add the fennel and stir to coat. Reduce the heat, cover, and cook, stirring occasionally, until very tender, about 30 minutes. Serve, sprinkled with the pepper.

Per serving: 63 Calories, 4 g Total Fat, 1 g Saturated Fat, 13 mg Cholesterol, 570 mg Sodium, 3 g Total Carbohydrate, 1 g Dietary Fiber, 5 g Protein, 54 mg Calcium.

POINTS *per serving: 1.*

D i G i o r n o   Cooked over low heat, fennel releases enough liquid so there's no need to add braising liquid. Just stir every so often to be sure it isn't sticking; lower the heat if necessary.

Braised Cauliflower

If you're bored of steamed vegetables, give braising a try. This cooking method not only retains nutrients but also lets you alter the flavor by braising in different liquids and by adding ingredients to the liquid.

Makes 6 servings

2 teaspoons olive oil

1¹/₂ pounds cauliflower, cut into florets (about 6 cups)

2 garlic cloves, minced

1 small onion, sliced

¹/₂ cup water

2 plum tomatoes, seeded and chopped

2 tablespoons large capers, drained and chopped

¹/₈ teaspoon freshly ground pepper

Heat a nonstick skillet. Swirl in the oil, then add the cauliflower, garlic, and onion. Sauté until the vegetables begin to brown. Add the water and cook, covered, until the water evaporates and the cauliflower is fork-tender, about 10 minutes. Uncover and add the tomatoes, capers, and pepper. Cook, stirring constantly, until the tomatoes begin to break down, about 3 minutes.

Per serving: 55 Calories, 2 g Total Fat, 0 g Saturated Fat, 0 mg Cholesterol, 142 mg Sodium, 9 g Total Carbohydrate, 4 g Dietary Fiber, 3 g Protein, 33 mg Calcium.

POINTS *per serving: 0.*

Di Giorno   Large Italian capers are more robustly flavored than the small French nonpareils are; their assertiveness complements the natural sweetness of the cauliflower.

Drunken Escarole

Braising greens in wine is popular in several regions of Italy. This Tuscan preparation uses Chianti, a sturdy red wine, superior bottles of which will be marked *riserva*. Escarole is a mild green—not as sweet as spinach, but less bitter than many greens, including curly endive and chard. It can be eaten raw in a salad or cooked in a variety of ways.

Makes 4 servings

1 teaspoon olive oil

2 large garlic cloves, minced

1 bunch escarole, cleaned and chopped

$1/2$ cup Chianti or other dry red wine

$1/8$ teaspoon salt

$1/8$ teaspoon freshly ground pepper

Heat a nonstick skillet. Swirl in the oil, then add the garlic. Sauté until fragrant. Add the escarole and wine. Cook, covered, until wilted, about 5 minutes. Uncover and cook, stirring constantly, until most of the liquid evaporates. Stir in the salt and pepper.

Per serving: 48 Calories, 1 g Total Fat, 0 g Saturated Fat, 0 mg Cholesterol, 93 mg Sodium, 4 g Total Carbohydrate, 3 g Dietary Fiber, 1 g Protein, 50 mg Calcium.

POINTS per serving: 0.

Eggplant Torta

Torta means "cake" in Italian. When the baked eggplant slices are piled in a circle and covered with tomatoes, herbs, and grated Parmesan cheese, that's just what it looks like.

Makes 4 servings

1 (1-pound) eggplant, peeled and cut into $1/4$ -inch slices

$3/4$ cup Tomato-Herb Sauce (page 61), heated

2 tablespoons grated Parmesan cheese

$1/4$ cup minced basil

1. Preheat oven to 400°F. Spray 2 baking sheets with nonstick spray. Arrange the eggplant slices in a single layer on the baking sheets. Bake until tender, 15–20 minutes.

2. Arrange one-third of the eggplant slices in an 8-inch circle on a plate. Spread $1/4$ cup of the sauce over the eggplant; sprinkle with one-third of the cheese. Repeat the layers, finishing with the last of the cheese. Sprinkle the top of the torta with the basil. When ready to serve, cut into 4 wedges with a serrated knife.

Per serving: 85 Calories, 4 g Total Fat, 1 g Saturated Fat, 4 mg Cholesterol, 159 mg Sodium, 10 g Total Carbohydrate, 2 g Dietary Fiber, 4 g Protein, 145 mg Calcium.

POINTS per serving: 2.

Di Giorno   Here's an easy way to check eggplants for ripeness: Press them with your finger. If an impression remains, they're ready to eat. If their flesh springs back, you'll need to wait.

Eggplant Parmigiana

Although the name of this dish might lead you to conclude it is from Parma, a city in northern Italy, it is definitely southern. In fact, some culinary scholars think that *parmigiana* is a corruption of the Sicilian dialectical word *palmigiana,* which means shuttered, perhaps referring to the overlapping layers of the vegetable. Regardless, you'll want to make a double batch: Reheat the leftovers and pile on crusty Italian bread for a fantastic sandwich.

Makes 4 servings

1 (1-pound) eggplant, peeled and cut into 1/4-inch slices

1/2 teaspoon salt

1 1/2 cups Tomato-Herb Sauce (page 61)

6 tablespoons plain dried bread crumbs

3/4 cup shredded skim-milk mozzarella cheese

1. Set the eggplant in a single layer on paper towels and sprinkle with the salt, cover with more paper towels. Let stand 30 minutes, then pat dry with paper towels.

2. Preheat the oven to 350°F. Spray 2 baking sheets and an 8-inch square baking dish with nonstick spray. Arrange the eggplant slices in a single layer on the baking sheets. Bake until tender, 15–20 minutes.

3. Spread one-fourth of the tomato sauce in the baking dish. Top with some of the eggplant slices in a single layer, slightly overlapping if necessary. Sprinkle with one-third of the bread crumbs, one-fourth of the cheese, and another one-fourth of the sauce. Repeat the layers, finishing with the cheese. Cover with foil and bake until heated through and bubbling, 30–40 minutes. Remove the foil; increase the oven temperature to 400°F and bake until the top is slightly crisp, about 15 minutes longer. Serve hot or warm.

Per serving: 155 Calories, 5 g Total Fat, 1 g Saturated Fat, 2 mg Cholesterol, 360 mg Sodium, 20 g Total Carbohydrate, 3 g Dietary Fiber, 10 g Protein, 232 mg Calcium.

POINTS *per serving: 3.*

D i G i o r n o   Eggplant is a member of the nightshade family, and when it was introduced to Europe during the Middle Ages, Europeans thought eating it could cause insanity (perhaps because it's related to the poisonous belladonna, or possibly because early varieties were very bitter). Though it's almost always prepared as a vegetable, eggplant is actually a fruit, specifically a berry. If you like, make individual servings: Just assemble the layers in separate piles on a jelly-roll pan.

*Eggplant
Parmigiana*

Leek Sformato

The Piedmontese love savory egg yolk-based flans; we use buttermilk and egg substitute for richness instead. Don't worry if the pie puffs up in the oven; it will fall naturally as it cools.

Makes 6 servings

2 teaspoons olive oil

4 leeks, cleaned and sliced crosswise

1 head radicchio, cleaned and sliced

1/2 cup low-fat buttermilk

3/4 cup fat-free egg substitute

1/4 teaspoon salt

1/8 teaspoon ground white pepper

1 tablespoon all-purpose flour

1. Heat the oil in a nonstick skillet. Add the leeks and radicchio, reduce the heat and cook, covered, stirring occasionally, until very wilted, 18–20 minutes.

2. Meanwhile, adjust the racks to divide the oven into thirds and preheat to 375°F. Spray a 9-inch glass pie plate with nonstick spray. Transfer the vegetables to the pie plate.

3. Whisk together the buttermilk and egg substitute. Add the salt and pepper, then whisk in the flour. Pour over the vegetables. Set the pie plate on the upper rack of the oven and bake until lightly browned and a knife tip inserted in the center comes out clean, about 30 minutes. Let stand 10 minutes before serving.

Per serving: 91 Calories, 2 g Total Fat, 0 g Saturated Fat, 1 mg Cholesterol, 193 mg Sodium, 13 g Total Carbohydrate, 2 g Dietary Fiber, 6 g Protein, 90 mg Calcium.

POINTS per serving: 2.

eleven

bread and pizza

Italian Loaf

This is a classic Italian bread, comprised basically of flour, water, yeast, and a bit of salt. For a crisper loaf, preheat a baking stone in the oven and place the bread onto the stone.

Makes 48 servings

1 1/4 cups warm (110–115°F) water

1/2 teaspoon sugar

1 teaspoon quick-rise yeast

4 cups unbleached all-purpose flour

1 teaspoon salt

1/4 cup room-temperature water

1 1/2 tablespoons semolina flour

1. To make the sponge, combine the warm water and sugar in a large bowl. Whisk in the yeast and let stand until foamy, about 10 minutes. Stir in 2 cups of the all-purpose flour, 1 cup at a time. Cover tightly with plastic wrap and set in a warm spot until the sponge is bubbling and has tripled in size and then receded in the center, 8–9 hours.

2. Scrape the sponge into a food processor. Add the remaining 2 cups of all-purpose flour and the salt and pulse about 15 times to mix. With the machine running, slowly add the room-temperature water through the feed tube. After the dough forms a ball, continue to run about 30 seconds to knead.

3. Spray a large bowl with nonstick spray; put the dough in the bowl. Cover again with plastic wrap and let the dough rise in a warm spot until it doubles in size, about 1 1/2 hours.

4. Line a baking sheet with baker's parchment or wax paper and sprinkle with the semolina. Cut the dough in half and form each half into a 12-inch loaf, about 2 inches high. Set on the baking sheet, cover loosely, and return to the warm spot until doubled again, about 1 hour. Preheat the oven to 425°F.

5. Spray the loaves lightly with water. Bake 5 minutes, spray again, and bake until the loaves are golden and sound hollow when tapped, about 25 minutes longer. Transfer to a rack to cool, then cut each loaf into 24 slices.

Per serving: 40 Calories, 0 g Total Fat, 0 g Saturated Fat, 0 mg Cholesterol, 49 mg Sodium, 8 g Total Carbohydrate, 0 g Dietary Fiber, 1 g Protein, 2 mg Calcium.

POINTS *per serving: 1.*

Di Giorno   If you don't have a water mister, you can provide the needed moisture by placing an aluminum pie plate containing two ice cubes on the oven floor when you put the bread into the oven, then adding two more cubes five minutes later.

Semolina Bread

Semolina is the flour made from very hard wheat that's used in high-quality and imported pasta. It is available at natural food stores and Italian markets, and some large supermarkets.

Makes 14 servings

1 cup + 1 tablespoon warm (105–115°F) water

$^1/_2$ teaspoon sugar

1 ($^1/_4$-ounce) packet active dry yeast

2 cups bread flour

1 cup semolina flour

1 teaspoon salt

2 teaspoons olive oil

1 tablespoon cornmeal

1 tablespoon sesame seeds

1. Combine the water and sugar in a small bowl. Sprinkle in the yeast. Let stand until foamy, about 5 minutes. Combine both flours and the salt in food processor. With the machine running, scrape the yeast mixture and the oil through the feed tube. After the dough forms a ball, continue to run about 40 seconds to knead.

2. Spray a large bowl with nonstick spray; put the dough in the bowl. Cover tightly with plastic wrap and let rise in a warm spot until it doubles in size, about 1$^1/_2$ hours.

3. Sprinkle a baking sheet with the cornmeal. On a lightly floured counter, knead the dough briefly, then roll into a 2-inch thick rope. Coil the rope into an inverted S shape and place on the baking sheet. Cover loosely and return to the warm spot until doubled again, 1–1$^1/_2$ hours. Adjust the racks to divide the oven in half and preheat to 425°F.

4. Spray the loaf with water and sprinkle with the sesame seeds. Place on the middle rack. Spray the oven walls with water and close the oven door. After 30 seconds, spray the walls of the oven again. Bake until the crust is golden and an instant-read thermometer reaches 200–210°F, about 30 minutes. Remove the bread from the baking sheet and cool slightly on a wire rack.

Per serving: 130 Calories, 2 g Total Fat, 0 g Saturated Fat, 0 mg Cholesterol, 158 mg Sodium, 24 g Total Carbohydrate, 1 g Dietary Fiber, 4 g Protein, 13 mg Calcium.

POINTS *per serving: 3.*

D i G i o r n o   Although it may seem like a strange thing to do, be sure to spray the bread and the inside of the heated oven with water—the steam that's created is the secret to a crisp crust.

Olive Bread

Commonly available kalamata olives, packed in vinegar, are very similar to Sicilian vinegar-cured olives.

Makes 24 servings

¹/₄ cup warm (110–115°F) water

¹/₂ teaspoon sugar

1 (¹/₄-ounce) packet quick-rise yeast

3 cups unbleached all-purpose flour

1 teaspoon salt

12 large kalamata olives, pitted

2 teaspoons olive oil

³/₄ cup + 2 tablespoons room-temperature water

1 tablespoon semolina flour

1 egg white, beaten

1. Combine the warm water and sugar in a small bowl. Whisk in the yeast and let stand until foamy, about 3 minutes. Put the all-purpose flour and salt into a food processor and mix for 10 seconds. Add the olives and olive oil and process to chop the olives, about 1 minute. Scrape in the yeast mixture. With the machine running, pour the room-temperature water through the feed tube. After the dough forms a ball, continue to run about 45 seconds to knead.

2. Transfer the dough to a bowl, cover tightly with plastic wrap and set in a warm spot until the dough has almost doubled in size and no longer springs back to the touch, 1¹/₂–2 hours.

3. Line a baking sheet with baker's parchment or wax paper and sprinkle with the semolina. Set the dough on the baking sheet and form into 12 × 5-inch oval, about 1 inch high. Cover loosely and return to the warm spot to rise 45 minutes. Preheat the oven to 450°F.

4. Brush the bread with the egg white. Bake 10 minutes, reduce the oven temperature to 400°F, and bake until the loaf sounds hollow when tapped, about 30 minutes longer. Transfer to a rack to cool, then cut into 24 slices.

Per serving: 80 Calories, 2 g Total Fat, 0 g Saturated Fat, 0 mg Cholesterol, 196 mg Sodium, 13 g Total Carbohydrate, 1 g Dietary Fiber, 2 g Protein, 5 mg Calcium.

POINTS *per serving: 2.*

Breadsticks

Rosemary bread is so prevalent in Tuscany that the word *ramerino* refers to both the herb and the loaf. For variety, replace the rosemary with Parmesan cheese, or omit any mix-ins from the dough and sprinkle the breadsticks with sesame, poppy, or fennel seeds.

Makes 24 servings

3/4 cup warm (105–115°F) water

1 (1/4-ounce) packet active dry yeast

1/2 teaspoon sugar

2 3/4 cups bread flour

1/2 teaspoon minced fresh rosemary leaves, or 1 tablespoon dried rosemary leaves, crumbled

1 teaspoon salt

2 tablespoons olive oil

1. Put the warm water in a large bowl and sprinkle in the yeast and sugar. Let stand until foamy, about 5 minutes. Combine the flour, rosemary, and salt in a food processor. With the machine running, scrape the yeast mixture and the oil through the feed tube just until the dough forms a ball. Knead the dough by pulsing until it is no longer sticky and is smooth and elastic.

2. Sprinkle about 2 tablespoons of flour onto a large cutting board. Put the dough on the board and roll into a 10 × 6-inch rectangle. Cover loosely and let rise in a warm spot until it doubles in size, about 1 hour. Preheat the oven to 450°F. Spray 2 baking sheets with nonstick spray.

3. Cut the dough crosswise into 24 strips. Keeping the dough you aren't working with covered loosely, roll each strip into a 1/2-inch rope. Set the ropes about 1 inch apart on the baking sheets (the ropes will shrink to approximately 8-inch lengths). Bake until golden, about 18 minutes. Cool completely on a wire rack. Store in an airtight container.

Per serving: 71 Calories, 2 g Total Fat, 0 g Saturated Fat, 0 mg Cholesterol, 92 mg Sodium, 12 g Total Carbohydrate, 0 g Dietary Fiber, 2 g Protein, 5 mg Calcium.

POINTS *per serving: 2.*

Grissini

These crisp breadsticks, a specialty of Turin, can sometimes measure up to three feet in length. To make very long, thin grissini, cut the dough into only six pieces and work each through the fettuccine cutters of a pasta machine instead of fashioning by hand.

Makes 24 servings

1³/4 cups unbleached all-purpose flour

1 teaspoon quick-rise yeast

1 teaspoon salt

2 teaspoons grated Parmesan cheese

³/4 cup very hot tap water

3 tablespoons semolina flour

1. Combine the all-purpose flour, yeast, salt, and cheese in a food processor and process 1–2 minutes to mix. With the machine running, add the water through the feed tube. After the dough forms a ball, continue to run about 45 seconds to knead.

2. Spray a bowl with nonstick spray; put the dough in the bowl. Cover tightly with plastic wrap and let the dough rise in a warm spot until it doubles in size, about 1 hour. Preheat the oven to 400°F.

3. On a lightly floured counter, form the dough into a 12 × 5-inch rectangle and cut the rectangle into forty-eight 5-inch strips, then roll each to stretch it to 10–12 inches. Sprinkle the semolina on a baking sheet and place the strips on the sheet. Bake until golden, about 15 minutes. Transfer to a rack to cool.

Per serving: 39 Calories, 0 g Total Fat, 0 g Saturated Fat, 0 mg Cholesterol, 100 mg Sodium, 8 g Total Carbohydrate, 0 g Dietary Fiber, 1 g Protein, 4 mg Calcium.

POINTS per serving: 1.

D i   G i o r n o   For a dramatic presentation that's especially nice at a cocktail party or on a buffet, stand these in a small vase or glass.

Easter Bread

Also called *colomba pasquale* or "dove bread," this Easter version of panettone has much in common with that Christmas bread: Both breads hail from Lombardy, and they're made from similar dough. If you like, knead in $1/4$ cup blanched chopped almonds with the candied citron and raisins.

Makes 40 servings

- $3/4$ **cup bread flour**
- $1/2$ **cup + 1 tablespoon sugar**
- **1 ($1/4$-ounce) packet quick-rise yeast**
- $1/2$ **cup very hot tap water**
- **2 eggs, beaten**
- **2 tablespoons unsalted butter, melted**
- $1/4$ **cup fat-free milk**
- **1 tablespoon vanilla extract**
- **3 cups unbleached all-purpose flour**
- $1/2$ **teaspoon salt**
- **1 teaspoon grated orange zest**
- **1 teaspoon grated lemon zest**
- $1/2$ **cup finely chopped candied citron**
- $1/2$ **cup seedless raisins**
- **1 egg white, beaten with 2 tablespoons water**

1. Whisk together the bread flour, 1 tablespoon of the sugar, and the yeast in a large bowl. Add the water and stir to create a thick, pasty dough. Cover tightly with plastic wrap and set aside in a warm spot until it doubles in size, 30–45 minutes.

2. Whisk together the eggs, butter, milk, and vanilla in another bowl. Combine the all-purpose flour, salt, orange zest, and lemon zest in a food processor and pulse to mix. Scrape in the yeast mixture. With the machine running, add the egg mixture through the feed tube. After the dough forms a ball, continue to run about 30 seconds to knead. Turn out the dough on a lightly floured counter and knead in the candied citron and raisins.

3. Spray a large bowl and a sheet of plastic wrap with nonstick spray; put the dough in the bowl. Cover tightly with the plastic wrap and let the dough rise in a warm spot until it doubles in size and no longer springs back to the touch, 1–1$1/4$ hours.

4. Line a baking sheet with baker's parchment or wax paper. Divide the dough in half and form each half into a 12 × 4-inch oval. Place one half on the sheet on the diagonal. Lay the second across it like an "X" and make indentations in the bottom layer of dough where the two pieces meet. Cover loosely and return to the warm spot until doubled again, 1–2 hours. Preheat the oven to 375°F.

5. Brush the bread with the egg wash. Bake until the loaf becomes golden and firm to the touch and a tester inserted into the center comes out clean, about 25 minutes. Transfer to a rack to cool. Cut into 40 slices.

Per serving: 81 Calories, 1 g Total Fat, 0 g Saturated Fat, 12 mg Cholesterol, 43 mg Sodium, 16 g Total Carbohydrate, 0 g Dietary Fiber, 2 g Protein, 9 mg Calcium.

***POINTS** per serving: 2.*

Pasqua e Natale: Easter and Christmas in Italy

Italy's celebrations surrounding Easter and Christmas have their roots in the agricultural calendar—a holdover from pagan times. Like the planting seasons, scarcity alternates with abundance: Christmas, like the pagan Saturnalia it replaced, brings a welcome feast during the darkest days of winter when the earth lies fallow. Likewise, before beginning the 40-day Lenten cycle of meatless eating, Christians celebrate *Carnevale* (literally "goodbye, meat!") with grand feasts and parties—and the long, meatless stretch that follows culminates in another glorious feast day, Easter.

The foods eaten during these celebrations vary from region to region and are influenced by geography; Lombardy and Piedmont, where rice is grown, feature more rice-based dishes; polenta is prominent in Emilia-Romagna, where corn is easiest to grow. Chestnuts are used like flour in the mountain regions, where wheat-growing land is scarce. But with religion as a great unifier, many holiday dishes share the same themes.

Christmas

Christmas begins with *La Vigilia*, the Christmas eve "vigil" of waiting for Christ's birth—a meatless day with nothing abstemious about it. In the seafood-rich south, a dinner comprising a specific number of fish is served—sometimes seven varieties, to honor the seven virtues, or nine (the Holy Trinity times three). Eel, an ancient symbol of immortality, is always included. In the north, preserved fish like anchovies or salt cod are more available, and find their way into dishes such as Piedmont's *lasagne di natale*, layers of pasta with anchovies and butter.

On Christmas Day, meat returns to the table. The meal starts with a soup of meat-filled *cappelletti* ("little hats") pasta in broth, prepared on Christmas Eve—it's good luck to eat at least twelve cappelletti. Then a roast capon or turkey, stuffed according to region—chestnuts and fruit in Milan, for example, or pancetta and bread crumbs in Rome. Sweet Christmas "breads" studded with fruits, nuts, and other symbols of fertility are another tradition, to ensure a sweet (and fertile) new year: In Tuscany, it's *panpepato* ("peppery bread") redolent of cloves, ginger, and cinnamon. In Rome, it's *pangiallo,* a sturdy fruitcake glazed with sugar syrup. Milan has its famous panettone, a towering cake with citron and candied fruit baked inside.

Other Christmas treats are more subject to regional variations. Neapolitans enjoy *struffoli,* small nubbins of fried dough drizzled with honey; their Perugian counterparts nibble *pinoccate,* a pine nut confection. In Parma, hot chestnuts are plucked from the roasting pan, shelled and dropped into sweet red wine. Calabrians make *chinuille,* sweet ravioli filled with chestnuts, cocoa, candied fruit, and ricotta, then deep-fried and smothered with honey.

Easter

Easter takes place after the spring equinox, when the land is becoming fertile again, and it is full of symbols of rebirth and fertility, like fruits, beans, rice, nuts, wheat grains, and particularly eggs. Hard-cooked eggs may be eaten to break the Lenten fast, and lavishly decorated chocolate eggs are traditional gifts. Tuscans enjoy eggy *schiacciata* bread, while southern Italians insert hard-cooked eggs into bread dough and bake it into symbolic shapes, such as doves or wreaths. In Naples, everyone eats *pastiera*—a tart made of soft new wheat berries, eggs, and ricotta, while in rice-growing Modena, *torta di riso,* an almond-studded rice pudding, is served.

Lamb is the traditional Easter centerpiece throughout Italy. Herbs and spring vegetables flavor other offerings, from the herbed rice *torta* (cake) served in Piedmont or the egg-and-Swiss chard–filled *torta pasqualina* of Liguria.

Panettone

This centuries-old Milanese Christmas bread marked the holiday season because most peasants could not afford the extravagant ingredients more than once a year. Traditionally made with candied orange and lemon peel, and candied citron, our recipe uses a candied fruit and peel mixture, such as you would use for fruitcake, is substituted.

Makes 10 servings

$^1/_2$ cup bread flour

$^1/_3$ cup fat-free milk

1 ($^1/_4$-ounce) packet active dry yeast

2 cups + 2 tablespoons unbleached all-purpose flour

$^1/_4$ cup sugar

$^1/_2$ teaspoon salt

2 teaspoons lemon zest

$^1/_2$ cup finely chopped candied fruit and peel

$^3/_4$ cup golden raisins

2 eggs, beaten

4 tablespoons unsalted butter, melted and cooled

1 teaspoon vanilla extract

$^1/_4$ teaspoon anise extract

$^1/_4$ cup water

1. Put the bread flour in a large bowl. Warm the milk to 110–115°F. Remove from the heat and whisk in the yeast, then pour over the flour. Stir to create a paste. Cover with plastic wrap and set aside in a warm spot until the sponge has doubled in size, $1^1/_4$–$1^1/_2$ hours.

2. Combine 2 cups of the all-purpose flour, the sugar, salt, and lemon zest in a food processor fitted with the plastic blade. Pulse to mix. Add the sponge, candied fruit and peel, and raisins. With the machine running, add the eggs, butter, vanilla, anise extract, and water through the feed tube. Turn the dough out onto a work surface and knead in the remaining 2 tablespoons of all-purpose flour.

3. Spray a large bowl with nonstick spray; put the dough in the bowl. Cover tightly with plastic wrap and return to the warm spot until doubled in size, $1^1/_2$–2 hours. Place the dough in a lightly greased panettone mold or 6-inch soufflé dish. Spray a sheet of plastic wrap lightly with nonstick spray and set over the mold; let rise $1^1/_2$–2 hours longer. Preheat the oven to 375°F.

4. Cut an "X" into the top of the dough. Bake until the panettone is well browned and a tester comes out clean, about 40 minutes. Cool in the mold on a rack about 15 minutes, then unmold and cool completely on the rack.

Per serving: 276 Calories, 6 g Total Fat, 3 g Saturated Fat, 55 mg Cholesterol, 153 mg Sodium, 50 g Total Carbohydrate, 2 g Dietary Fiber, 6 g Protein, 33 mg Calcium.

POINTS *per serving: 6.*

D i   G i o r n o   In addition to a panettone mold or a soufflé dish, you can make the panettone in a rinsed and dried 23-ounce coffee can. Be sure to use a plastic blade to make the dough; a food processor's metal blade will shred the raisins and candied fruit.

Panettone

Basic Pizza Dough

This dough freezes beautifully. If you need only one crust, wrap half of the dough in plastic and refrigerate for up to three days, or freeze for up to one month. Thaw it in the refrigerator overnight.

Makes 2 (12-inch) pizza crusts (8 servings per crust)

4 cups unbleached all-purpose flour

1 (1/4-ounce) packet active dry yeast

1/2 teaspoon salt

1 1/4 cups hot (120–130°F) water

1. Combine 2 cups of the flour, the yeast, and salt in a large bowl. With an electric mixer, slowly beat in the water. Beat 2 minutes, scraping the sides of the bowl occasionally with a rubber spatula. With the mixer on medium speed, add in 1/2 cup of the remaining flour, beating until the dough is stiff, about 2 minutes. With a wooden spoon, stir in the remaining flour, working in as much as possible with your hands when the dough becomes too stiff to stir.

2. Spray a large bowl with nonstick spray; put the dough in the bowl. Cover tightly with plastic wrap and let the dough rise in a warm spot until it doubles in size, about 1 hour.

3. Divide the dough in half (refrigerate or freeze one half at this point, if you like). Use as directed in the recipe.

Per serving: 130 Calories, 0 g Total Fat, 0 g Saturated Fat, 0 mg Cholesterol, 69 mg Sodium, 27 g Total Carbohydrate, 1 g Dietary Fiber, 4 g Protein, 6 mg Calcium.

POINTS per serving: 2.

Di Giorno   If you like whole-wheat bread, try whole-wheat pizza crust: Replace 1 1/2 cups of the all-purpose flour with whole-wheat flour.

Potato and Smoked Mozzarella Pizza

In Apulia, they form mashed potatoes into a crust and top it with smoked mozzarella and herbs. This variation uses a traditional crust, with sliced potatoes as a topping. It's a slightly unusual but altogether delicious pizza.

Makes 4 servings

1/2 cup hot (120–130°F) water

1/2 teaspoon sugar

1 (1/4-ounce) packet quick-rise yeast

1 1/4 cups unbleached all-purpose flour

1/2 teaspoon salt

1 medium all-purpose potato, peeled, thinly sliced, and dropped into cold water

2 teaspoons extra-virgin olive oil

1/4 teaspoon kosher salt

3 ounces smoked mozzarella cheese, shredded (about 3/4 cup)

Freshly ground pepper, to taste

1. To make the dough, combine the water and sugar in a small bowl. Whisk in the yeast and let stand until foamy, about 5 minutes. Combine the flour and salt in a food processor. With the machine running, scrape the yeast mixture through the feed tube. After the dough forms a ball, continue to run about 30 seconds to knead.

2. Spray a large bowl with nonstick spray; put the dough in the bowl. Cover tightly with plastic wrap and let rise in a warm spot until it doubles in size, about 30 minutes.

3. Meanwhile, drain the potato; pat dry with paper towels. Combine the potato, oil, and kosher salt. Preheat the oven to 425°F.

4. Work the dough into a 12-inch circle on a nonstick baking sheet or pizza pan. Sprinkle with half the cheese and top with the potatoes, arranging them in a single layer. Sprinkle with the remaining cheese and pepper. Bake until the crust is crisp and lightly browned, about 18 minutes.

Per serving: 283 Calories, 9 g Total Fat, 4 g Saturated Fat, 30 mg Cholesterol, 615 mg Sodium, 39 g Total Carbohydrate, 2 g Dietary Fiber, 11 g Protein, 125 mg Calcium.

POINTS *per serving: 6.*

Quick Olive Pizza

Pizza's success often depends on the heat of the oven. Because your oven may take a while to reach 500°F, start preheating it while the dough rises.

Makes 8 servings

¹/₂ cup + 2 tablespoons hot (120–130°F) water

¹/₂ teaspoon sugar

1 (¹/₄-ounce) packet quick-rise yeast

1¹/₂ cups unbleached all-purpose flour

¹/₂ teaspoon salt

1 cup prepared pizza-style tomato sauce

12 large kalamata olives, pitted and chopped

1. To make the dough, combine the water and sugar in a small bowl. Whisk in the yeast and let stand until foamy, about 5 minutes. Combine the flour and salt in a food processor. With the machine running, scrape the yeast mixture through the feed tube. After the dough forms a ball, continue to run 30 seconds to knead.

2. Spray a large bowl with nonstick spray; put the dough in the bowl. Cover tightly with plastic wrap and let rise in a warm spot until it doubles in size, about 30 minutes. Preheat the oven to 500°F.

3. Work the dough into a 12-inch circle on a nonstick baking sheet or pizza pan. Spoon the tomato sauce over the dough; top with the olives. Bake until the crust is crisp and lightly browned, about 10 minutes.

Per serving: 134 Calories, 3 g Total Fat, 0 g Saturated Fat, 0 mg Cholesterol, 392 mg Sodium, 23 g Total Carbohydrate, 1 g Dietary Fiber, 4 g Protein, 5 mg Calcium.

***POINTS** per serving: 3.*

Pizza alla Marinara

On nights when you're craving pizza but still want to avoid excess fat and calories, whip up this authentic pizza.

Makes 8 servings

¹/₂ cup + 1 tablespoon warm (105–115°F) water

¹/₂ teaspoon sugar

1 (¹/₄-ounce) packet active dry yeast

1¹/₂ cups unbleached all-purpose flour

1 onion, finely chopped

4 teaspoons olive oil

1 (14¹/₂-ounce) can Italian plum tomatoes (no salt added), chopped

1 teaspoon dried oregano

¹/₄ teaspoon salt

2 tablespoons grated pecorino Romano cheese

¹/₂ cup shredded skim-milk mozzarella cheese

1. To make the dough, combine the water and sugar in a small bowl. Whisk in the yeast and let stand until foamy, about 5 minutes. Put the flour in a food processor. With the machine running, scrape the yeast mixture through the feed tube. After the dough forms a ball, continue to run 30 seconds to knead.

2. Spray a large bowl with nonstick spray; put the dough in the bowl. Cover tightly with plastic wrap and let rise in a warm spot until it doubles in size, about 1 hour.

3. Meanwhile, make the sauce. Combine the onion and oil in a saucepan over low heat. Cover and cook 5 minutes. Add the tomatoes, oregano, and salt. Keep uncovered and cook, stirring occasionally, 15 minutes longer. Set aside to cool.

4. Work the dough into a 12-inch circle on a nonstick baking sheet or pizza pan. Cover loosely and return to the warm spot 30 minutes. Preheat the oven to 500°F.

5. Spoon the sauce over dough, then sprinkle with the cheeses. Bake until the crust is lightly browned and the cheeses melt, 10–12 minutes.

Per serving: 146 Calories, 4 g Total Fat, 0 g Saturated Fat, 4 mg Cholesterol, 166 mg Sodium, 22 g Total Carbohydrate, 1 g Dietary Fiber, 7 g Protein, 106 mg Calcium.

POINTS *per serving: 3.*

Artichoke and Red Pepper Whole-Wheat Pizza

A blue cheese like Gorgonzola doesn't melt. It will soften slightly, but not as much as mozzarella does.

Makes 6 servings

$1/2$ cup + 1 tablespoon warm (105–115°F) water

$1/2$ teaspoon sugar

1 ($1/4$-ounce) packet active dry yeast

1 cup bread flour

$1/2$ cup whole-wheat flour

$1/4$ teaspoon salt

2 cups drained canned or thawed frozen artichoke hearts, chopped

1 red bell pepper, seeded and julienned

1 tablespoon olive oil

2 ounces Gorgonzola cheese, crumbled (about $1/2$ cup)

Freshly ground pepper, to taste

1. To make the dough, combine the water and sugar in a small bowl. Whisk in the yeast and let stand until foamy, about 5 minutes. Combine both flours and half of the salt in a food processor. With the machine running, scrape the yeast mixture through the feed tube. After the dough forms a ball, continue to run about 30 seconds to knead.

2. Spray a large bowl with nonstick spray; put the dough in the bowl. Cover tightly with plastic wrap and let rise in a warm spot until it doubles in size, about 1 hour.

3. Work the dough into a 12-inch circle on a nonstick baking sheet or pizza pan. Cover loosely and return to the warm spot 30 minutes. Preheat the oven to 500°F.

4. Combine the artichokes, bell pepper, oil, and the remaining salt. Spoon over the dough; sprinkle with the cheese and pepper. Bake until the crust is lightly browned, about 10 minutes.

Per serving: 197 Calories, 6 g Total Fat, 2 g Saturated Fat, 9 mg Cholesterol, 237 mg Sodium, 30 g Total Carbohydrate, 4 g Dietary Fiber, 8 g Protein, 73 mg Calcium.

POINTS per serving: 4.

D i G i o r n o   If you have a choice, bake your pizza on a dark heavy pan. Darker metals absorb heat evenly and rapidly, so your crust will be crisp and brown.

Pizza Problems, Solved

Problem: The dough tears as you stretch it out.

Solution: You're overworking the dough. Cover it with a damp towel and let it rest 15–20 minutes at room temperature. This helps to relax the gluten—the protein in flour that gives dough its elasticity.

Problem: Your pizza crust isn't crisp on the bottom like restaurant pizza.

Solution: Authentic pizzas are made in wood-burning ovens lined with fire bricks, reaching temperatures as high as 700°F—not usually possible in home kitchens. You can use a pizza pan with holes in the bottom, but by lining the bottom of your oven with heat-retaining pizza bricks or stones, you can come closer to the fabulously crisp-bottomed crust Neapolitans savor. Cook the pizza directly on the preheated bricks for best results.

Problem: Your pizza sticks to the pizza peel.

Solution: A pizza or baker's peel—a long-handled, flat, wooden paddle—allows you to slide a pie directly into the oven, but it can be tricky to use. First, sprinkle the peel liberally with cornmeal before placing the dough on it, to prevent sticking. Second, don't let the pizza sit on the peel for long. Work quickly as you top the pie on the peel, then slide it immediately into the oven.

Problem: Your deep-dish pizza crust is heavy and doughy.

Solution: Try a softer dough. Some deep-dish pizza recipes call for eggs, cornmeal, and other nontraditional ingredients, which produce a tender, biscuitlike crust. Refrigerated French bread dough (not pizza dough) would be a good substitute.

Problem: Your pizza has a soggy crust and runny sauce, and the toppings aren't cooked through.

Solution: Certain toppings release water or fat when they are cooked. Vegetables like onions, spinach, broccoli, artichoke hearts, and mushrooms should be sautéed or steamed. (Frozen vegetables don't need to be cooked, but they should be thawed and thoroughly drained or squeezed dry.) Ground beef or poultry and bulk sausage should be browned and drained—not only will you reduce their water content, you'll also cut fat.

Roasted Vegetable Pizzas

A pizza pan with air holes in the bottom will help the crust to crisp. You can also place the pizza directly onto a preheated baking stone for the crispiest results.

Makes 16 servings

1 (1-pound) eggplant, cut into chunks

3 medium zucchini, cut into chunks

1 onion, sliced

2 teaspoons olive oil

4 plum tomatoes, cut into 1/4-inch slices

1 recipe (about 2 pounds) Basic Pizza Dough (page 270)

1 (15-ounce) container nonfat ricotta cheese

1/4 cup chopped basil

1. Preheat the oven to 350°F. In a large bowl, combine the eggplant, zucchini, and onion. Add the oil and toss to coat. Transfer the mixture to a baking sheet and bake 15 minutes. Toss the mixture, add the tomatoes and bake until the vegetables just begin to brown, about 15 minutes longer. Remove from the oven and increase the oven temperature to 450°F.

2. Work the dough into two 12-inch circles on nonstick baking sheets or pizza pans. Prick all over with the tines of a fork. Bake until the dough begins to puff, about 5 minutes.

3. Thoroughly blend the ricotta and basil. Spread evenly over each crust. Scatter the vegetables on top. Bake until golden brown, about 10 minutes.

Per serving: 175 Calories, 1 g Total Fat, 0 g Saturated Fat, 0 mg Cholesterol, 69 mg Sodium, 32 g Total Carbohydrate, 2 g Dietary Fiber, 9 g Protein, 46 mg Calcium.

POINTS *per serving: 3.*

Roasted Vegetable Pizza

Portobello Pizza

Stemmed and sliced white or cremini mushrooms, or stemmed shiitake mushrooms may be substituted for any or all of the portobellos.

Makes 8 servings

1/2 recipe (about 1 pound) Basic Pizza Dough (page 270)

3 tablespoons crumbled Gorgonzola cheese

1 cup nonfat ricotta cheese

2 tablespoons fat-free milk

6 ounces portobello mushrooms, cleaned, stemmed, and cut into 1/4-inch slices

1 tablespoon chopped rosemary

1. Preheat the oven to 450°F. Work the dough into a 12-inch circle on a nonstick baking sheet or pizza pan. Prick all over with the tines of a fork. Bake until the dough begins to puff, about 5 minutes. Spray the crust with nonstick spray.

2. Thoroughly blend the Gorgonzola, ricotta, and milk. Spread evenly over the crust. Cover with mushroom slices, scatter the rosemary on top, and lightly spray the pizza again. Bake until golden brown, 10–12 minutes.

Per serving: 174 Calories, 1 g Total Fat, 1 g Saturated Fat, 3 mg Cholesterol, 152 mg Sodium, 29 g Total Carbohydrate, 2 g Dietary Fiber, 10 g Protein, 73 mg Calcium.

POINTS *per serving: 3.*

D i G i o r n o   You can buy packages of presliced portobellos, but take a good look at them. They tend to be sliced rather thickly (usually about 1/2 inch), which means that you'll have to cut each slice in half.

Pizza Florentine

Dishes prepared *alla fiorentina*, or in the style of Florence, feature spinach and are often topped with cheese and lightly browned. Use fresh and not frozen spinach for this pizza, and leave some water clinging to the leaves after rinsing them to promote quick steaming.

Makes 8 servings

1 (10-ounce) bag triple-washed spinach, cleaned (do not dry)

1/2 recipe (about 1 pound) Basic Pizza Dough (page 270)

1/3 cup crumbled fat-free feta cheese with herbs

1/2 cup shredded part-skim mozzarella cheese

1. Preheat the oven to 450°F.

2. Heat a nonstick skillet. Add the spinach and cook, covered, until wilted, about 2 minutes. Remove from the heat and let cool, then squeeze dry and coarsely chop.

3. Work the dough into a 12-inch circle on a nonstick baking sheet or pizza pan. Prick all over with the tines of a fork. Bake until the dough begins to puff, about 5 minutes. Spread the spinach over the crust. Scatter the feta, then the mozzarella, over the spinach and lightly spray the pizza with nonstick spray. Bake until the cheese is melted and browned, 11–12 minutes.

Per serving: 167 Calories, 1 g Total Fat, 1 g Saturated Fat, 7 mg Cholesterol, 174 mg Sodium, 29 g Total Carbohydrate, 2 g Dietary Fiber, 7 g Protein, 110 mg Calcium.

***POINTS** per serving: 3.*

Di Giorno   Partially baking the pizza crust helps to keep it from getting soggy; this technique is especially necessary when your toppings have a high water content (like spinach).

Three-Cheese Pizza

What, no tomato sauce? Indeed, a tomatoless pie like this is known as *pizza bianca*, or white pizza. It's a particular favorite in Rome.

Makes 6 servings

$1/4$ cup + 2 tablespoons hot (120–130°F) water

$1/2$ teaspoon sugar

1 ($1/4$-ounce) packet active dry yeast

1 cup unbleached all-purpose flour

$1/4$ cup oat bran

$1/2$ teaspoon salt

1 tablespoon + 1 teaspoon olive oil

1 cup nonfat ricotta cheese

2 tablespoons grated Parmesan cheese

$1^1/2$ ounces fontina cheese, grated (about $1/3$ cup)

1 large garlic clove, thinly sliced

Salt and freshly ground pepper, to taste

1. To make the dough, combine the water and sugar in a small bowl. Whisk in the yeast and let stand until foamy, about 5 minutes. Combine the flour, oat bran, and salt in a food processor. With the machine running, add 1 tablespoon of the oil, then scrape the yeast mixture through the feed tube. After the dough forms a ball, continue to run about 30 seconds to knead.

2. Spray a large bowl with nonstick spray; put the dough in the bowl. Cover tightly with plastic wrap and let rise in a warm spot until it doubles in size, about 1 hour.

3. Spoon the ricotta into a coffee filter or cheesecloth-lined strainer and set over a bowl; let drain 15 minutes. Discard the liquid in the bowl. Preheat the oven to 425°F.

4. Work the dough into a 10-inch circle on a nonstick baking sheet or pizza pan. Spread the ricotta over the dough. Sprinkle with the Parmesan, fontina, garlic, and salt and pepper; drizzle with the remaining oil. Bake until the crust is lightly browned, about 18 minutes.

Per serving: 209 Calories, 11 g Total Fat, 5 g Saturated Fat, 28 mg Cholesterol, 402 mg Sodium, 20 g Total Carbohydrate, 1 g Dietary Fiber, 10 g Protein, 169 mg Calcium.

POINTS *per serving: 5.*

Di Giorno   If you don't have a pizza cutter, use kitchen shears to cut your pizza into wedges.

Shrimp Pizza

Shellfish pizza is extremely popular in Venice, where the shellfish are sometimes left in their shells. For a stronger roasted garlic flavor, use up to 12 garlic cloves.

Makes 8 servings

1/2 recipe (about 1 pound) Basic Pizza Dough (page 270)

8 garlic cloves, roasted (page 5) and peeled

2 plum tomatoes, thinly sliced

3/4 pound medium shrimp, peeled and deveined

2/3 cup shredded part-skim mozzarella cheese

2 tablespoons sliced basil

1. Preheat the oven to 450°F.

2. Work the dough into a 12-inch circle on a nonstick baking sheet or pizza pan. Prick all over with the tines of a fork. Bake until the dough begins to puff, about 5 minutes. Spread the roasted garlic over the crust. Scatter the tomatoes and shrimp on top, then sprinkle with the cheese and the basil. Bake until the shrimp are cooked through and the cheese melts, 9–10 minutes.

Per serving: 209 Calories, 2 g Total Fat, 1 g Saturated Fat, 70 mg Cholesterol, 184 mg Sodium, 29 g Total Carbohydrate, 1 g Dietary Fiber, 16 g Protein, 104 mg Calcium.

POINTS per serving: 4.

Deep-Dish Sausage Pizza

Although most North Americans might associate deep-dish pizza with the Windy City, Italians know it as *pizza alla siciliana*, or Sicilian pizza. This thick-crust pizza is baked in a square pan, topped with tomato sauce and, frequently, anchovies.

Makes 4 servings

1 teaspoon cornmeal

1/4 recipe (about 1/2 pound) Basic Pizza Dough (page 270)

1/2 cup tomato sauce (no salt added)

1/2 green bell pepper, seeded and sliced

1 small onion, thinly sliced

1 cup cooked crumbled Italian pork sausage (about 1/4 pound)

1/3 cup shredded part-skim mozzarella cheese

2 tablespoons minced basil

Freshly ground pepper, to taste

1 garlic clove, minced

1. Preheat the oven to 450°F. Sprinkle an 8-inch square baking pan with the cornmeal.

2. On a lightly floured counter, stretch the dough into a 10-inch square. Fit it into the baking pan, pressing the edges against the sides of the pan to form a rim.

3. Spread the tomato sauce over the dough. Top with the bell pepper and onion, then sprinkle with the sausage, cheese, basil, pepper, and garlic. Bake until the crust is browned and the cheese melts, about 20 minutes.

Per serving: 295 Calories, 11 g Total Fat, 4 g Saturated Fat, 28 mg Cholesterol, 630 mg Sodium, 33 g Total Carbohydrate, 2 g Dietary Fiber, 14 g Protein, 93 mg Calcium.

POINTS per serving: 6.

D i G i o r n o   We've reduced the fat from the pizzeria classic considerably, but if you want to reduce it even further, rinse the sausage under hot water after cooking it.

Deep-Dish Sausage Pizza

Focaccia Dough

A Genoese invention, focaccia is thicker and chewier than pizza and usually has somewhat fewer toppings. Using quick-rise yeast in this easy dough eliminates the need to proof the yeast and cuts the time for the first rise in half.

Makes 16 servings

1 (1/4-ounce) packet quick-rise yeast

1 teaspoon sugar

1 tablespoon olive oil

2 1/2 cups unbleached all-purpose flour

1 cup very hot tap water

1. Combine the yeast, sugar, salt, oil, and flour in a food processor. With the machine running, pour the water through the feed tube. After the dough forms a ball, continue to run about 1 minute to knead.

2. Spray a large bowl with nonstick spray; put the dough in the bowl. Cover tightly with plastic wrap and let the dough rise in a warm spot until it doubles in size, about 45 minutes.

3. Use the dough as directed in the recipe.

Per serving: 81 Calories, 1 g Total Fat, 0 g Saturated Fat, 0 mg Cholesterol, 1 mg Sodium, 15 g Total Carbohydrate, 1 g Dietary Fiber, 2 g Protein, 3 mg Calcium.

POINTS per serving: 2.

Rosemary Focaccia

Instead of layering the focaccia with whole rosemary sprigs in the original Italian style, this very thick focaccia has chopped rosemary kneaded into the dough. In Genoa, bakers would dimple the focaccia with their fingertips rather than with the end of a wooden spoon.

Makes 24 servings

- 1/4 cup warm (110–115°F) water
- 1 tablespoon honey
- 1 (1/4-ounce) packet quick-rise yeast
- 3 1/4 cups unbleached all-purpose flour
- 1 1/2 tablespoons chopped rosemary
- 1/2 tablespoon table salt
- 3/4 cup room-temperature water
- 1 egg white, beaten with 1 1/2 tablespoons water
- 1 tablespoon crystal sea salt or 1/2 tablespoon kosher salt

1. Combine the warm water and honey in a small bowl. Whisk in the yeast and let stand until foamy, about 10 minutes. Combine the flour, rosemary, and table salt in a food processor and process for 1 minute, then scrape in the yeast mixture. With the machine running, drizzle the room-temperature water through the feed tube. After the dough forms a ball, continue to run about 1 minute to knead.

2. Spray a large bowl with nonstick spray; put the dough in the bowl. Cover loosely and let the dough rise in a warm spot until it doubles in size and no longer springs back to the touch, about 45 minutes.

3. Spray a 9 1/4 × 13 1/4-inch baking sheet with nonstick spray. Work the dough into the pan, stretching it into the corners. Cover again and set aside 15 minutes. Dimple the dough with a wooden spoon handle, brush with the egg wash, and sprinkle with the sea salt. Preheat the oven to 350°F.

4. Bake until golden, about 45 minutes. Cool in the pan on a rack 5 minutes before cutting.

Per serving: 66 Calories, 0 g Total Fat, 0 g Saturated Fat, 0 mg Cholesterol, 436 mg Sodium, 14 g Total Carbohydrate, 1 g Dietary Fiber, 2 g Protein, 5 mg Calcium.

POINTS *per serving: 1.*

Gorgonzola Focaccia

Named for the town in Lombardy where it originated, Gorgonzola is a rich and pungent blue cheese. One of the best Gorgonzolas, BelGioioso, is now made in Wisconsin. Like Parmesan, Gorgonzola has such a strong flavor that a very little bit added to nonfat ricotta and fat-free milk makes a flavorful spread. Make extras of the spread to use on grilled portobello mushroom panini or as a salad dressing.

Makes 16 servings

- 1 large red onion, halved lengthwise, then thinly sliced crosswise
- 1/2 cup nonfat ricotta cheese
- 1/4 cup Gorgonzola cheese
- 2 tablespoons fat-free milk
- 1 recipe Focaccia Dough (page 284)

1. Preheat the oven to 425°F. Line a baking dish with foil and put the onions into it. Bake 3 minutes, stir, and continue to bake until softened, about 3 minutes longer. Turn off the oven.

2. Meanwhile, blend the ricotta, Gorgonzola, and milk.

3. Spray an 11 × 15-inch baking sheet with nonstick spray. Work the dough into the pan, pushing it into the corners. Dimple the dough with a wooden spoon handle and prick all over with the tines of a fork. Spread with the cheese mixture, then scatter the onions on top. Cover loosely and let rise in a warm spot about 45 minutes. Preheat the oven to 425°F.

4. Bake until the focaccia is puffed and browned, about 20 minutes. Cool in the pan on a rack 5 minutes before cutting.

Per serving: 97 Calories, 2 g Total Fat, 1 g Saturated Fat, 2 mg Cholesterol, 37 mg Sodium, 16 g Total Carbohydrate, 1 g Dietary Fiber, 4 g Protein, 24 mg Calcium.

POINTS per serving: 2.

Parmesan Focaccia

Focaccia is basically pizza dough with ingredients mixed in or, sometimes, sprinkled on top. This very basic focaccia makes an excellent *panino*.

Makes 24 servings

1 1/2 cups warm (105–115°F) water

1 (1/4-ounce) packet active dry yeast

1 teaspoon sugar

4 cups unbleached all-purpose flour

1 1/2 teaspoons dried oregano

1 teaspoon salt

2 tablespoons olive oil

1/4 cup grated Parmesan cheese

1. To make the dough, combine $1/2$ cup of the water and the yeast in a small bowl. Stir in the sugar. Let stand until foamy, about 5 minutes. Combine the flour, oregano, and salt in a food processor. With the machine running, scrape in the yeast mixture, 1 tablespoon oil, and remaining water. After the dough forms a ball, continue to run about 30 seconds to knead. Turn out the dough onto a lightly floured counter and knead until smooth and elastic, about 1 minute.

2. Spray a large bowl with nonstick spray; put the dough in the bowl. Cover tightly with plastic wrap and let rise in a warm spot until it doubles in size, about 1 hour.

3. Spray a jelly-roll pan with nonstick spray. Work the dough into the pan, stretching it to fit in the corners. Dimple the dough with a wooden spoon handle and prick all over with the tines of a fork. Cover loosely and set aside in a warm spot 30 minutes. Adjust the racks to divide the oven in half and preheat to 450°F.

4. Brush the remaining tablespoon of oil over the dough. Bake 10 minutes; reduce the oven temperature to 400°F. Sprinkle with the cheese; bake until crisp and browned, about 15 minutes longer. Cool in the pan on a rack 5 minutes before cutting.

Per serving: 105 Calories, 2 g Total Fat, 1 g Saturated Fat, 1 mg Cholesterol, 125 mg Sodium, 18 g Total Carbohydrate, 1 g Dietary Fiber, 3 g Protein, 30 mg Calcium.

***POINTS** per serving: 2.*

Di Giorno   To make the dough by hand, combine $1/2$ cup of the water and the yeast in a large bowl; stir in the sugar. Let stand until foamy. Stir in 1 tablespoon of the oil and the remaining water. Add 4 cups of the flour, the oregano, and salt; stir until a soft dough forms. Sprinkle a work surface with 1 tablespoon of the remaining flour. Turn out the dough and knead about 10 minutes, adding all but 1 teaspoon of the remaining flour as needed, until the dough is smooth and elastic. Continue with the recipe at Step 3, but be warned: Using a food processor heats up the dough, so handmade dough may need up to twice as long to double in size.

Mixed Bell Pepper Focaccia

The word *focaccia* comes from the Latin *focolare*, which means hearth: *Focacce*, which predate ovens, were originally cooked in the fireplace. If you have a baking stone, preheat it and set the focaccia on it for a crustier, more authentic focaccia. To make a Neapolitan-style focaccia, omit the basil and toss the bell peppers and oil with two teaspoons of anchovy paste.

Makes 16 servings

2 red bell peppers

2 yellow bell peppers

2 tablespoons thinly sliced basil

2 1/2 teaspoons olive oil

1 recipe Focaccia Dough (page 284)

1. Preheat the broiler. Line a baking sheet with foil and set the bell peppers on the foil. Broil the peppers 2–3 inches from the heat, turning frequently with tongs, until charred, about 10 minutes. Fold up the foil to seal the peppers and let stand about 10 minutes, then rub off the skins. Seed and slice the peppers and put them into a bowl, then stir in the basil and 2 teaspoons of the oil.

2. Spray an 11 × 15-inch baking sheet with nonstick spray. Work the dough into the pan, stretching it into the corners. Dimple the dough with a wooden spoon handle and prick all over with the tines of a fork. Spread the bell pepper mixture over the surface, cover loosely, and set aside in a warm spot about 45 minutes. Preheat the oven to 425°F.

3. Bake the focaccia until the crust is golden and crisp around the edges, and the bell peppers lightly browned, about 30 minutes. Brush the exposed edges with the remaining $1/2$ teaspoon olive oil. Cool in the pan on a rack about 5 minutes before cutting.

Per serving: 92 Calories, 2 g Total Fat, 0 g Saturated Fat, 0 mg Cholesterol, 1 mg Sodium, 17 g Total Carbohydrate, 1 g Dietary Fiber, 2 g Protein, 5 mg Calcium.

POINTS *per serving: 2.*

Mixed Bell Pepper Focaccia

Perfect Panini

*P*anini ("small breads") are very thin grilled sandwiches that Italians practically live on. They're easy to make: Simply cut a piece of focaccia in half horizontally, apply a thin layer of a flavorsome spread, then add the fillings (see our recommendations, below). Lightly brush the outside of the focaccia with olive oil and grill in a dark heavy skillet, pressing frequently with a spatula. Depending on your focaccia's topping, you may wish to have the topping face inward when you put the sandwich together. See the index for page numbers of recipes.

- Spread Cannellini and Rosemary Spread on Rosemary Focaccia; top with prosciutto.

- Spread a very thin layer of Anchovy Spread on Mixed Bell Pepper Focaccia; top with very thin slices of Braised Veal Roast.

- Spread arugula pesto on Parmesan Focaccia; top with slices of milk-braised turkey (see Milk-Braised Turkey with Arugula Pesto).

- Squeeze the pulp from Roasted Garlic onto Parmesan Focaccia; top with sliced tomato.

- Layer slices of Chicken Breast in Tuna Sauce on Parmesan Focaccia; use the tuna sauce as a spread.

- Spread pesto on Gorgonzola Focaccia; top with sliced tomato and Roasted Basil Chicken.

- Squeeze the pulp from Roasted Garlic onto Rosemary Focaccia; top with slices of Fennel-Roasted Capon and Asiago Cheese.

Calzone Dough

Calzoni were originally shaped in long rectangles, hence their name which means "trouser legs." They are now shaped as half moons, leading the Apulians to call them *cappelli degli gendarmi*, or "gendarmes' hats."

Makes 6 servings

2 3/4 cups bread flour

1 cup whole-wheat flour

2 teaspoons sugar

1 teaspoon salt

1 (1/4-ounce) packet quick-rise yeast

1 egg

1/2 tablespoon olive oil

1 1/4 cups very hot tap water

1. Combine both flours, the sugar, salt, and yeast in a food processor and process about 1 minute to mix. Add the egg and oil. With the machine running, drizzle the water through the feed tube. After the dough forms a ball, continue to process about 30 seconds to knead.

2. Spray a large bowl with nonstick spray; put the dough in the bowl. Cover tightly with plastic wrap and let the dough rise in a warm spot until it doubles in size, about 1 hour.

3. Use the dough as directed in the recipe.

Per serving: 326 Calories, 3 g Total Fat, 1 g Saturated Fat, 35 mg Cholesterol, 401 mg Sodium, 62 g Total Carbohydrate, 4 g Dietary Fiber, 12 g Protein, 21 mg Calcium.

POINTS per serving: 6.

D i G i o r n o   Covering the bowl tightly with plastic wrap means you don't have to worry about drafts interfering with the dough's rising.

Ham and Cheese Calzones

Prosciutto is sometimes called Parma ham. Select prosciutto imported from Italy, preferably prosciutto di Parma. This is rather like an Italian grilled ham and cheese.

Makes 6 servings

1/2 cup chopped arugula

1 1/2 cups nonfat ricotta cheese

1/2 cup shredded part-skim mozzarella cheese

4 slices prosciutto (about 2 ounces), chopped

2 large scallions, sliced

1 teaspoon salt

1/4 teaspoon freshly ground pepper

1 recipe Calzone Dough (page 276)

1 egg white, beaten with 1 tablespoon water

1. Preheat the oven to 400°F. Spray a baking sheet with nonstick spray.

2. Thoroughly combine the arugula, ricotta, mozzarella, prosciutto, scallions, salt, and pepper.

3. Cut the dough into 6 pieces and work each into a 6-inch circle, about 1/4-inch thick. Mound about 1/3 cup of the filling over half of each circle, then brush the rims lightly with some of the egg wash. Fold the dough over the filling, crimp the edges together, and brush the exposed surface with the remaining wash. Set the calzones on the baking sheet and prick each 4 times with the tines of a fork. Bake until golden, 20–23 minutes. Cool on a rack about 5 minutes before serving.

Per serving: 426 Calories, 7 g Total Fat, 2 g Saturated Fat, 46 mg Cholesterol, 998 mg Sodium, 65 g Total Carbohydrate, 4 g Dietary Fiber, 26 g Protein, 158 mg Calcium.

POINTS per serving: 8.

Chicken Calzones

No leftover chicken on hand? Simply poach an 8-ounce skinless, boneless chicken breast in 1 cup simmering chicken broth (dissolve 1 chicken bouillon cube in 1 cup simmering water) for 10 minutes; it should be white throughout. The sun-dried tomatoes will soften slightly as the calzone is baked, but you'll have better results if you start with very soft, pliable sun-dried tomatoes. If yours are fairly brittle, soak them in $1/4$ cup boiling water for five minutes.

Makes 6 servings

$1^1/2$ **cups chopped cooked chicken breast (about 6 ounces)**

2 scallions, sliced

1 (10-ounce) box frozen chopped spinach, thawed and squeezed dry

2 tablespoons chopped sun-dried tomatoes

2 tablespoons chopped basil

2 tablespoons chopped flat-leaf parsley

$2/3$ **cup nonfat ricotta cheese**

1 egg

1 teaspoon salt

$1/4$ **teaspoon freshly ground pepper**

1 recipe Calzone Dough (page 291)

1 egg white, beaten with 1 tablespoon water

1. Preheat the oven to 400°F. Spray a baking sheet with nonstick spray.

2. Thoroughly combine the chicken, scallions, spinach, tomatoes, basil, parsley, ricotta, egg, salt, and pepper.

3. Cut the dough into 6 pieces and work each into a 6-inch circle, about $1/4$-inch thick. Mound a generous $1/4$ cup of the filling over half of each circle, then brush the rims lightly with the egg wash. Fold the dough over the filling, crimp the edges together, and brush the exposed dough with the remaining wash. Set the calzones on the baking sheet and prick each twice with the tines of a fork. Bake until golden, 20–22 minutes. Cool on a rack 7–8 minutes before serving.

Per serving: 427 Calories, 5 g Total Fat, 1 g Saturated Fat, 95 mg Cholesterol, 903 mg Sodium, 66 g Total Carbohydrate, 6 g Dietary Fiber, 28 g Protein, 120 mg Calcium.

POINTS per serving: 8.

Pepperoni Stromboli

Much like *calzoni*, *stromboli*—named for an island near Naples—encase a filling (usually meat) in a thin pizzalike dough. Turkey pepperoni has a fraction of the fat of real pepperoni, but it's salty and spicy enough that no additional salt or pepper is necessary.

Makes 6 servings

1/2 teaspoon olive oil

1 yellow bell pepper, seeded and chopped

1 small red onion, chopped

2 ounces turkey pepperoni (about 34 small rounds), chopped

1/2 cup nonfat ricotta cheese

1/2 cup shredded part-skim mozzarella cheese

1/4 cup chopped flat-leaf parsley

1 recipe Calzone Dough (page 276)

1 egg white, beaten with 1 tablespoon water

1. Preheat the oven to 400°F. Spray a baking sheet with nonstick spray.

2. Heat a nonstick skillet. Swirl in the oil, then add the bell pepper and onion. Sauté until the onion just begins to brown. Transfer to a bowl and mix in the pepperoni, ricotta, mozzarella, and parsley.

3. Cut the dough into 6 pieces and work each into a 6-inch square, about 1/4-inch thick. Mound 1/2 cup of the filling in the middle of each square, then brush the edges with the egg wash and fold the dough over the filling. Set the stromboli, seam-side down, on the baking sheet. Cut 2 vent slits in each with the tip of a sharp knife. Bake until golden, about 20 minutes. Cool on a rack about 10 minutes before serving.

Per serving: 403 Calories, 7 g Total Fat, 2 g Saturated Fat, 47 mg Cholesterol, 544 mg Sodium, 66 g Total Carbohydrate, 5 g Dietary Fiber, 20 g Protein, 121 mg Calcium.

POINTS *per serving: 8.*

twelve

desserts

Sorbetto di Limone

Lemon trees grow everywhere in southern Italy and Sicily—in fact, at one point, citrus was Sicily's second most important crop (wheat was first). Serve this refreshing sorbet with fresh grapes or sesame biscotti for a Sicilian-inspired dessert.

Makes 12 servings

1 cup sugar

4 cups water

1 teaspoon grated lemon zest

1 cup fresh lemon juice

1. Bring the sugar and water to a boil in a medium saucepan. Reduce the heat and simmer, stirring occasionally, until the sugar dissolves. Remove from the heat and stir in the lemon zest and juice. Cool 30 minutes, then cover and refrigerate for at least 3 hours or overnight.

2. Transfer the mixture to an ice cream maker and freeze according to the manufacturer's instructions.

Per serving: 70 Calories, 0 g Total Fat, 0 g Saturated Fat, 0 mg Cholesterol, 0 mg Sodium, 18 g Total Carbohydrate, 0 g Dietary Fiber, 0 g Protein, 2 mg Calcium.

POINTS per serving: 1.

Espresso Granita

Granitas have a coarser, grainier texture than sorbets. If you prefer a smoother dessert, omit Step 3 and prepare the espresso mixture in an ice cream maker.

Makes 7 servings

2 cups brewed decaffeinated espresso or dark roast coffee, chilled

¹/₃ cup sugar

2 teaspoons lemon zest

1. Freeze an 8-inch square metal baking pan and a metal fork overnight.

2. Combine the espresso and sugar, whisking until the sugar dissolves. Stir in the lemon zest.

3. Pour into the baking pan. Freeze, stirring with the chilled fork, every 20 minutes, until the mixture is frozen but still grainy, about 2 hours. Cover with foil and keep frozen until ready to serve.

Per serving: 38 Calories, 0 g Total Fat, 0 g Saturated Fat, 0 mg Cholesterol, 1 mg Sodium, 10 g Total Carbohydrate, 0 g Dietary Fiber, 0 g Protein, 2 mg Calcium.

POINTS per serving: 1.

Di Giorno   Although granitas do have a coarser texture than other frozen desserts, you'll want to be sure to chill the sugar syrup rapidly to keep the ice crystals from becoming too big. Metal gets colder faster than glass or plastic, and it stays colder longer (think about touching the different materials on a cold winter day). Be sure to protect your hands with gloves or oven mitts when you stir the granita! Frequently stirring keeps the ice crystals small.

Gelato Affogato

The hot espresso "drowns" the yogurt just enough to give it the texture of a coffee float. Although *gelato* is the italian word for ice cream, this dessert still has fabulous flavor with frozen yogurt.

Makes 4 servings

1 tablespoon slivered lemon zest

1/4 cup water

1 teaspoon sugar

1 (16-fluid ounce) container sugar-free vanilla or coffee nonfat frozen yogurt

1/2 cup brewed decaffeinated espresso

1. Bring the lemon zest and water to a boil in a small saucepan. Remove from the heat and let stand 10 minutes. Pat the lemon zest dry with a paper towel, then set it on wax paper and sprinkle it with the sugar. Let stand at least 30 minutes.

2. Scoop 1/2 cup of frozen yogurt into each of 4 dessert dishes; pour 2 tablespoons espresso over each. Garnish with the candied lemon zest and any remaining sugar. Serve at once.

Per serving: 56 Calories, 0 g Total Fat, 0 g Saturated Fat, 2 mg Cholesterol, 66 mg Sodium, 10 g Total Carbohydrate, 0 g Dietary Fiber, 5 g Protein, 153 mg Calcium.

POINTS per serving: 1.

Orange Panna Cotta

Traditionally made with heavy cream, this classic custard dessert is a fat and cholesterol minefield. Using gelatin to help thicken the milk lowers the fat and cholesterol, but the flavor and texture are virtually the same as the original.

Makes 4 servings

2 cups low-fat (1%) milk

1 (1/4-ounce) envelope unflavored gelatin

1/4 cup sugar

1 teaspoon vanilla extract

1 teaspoon orange extract

1 teaspoon grated orange zest

Pinch salt

1/2 cup frozen light whipped topping

Ground cinnamon

1. Combine the milk and gelatin in a nonstick saucepan; let stand until the gelatin softens, about 5 minutes. Cook over low heat, stirring constantly, until the gelatin dissolves completely, about 5 minutes. Whisk in the sugar, both extracts, the orange zest, and salt; bring to a simmer, stirring frequently. Pour evenly into 4 small ramekins. Cool slightly, then cover and refrigerate overnight.

2. To serve, top each with 2 tablespoons whipped topping and a sprinkling of cinnamon.

Per serving: 134 Calories, 2 g Total Fat, 2 g Saturated Fat, 5 mg Cholesterol, 96 mg Sodium, 21 g Total Carbohydrate, 0 g Dietary Fiber, 5 g Protein, 152 mg Calcium.

POINTS per serving: 3.

Tiramisù

Although tiramisù was created just in the 1960s at a restaurant in the Veneto, it's become one of the most popular and classic of all Italian desserts. Don't confuse ladyfinger biscuits with the soft, spongecake-like ladyfingers. The biscuits are the crisp Italian cookies called *savoiardi*, which you can find in the Italian food section of your supermarket. For a pretty presentation, reserve some of the biscuits to arrange on the diagonal around a glass dish.

Makes 8 servings

12 ladyfinger biscuits

1/4 cup brewed decaffeinated espresso or strong coffee, cooled

1/2 cup warm (105–115°F) water

2 tablespoons + 2 teaspoons powdered egg whites

1 1/3 cups nonfat ricotta cheese

1/3 cup fat-free egg substitute

1/2 cup mascarpone cheese

2 tablespoons sugar

1/2 teaspoon vanilla extract

2 teaspoons unsweetened cocoa powder

1. Dip each biscuit into the espresso and place in a single layer in an 8-inch square glass or ceramic baking dish.

2. Combine the water and powdered egg whites in a large stainless steel bowl, stirring gently until the powder dissolves, 3–4 minutes. With an electric mixer, beat at medium-high speed until stiff peaks form, 5–7 minutes.

3. In another large bowl, beat together the ricotta, egg substitute, mascarpone, sugar, and vanilla. Stir in about one third of the beaten egg whites, then gently fold in the remainder with a rubber spatula. Pour over the ladyfingers. Cover and refrigerate 6–8 hours. Sprinkle with the cocoa just before serving.

Per serving: 182 Calories, 8 g Total Fat, 0 g Saturated Fat, 80 mg Cholesterol, 117 mg Sodium, 15 g Total Carbohydrate, 0 g Dietary Fiber, 10 g Protein, 213 mg Calcium.

***POINTS** per serving: 4.*

Di Giorno   These egg whites are not cooked. For food safety, use salmonella-negative powdered egg whites (available in the baking section of many supermarkets) and water or pasteurized egg whites (near the egg substitutes in the dairy case). To get the most volume when you beat the egg whites, make sure the stainless steel bowl and the beaters are very clean and completely dry.

Tiramisù

Zabaglione

Zabaglione, also called *zabaione*, hails from Piedmont, where it is made with Barolo wine. Throughout the rest of Italy, Marsala is used. It is traditionally spooned over bowls of sliced fruit.

Makes 6 servings

4 egg yolks

¹/₄ cup sugar

¹/₄ cup dry Marsala wine or Frangelico liqueur

Combine the egg yolks, sugar, and wine or liqueur in the top of a double boiler over simmering water or in a glass bowl suspended over a saucepan of simmering water. Cook, beating constantly with an electric mixer at medium speed, until thick enough that the beaters trail ribbons over the top, 4–5 minutes.

Per serving: 87 Calories, 3 g Total Fat, 1 g Saturated Fat, 142 mg Cholesterol, 6 mg Sodium, 10 g Total Carbohydrate, 0 g Dietary Fiber, 2 g Protein, 16 mg Calcium.

POINTS per serving: 2.

Di Giorno   If you use a glass bowl suspended over water, make sure to select a heat-resistant bowl and take care that the water does not touch the bottom of it.

Budino di Ricotta

This old-fashioned almond-ricotta pudding is a cross between a flan and a soufflé.

Makes 8 servings

1 (15-ounce) container part-skim ricotta cheese

8 (1-inch diameter) amaretti cookies, crushed

4 eggs, separated (at room temperature)

¹/₄ cornstarch

2 tablespoons amaretto liqueur

¹/₈ teaspoon cream of tartar

¹/₄ cup sugar

1. Adjust the racks to divide the oven in half and preheat to 375°F. Spray a 6-cup soufflé dish with nonstick spray.

2. Combine the ricotta, cookies, egg yolks, cornstarch, and amaretto in a large bowl.

3. With an electric mixer at high speed, beat the egg whites and cream of tartar until foamy. Beat in the sugar, 1 tablespoon at a time, until the whites are stiff and glossy but not dry. Gently fold the egg whites, one-third at a time, into the ricotta mixture until no white streaks remain.

4. Spoon the batter into the soufflé dish. Place it in a roasting pan, then set the pan on the center oven rack. Pour boiling water into the roasting pan to come halfway up the side of the soufflé dish. Bake until puffed and golden, about 45 minutes. Serve warm.

Per serving: 198 Calories, 8 g Total Fat, 4 g Saturated Fat, 125 mg Cholesterol, 111 mg Sodium, 19 g Total Carbohydrate, 0 g Dietary Fiber, 10 g Protein, 180 mg Calcium.

POINTS per serving: 5.

D i G i o r n o *Amaretti* means "little bitter cookies"; they are basically almond-flavored macaroons. If you cannot find them in your supermarket or an Italian grocery, they're easy enough to make (see page 313).

Torta di Ricotta

American-style cheesecake gets its light yet rich texture from cream cheese, but this classic dessert uses ricotta cheese—it's denser, like a flourless cake.

Makes 12 servings

12 (2 1/2-inch square) graham crackers, made into fine crumbs

3 cups part-skim ricotta cheese

1/2 cup nonfat cream cheese

1/2 cup sugar

1/4 cup cornstarch

2 teaspoons grated orange zest

4 eggs

1 1/2 tablespoons dark rum

2 teaspoons vanilla extract

1. Preheat the oven to 300°F. Spray an 8-inch springform pan with nonstick spray. Pat the graham cracker crumbs into the bottom of the pan.

2. Combine the ricotta and cream cheese in a food processor. Sift in the sugar and cornstarch, then add the orange zest. Process until smooth.

3. Combine the eggs, rum, and vanilla. With the machine running, pour the egg mixture through the feed tube. Process until combined, scraping down the sides of the bowl as needed. Pour the batter into the pan. Bake until golden and puffed and a knife tip inserted in the center comes out clean, 1 1/2–2 hours. Cool in the pan on a rack 1 hour. Run a sharp knife around the inside of the pan to release the cake. Remove the ring and cool the cake completely on the rack. Wrap in foil and refrigerate overnight.

Per serving: 198 Calories, 7 g Total Fat, 4 g Saturated Fat, 91 mg Cholesterol, 186 mg Sodium, 20 g Total Carbohydrate, 0 g Dietary Fiber, 11 g Protein, 204 mg Calcium.

POINTS *per serving: 5.*

Gattò di Ricotta

Gattò di ricotta is the southern Italian version of cheesecake; it doesn't have a crust, and it's often flavored with orange. This Sicilian version is much lighter than what Americans are accustomed to or what would be made in the north of Italy, where the cake would be called a *torta* (see opposite).

Makes 10 servings

2 (15-ounce) containers nonfat ricotta cheese, drained

2 eggs

1 cup fat-free egg substitute

³/₄ cup sugar

¹/₄ cup all-purpose flour

¹/₈ teaspoon salt

1 tablespoon grated orange zest

1 tablespoon vanilla extract

1. Preheat the oven to 300°F. Spray a 9-inch springform pan with nonstick spray and dust it with flour.

2. Put the ricotta into a large bowl. With an electric mixer at low speed, beat just enough to break it up. Beat in the eggs, 1 at a time. Increase the mixer speed to high and drizzle in the egg substitute. Beat in the sugar, flour, and salt, then the orange zest and vanilla. Pour the batter into the pan and bake until golden and firm in the center and a tester inserted into the center of the cake comes out clean, about 1¹/₄ hours. Cool completely in the pan on a rack, then cover and refrigerate at least 1 hour before serving.

3. To serve, run a sharp knife around the inside of the pan to release the cake. Remove the ring before serving.

Per serving: 135 Calories, 1 g Total Fat, 0 g Saturated Fat, 43 mg Cholesterol, 103 mg Sodium, 20 g Total Carbohydrate, 0 g Dietary Fiber, 11 g Protein, 70 mg Calcium.

POINTS *per serving: 3.*

D i G i o r n o   The drier the ricotta cheese for this type of cake, the better. Shake the cheese in a strainer or, if you have the time, put it into a strainer lined with a coffee filter and drain in the refrigerator for up to eight hours.

Easter Pie

This unique cheese pie is made with barley, wheat berries, or rice; be sure to use pearl barley, not the quick-cooking variety. The sambuca lends just a hint of anise flavor to this Neapolitan classic.

Makes 10 servings

1/2 cup pearl barley

3 cups water

1 cup + 1 tablespoon sugar

1/4 cup finely chopped candied orange peel

2 prepared pie crusts

1 (15-ounce) container nonfat ricotta cheese

2 eggs

1/4 teaspoon cinnamon

1 teaspoon vanilla extract

1 1/2 tablespoons sambuca liqueur

1. Combine the barley and 2 cups of the water. Cover and soak at least 8 and up to 24 hours.

2. Transfer the barley to a strainer and rinse under cold water. Put in a nonstick saucepan, add the remaining 1 cup of water, and bring to a boil. Reduce the heat and simmer, covered, until all the water is absorbed, 30–40 minutes. Add 1 tablespoon of the sugar and the candied orange peel. Remove from the heat and let cool.

3. Preheat the oven to 350°F. Fit 1 pie crust into a 9-inch glass pie plate and pat it into place. Cut the second crust into eight 1-inch strips.

4. With an electric mixer at high speed, cream the ricotta and the remaining cup of sugar. Beat in the eggs, 1 at a time, then the cinnamon, vanilla, and sambuca. Stir in the barley mixture. Pour into the pie crust and lay 4 of the pie crust strips on top in each direction to create a crosshatch. Bake until the bottom crust is golden brown, about 1 hour. Cool in the pan on a rack.

Per serving: 304 Calories, 9 g Total Fat, 1 g Saturated Fat, 43 mg Cholesterol, 183 mg Sodium, 46 g Total Carbohydrate, 2 g Dietary Fiber, 10 g Protein, 60 mg Calcium.

POINTS *per serving: 6.*

Easter Pie

Chocolate Grappa Cake

This cake is actually better the day after you make it. Serve it, if you like, with orange segments and sprinkled with orange zest.

Cake:

1/4 cup + 2 tablespoons raisins

1/4 cup grappa (Italian brandy)

5 tablespoons unsalted margarine, at room temperature

2/3 cup sugar

2/3 cup fat-free egg substitute

1 teaspoon vanilla extract

2 1/4 cups all-purpose flour

1/3 cup unsweetened cocoa powder

3/4 teaspoon baking powder

1/2 teaspoon baking soda

1/4 teaspoon cinnamon

1/4 teaspoon salt

1 cup aspartame-sweetened vanilla nonfat yogurt

Syrup:

1/2 cup sugar

1/3 cup water

1. Soak the raisins in the grappa 30 minutes. Drain the raisins, reserving the grappa separately.

2. Adjust the racks to divide the oven in half and preheat to 350°F. Spray an $8^{1}/2 \times 4^{1}/2$-inch loaf pan with nonstick spray.

3. To make the cake, with an electric mixer at medium speed, cream the margarine. Gradually add the sugar and continue beating until light and fluffy, about 5 minutes; scrape down the sides of the bowl as necessary. Beat in the egg substitute and vanilla.

4. Combine the flour, cocoa powder, baking powder, baking soda, cinnamon, and salt. With the mixer at low speed, add the dry ingredients to the margarine mixture, then add the yogurt, then the flour. Fold in the raisins. Spoon the batter into the pan. Bake until a toothpick inserted in the center comes out clean, about 1 hour. Cool in the pan on a rack 15 minutes. Run a knife around the inside of the pan to release the cake, but do not remove.

5. To make the syrup, bring the sugar and water to a boil in a small saucepan; boil, without stirring, 1 minute. Remove from the heat and stir in the grappa. Pierce the cake in several places with a skewer. Pour the grappa syrup slowly over the cake until it is absorbed. Cool the cake completely. When ready to serve, remove the cake from the pan and cut into 12 slices.

Per serving: 251 Calories, 5 g Total Fat, 1 g Saturated Fat, 0 mg Cholesterol, 163 mg Sodium, 44 g Total Carbohydrate, 2 g Dietary Fiber, 5 g Protein, 57 mg Calcium.

POINTS *per serving: 5.*

D i G i o r n o   Grappa is an Italian brandy made from the skins, seeds, and pulp left after grapes are pressed for winemaking. Its fiery flavor makes it something of an acquired taste. Marc, a French *eau de vie* made in the same manner, can be substituted, or if you prefer a sweeter, subtler flavor, substitute Frangelico or Amaretto.

Chocolate Grappa Cake

Layered Polenta Cake

The bowl you use to beat the egg whites can affect their volume. Copper is best, since it reacts chemically with the egg whites to maximum volume, but copper bowls tend to be very pricey; stainless steel is much more affordable and does almost as good a job. Steer clear of glass (it's very slick, which makes it hard for the whites to climb up the sides), aluminum (it reacts with the whites to turn them off-white or grey), and plastic (it's porous, so traces of fat or other food may adhere to it, compromising the volume).

Makes 8 servings

1 cup yellow cornmeal

3/4 cup self-rising cake flour

1 teaspoon baking soda

1/4 teaspoon salt

2/3 cup granulated sugar

3 eggs, separated (at room temperature)

1/4 cup low-fat (1%) buttermilk

4 teaspoons vegetable oil

2 teaspoons vanilla extract

1/2 cup spreadable fruit

2 teaspoons confectioners' sugar

1. Preheat the oven to 350°F. Spray an 8-inch springform pan with nonstick spray.

2. Combine the cornmeal, flour, baking soda, and salt in a large bowl.

3. With an electric mixer at medium-high speed, cream 1/3 cup of the granulated sugar and the egg yolks until light and fluffy, about 5 minutes. Add the buttermilk, oil, and vanilla and beat 1 minute longer. Beat the egg yolk mixture into the cornmeal mixture.

4. In a stainless steel bowl with clean, dry beaters, beat the egg whites at high speed until foamy. Beat in the remaining 1/3 cup of sugar, 1 tablespoon at a time, until the whites are stiff and glossy but not dry. Gently fold the egg whites, one third at a time, into the batter until no white streaks remain.

5. Spoon the batter into the pan. Bake until the center is puffed and golden and a toothpick inserted in the center comes out clean, about 40 minutes. Cool in the pan on a rack 10 minutes. Run a sharp knife around the inside of the pan to release the cake. Remove the ring and cool the cake completely on rack.

6. With a serrated knife, cut the cake in half. Place the bottom half on a platter and spread with the spreadable fruit; cover with the top half and dust with confectioners' sugar.

Per serving: 266 Calories, 5 g Total Fat, 1 g Saturated Fat, 80 mg Cholesterol, 384 mg Sodium, 50 g Total Carbohydrate, 1 g Dietary Fiber, 5 g Protein, 21 mg Calcium.

***POINTS** per serving: 6.*

Cannoli

Sicilian in origin, cannoli are crisp pastry tubes filled with a sweetened ricotta mixture. Traditionally served at carnival time, cannoli were always sent as gifts in quantities of twelve, perhaps commemorating the number of Apostles. In this Neapolitan-style cannoli, the ricotta is flavored with chocolate and candied orange peel rather than the original orange water.

Makes 12 servings

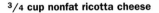

3/4 cup nonfat ricotta cheese

1/4 cup + 2 tablespoons confectioners' sugar

2 tablespoons finely chopped candied orange peel

1/2 teaspoon vanilla extract

1/2 tablespoon finely chopped bittersweet chocolate

12 mini cannoli shells

Thoroughly mix the ricotta cheese and sugar. Stir in the orange peel and vanilla, then fold in the chocolate. Stuff 4 teaspoons of the mixture into each of the cannoli shells, pushing the filling into the shell from both ends. Serve chilled or room temperature.

Per serving: 62 Calories, 1 g Total Fat, 1 g Saturated Fat, 0 mg Cholesterol, 7 mg Sodium, 9 g Total Carbohydrate, 0 g Dietary Fiber, 3 g Protein, 16 mg Calcium.

POINTS *per serving: 1*

D i   G i o r n o   In traditional cannoli recipes, getting the cannoli cream into the shells is an exercise in frustration, typically resulting in broken shells and short tempers. Part of the reason is that traditional recipes call for whole-milk ricotta to be drained in, then pressed through, a sieve to make it very dry; the thick cream is piped into the tubes. Our much less labor-intensive recipe starts with nonfat ricotta, which tends to be drier than the whole milk variety, and we push the filling into the shells, so it doesn't have to be quite so smooth (though our version still feels silky on the tongue).

Roasted Pears with Cannoli Cream

Both the pears and cannoli cream may be prepared and refrigerated, separately, overnight. To serve, bring to room temperature, then fill the pears and serve immediately.

Makes 4 servings

1 cup part-skim ricotta cheese

1/2 teaspoon cinnamon

4 firm small Bosc pears, cored and halved (do not peel)

1/4 cup confectioners' sugar

1/2 teaspoon vanilla extract

1 tablespoon mini chocolate chips

1. Spoon the ricotta into a coffee filter or cheesecloth-lined strainer; place over a bowl. Refrigerate, covered, 2 hours. Discard the liquid in the bowl.

2. Preheat the oven to 425°F. Spray a baking dish with nonstick spray.

3. Sprinkle 1/4 teaspoon of the cinnamon evenly over the cut sides of the pears. Set the pears, cut-side down, in the baking dish. Roast 30 minutes. Cool in the pan on a rack for 30 minutes.

4. To make the cannoli cream, whisk the ricotta, sugar, the remaining cinnamon, and the vanilla until well blended. Fold in the chips. Cover and let stand at room temperature 30 minutes. Spoon one heaping tablespoon into each pear half and serve at once.

Per serving: 227 Calories, 7 g Total Fat, 4 g Saturated Fat, 19 mg Cholesterol, 77 mg Sodium, 37 g Total Carbohydrate, 4 g Dietary Fiber, 8 g Protein, 189 mg Calcium.

POINTS *per serving: 4.*

Amaretti

Amaretti hail from Saronno, the town in Lombardy that is the birthplace of amaretto liqueur. Traditionally, these crisp little macaroons derive their flavor from apricot kernels as well as almonds. Our recipe gets all the flavor you'd want with a minimum of labor by using almond paste. Be sure you use canned almond paste, rather than the type in tubes—the two pastes have very different consistencies. Cookies made with paste from a tube will be much grainier.

Makes 45 servings

4 egg whites (about $^1/_2$ cup)

Pinch of salt

1 cup sugar

1 (8-ounce) can almond paste

1. Preheat the oven to 300°F. Line baking sheets with baker's parchment, or spray them liberally with nonstick spray and dust with flour.

2. With an electric mixer at medium speed, beat 2 of the egg whites (about $^1/_4$ cup) until frothy. Add the salt. With the machine running, slowly beat in $^1/_4$ cup of the sugar in a thin stream, beating until stiff, glossy peaks form, 2–3 minutes.

3. Combine the almond paste, the remaining 2 egg whites, and the remaining $^3/_4$ cup of sugar in a large bowl. Beat at medium speed until smooth, about 2 minutes. Beat in half of the egg white mixture, then the other half. Continue to beat a few seconds more to incorporate fully. Drop the batter by the teaspoonful on the baking sheets, leaving 1 inch between cookies. Bake until golden brown, about 40 minutes. Repeat with the remaining dough to make 90 cookies. Cool the cookies on racks.

Per serving: 42 Calories, 1 g Total Fat, 0 g Saturated Fat, 0 mg Cholesterol, 31 mg Sodium, 7 g Total Carbohydrate, 0 g Dietary Fiber, 1 g Protein, 9 mg Calcium.

***POINTS** per serving: 1.*

D i   G i o r n o   Don't be alarmed if the cookies make crackling sounds as they cool; this is a normal part of the drying process.

Chocolate-Almond Biscotti

In Italy, biscotti refers to all types of cookies, but is most often associated with the brittle, twice-baked treats. These cookies are perfect for dunking in a steaming cup of coffee. They'll keep for weeks stored in tightly sealed containers.

Makes 15 servings

1 cup sugar

2 cups all-purpose flour

3/4 cup unsweetened cocoa powder

2 teaspoons baking powder

1/2 teaspoon salt

3/4 cup whole almonds

1/4 cup honey

3/4 cup water

1 egg

1. Preheat the oven to 350°F. Line a large baking sheet with baker's parchment, nonstick plastic ovenware liner, or wax paper.

2. Whisk the sugar, flour, cocoa powder, baking powder, and salt in a large bowl. Stir in the almonds. Whisk the honey, water, and egg in a small bowl until frothy. Add to the dry ingredients, stirring to combine.

3. Gather the dough with lightly floured hands and transfer to a lightly floured counter. Divide the dough in half and work each into a 9 × 3-inch loaf, about 1 inch high. Transfer to the baking sheet and bake until risen and firm to the touch, about 35 minutes. Remove from the oven and let stand about 15 minutes. Cut each loaf into fifteen 1/2-inch slices, making 30 biscotti. Lay the slices on their sides on the baking sheet and bake 10 minutes, then turn the biscotti over and bake until very dry to the touch and slightly crisp, about 10 minutes longer. Cool completely on racks and store in an airtight container.

Per serving: 187 Calories, 5 g Total Fat, 1 g Saturated Fat, 14 mg Cholesterol, 148 mg Sodium, 35 g Total Carbohydrate, 3 g Dietary Fiber, 4 g Protein, 46 mg Calcium.

***POINTS** per serving: 4.*

Di Giorno   Here's a low-fat baking tip: Rather than melting squares of baking chocolate or using a mixture of melted butter and unsweetened cocoa powder, mix the cocoa powder with honey. The consistency will be virtually identical to melted chocolate (you may want to reduce the amount of sugar in your recipe slightly).

Anise Biscotti

Anise-flavored biscuits are popular in Piedmont and on the island of Sardinia. Pine nuts, or pignoli, are an essential component of pesto, but they're also used throughout Italy in all kinds of baked goods.

Makes 18 servings

2 1/4 cups all-purpose flour

1 teaspoon baking powder

1/2 teaspoon baking soda

1/2 teaspoon salt

1/3 cup pine nuts

1 cup sugar

3/4 cup fat-free egg substitute

2 teaspoons anise extract

1. Preheat the oven to 375°F. Line a large baking sheet with baker's parchment, nonstick plastic ovenware liner, or wax paper.

2. Whisk the flour, baking powder, baking soda, salt, and pine nuts together in a large bowl. Whisk the sugar, egg substitute, and anise extract in a small bowl. Add to the dry ingredients, stirring to combine.

3. Gather the dough with lightly floured hands and transfer to a lightly floured counter. Divide the dough in half, place the halves on the baking sheet, and work each into a 9 × 3-inch loaf, about 3/4-inch high. Bake until lightly golden and firm to the touch, about 25 minutes. Remove from the oven and let stand about 10 minutes. Cut each loaf into eighteen 1/2-inch slices, making 36 biscotti. Stand the biscotti upright on the baking sheet and bake until lightly browned, about 15 minutes. Cool the biscotti on racks and store in an airtight container.

Per serving: 122 Calories, 1 g Total Fat, 0 g Saturated Fat, 0 mg Cholesterol, 144 mg Sodium, 24 g Total Carbohydrate, 1 g Dietary Fiber, 3 g Protein, 25 mg Calcium.

POINTS *per serving: 2.*

Di Giorno   Toasting the biscotti standing upright yields a slightly softer cookie; if you prefer the very brittle variety, lay them down and toast for seven minutes on each side.

Venetian Cornmeal Cookies

Raisin-studded cornmeal cookies are called *zeletti* ("yellow ones") in the Venetian dialect. They are softer and more subtly colored than a similar polenta cookie with the same name that is made in Bologna.

Makes 72 servings

1¹/2 cups all-purpose flour

1 cup yellow cornmeal

³/4 teaspoon baking powder

¹/2 teaspoon salt

1 cup low-fat buttermilk

³/4 cup sugar

1 egg

¹/2 tablespoon vanilla extract

¹/2 teaspoon lemon extract

³/4 cup seedless raisins

1. Preheat the oven to 375°F. Lightly spray nonstick baking sheets with nonstick spray.

2. Whisk together the flour, cornmeal, baking powder, and salt. With an electric mixer at medium speed, beat the buttermilk and sugar in a large bowl until the sugar dissolves and the mixture is frothy. Beat in the egg, vanilla, and lemon extract. Stir in the flour mixture and the raisins.

3. Turn out the dough onto a floured counter and roll out to a thickness of $^1/4$ inch. Cut into $1^1/2$-inch squares, gathering and rerolling the scraps to use up the dough, making a total of 72 cookies. Transfer the cookies to the baking sheets and bake until golden brown, 12–14 minutes. Cool completely on racks and store in an airtight container.

Per serving: 32 Calories, 0 g Total Fat, 0 g Saturated Fat, 3 mg Cholesterol, 27 mg Sodium, 7 g Total Carbohydrate, 0 g Dietary Fiber, 1 g Protein, 8 mg Calcium.

POINTS *per serving: 1.*

index

The Regions of Italy

VALLE D'AOSTA

TRENTINO-ALTO ADIGE

FRIULI-VENEZIA GIULIA

LOMBARDY

PIEDMONT

VENETO

LIGURIA

EMILIA-ROMAGNA

TUSCANY

MARCHE

UMBRIA

LAZIO

ABRUZZO

MOLISE

SARDINIA

CAMPANIA

APULIA

BASILICATA

CALABRIA

SICILY